Y0-DNQ-091

BEING
AND
DEATH

BEING
AND
DEATH

An Outline of Integrationist Philosophy

BY JOSÉ FERRATER MORA

*Translated from the Spanish
with Extensive Revisions by the Author*

UNIVERSITY OF CALIFORNIA PRESS

BERKELEY AND LOS ANGELES 1965

UNIVERSITY OF CALIFORNIA PRESS, BERKELEY AND LOS ANGELES, CALIFORNIA
CAMBRIDGE UNIVERSITY PRESS, LONDON, ENGLAND

© 1965 BY THE REGENTS OF THE UNIVERSITY OF CALIFORNIA

TRANSLATED FROM *El Ser y la Muerte:*
Bosquejo de Filosofía integracionista
FIRST PUBLISHED IN MADRID BY AGUILAR, S. A. DE EDICIONES, 1962

PUBLISHED WITH THE ASSISTANCE OF A GRANT
FROM THE ROCKEFELLER FOUNDATION

LIBRARY OF CONGRESS CATALOG CARD NUMBER: 65-17450

PRINTED IN THE UNITED STATES OF AMERICA

PREFACE
to the American Edition

This book is basically a translation of a work which I originally wrote in Spanish, and which was published in 1962. It is not, however, a mere duplicate, in another tongue, of the original version. It differs from the latter in various important respects. To begin with, I have revised the text throughout in order to make it more concise without loss of meaning. I have added a number of paragraphs on some crucial points which I felt needed clarification. I have entirely rewritten half a dozen sections, and in many cases I have changed the order of presentation.

As a consequence, I hope that, while still fundamentally a translation, the book has been considerably improved. Indeed, if a new Spanish edition of the book is produced, I will probably rewrite large portions of it in accordance with the present English text.

I wish to express my thanks to Mr. Miguel González-Gerth for his help in the translation. I also wish to express to the University of California Press, and in particular to its Director, Mr. August Frugé, my sincere appreciation for issuing a book which, although on a topic of very general interest, remains a philosophic work, and makes no pretense of making difficult things easy. I should add that the book makes no pretense of making easy things difficult. From the point of view of its possible appeal to the public, making easy things difficult may be occasionally a more effective procedure than making difficult things easy or simply letting things be what they are. I know of not a few cases of works whose authors have succeeded in making easy things very arduous, and have subsequently enjoyed a wide reputation. To be sure, few people have read such works, but fewer still have dared confess that they did not. I have myself nothing against success—indeed, I sincerely hope that the present book will attain some measure of it—but I feel that, if it comes, it should be the result of understanding rather than of misunderstanding. Since in the world in which we live we have already had a good share of the latter, it may not seem too unreasonable to claim some of the former.

JOSÉ FERRATER MORA

Bryn Mawr College,
Pennsylvania

CONTENTS

INTRODUCTION   1

ONE: *Death in Inorganic Nature*   17

1. Quaestio de nomine; **2.** *Some Preliminary Difficulties;* **3.** *Science and Philosophy: A Digression;* **4.** *Some Theses on Inorganic Reality;* **5.** *Elements and Structures;* **6.** *The Basic Elements;* **7.** *Being "in Principle" and Being in Reality;* **8.** *Reality and Identity;* **9.** *The Two "Directions";* **10.** *The External and the Internal;* **11.** *Being and Meaning;* **12.** *Conclusion*

TWO: *Death in Organic Nature*   92

13. *Matter and Organism;* **14.** *Examination of Doctrines;* **15.** *The Nature of Organic Reality;* **16.** *From Ceasing to Dying;* **17.** *Death in Primary Organisms;* **18.** *Death in Superior Organisms;* **19.** *In Search of a Way Out*

THREE: *Human Death*   145

20. *Man and His Body;* **21.** *Biological Life and Human Life;* **22.** *Being, Becoming, Existing;* **23.** *Man as Selfhood and as*

Property; **24.** The Definition of Man; **25.** A Budget of Paradoxes; **26.** The Interiority of Death; **27.** The Experience of Death; **28.** Three Cases; **29.** "Literary" Testimony; **30.** The Attitudes Regarding Death; **31.** The Problem of One's Own Death; **32.** The Essence of Human Death

FOUR: *Death, Survival, and Immortality*   204

33. The Problem of Immortality; **34.** The Primitives; **35.** The Ancients; **36.** The Christians; **37.** The Philosophers; **38.** Rational Proofs; **39.** Empirical Proofs; **40.** Further Attempts; **41.** Conclusion

NOTES   243

INDEX   259

INTRODUCTION

The images elicited by the term 'death' are so diverse that they do not seem to mirror the same reality—or even the same process. Is death not conceived in various ways depending on learning, profession, temperament, and personal and social circumstances? Is it not confronted quite differently by the "primitive" and by the "civilized" man? By countryfolk and by city dwellers? By the extremely wealthy and the poverty-stricken? The "ages of man" only help multiply these images. An adolescent might envisage death as a welcome liberation from some cosmic evil; a young man might look at it as the glorious prize of an heroic act; a mature man may find himself suddenly plunged into disturbing thoughts of mortality while earning his daily bread. Thus the first difficulty encountered when we consider the problem of death concerns the possibility of unifying the above images in a single, all-embracing notion.

Let us assume that this has already been accomplished. Unfortunately, most of the problems raised by the meaning of 'death' remain as formidable as ever. Do "human death," as a single, all-embracing concept, and "organic death" have something in common? If 'to die' merely means 'to be no longer,' is it not reasonable to say that other realities besides human beings and organisms "die"? Can we ever discover a concept that comprehends so many diverse phenomena? Or granting that such a concept has been unearthed, will we not have dissolved once and for all the idea of human death in the much too general notions of "being no longer" and "passing away"?

The present book attempts to answer these questions. It advances the opinion that "death" is, indeed, a rather general concept, and that it should permit us to grasp the nature and meaning of all realities, whether inorganic, biological, or human. This is not to say that human death displays no characteristics of its own; the fact is, however, that human death cannot be adequately elucidated except against the background of the more general concept of "cessation." As I eventually hope to make clear, the death of human beings is a phenomenon both unique and common; in point of fact, unique only because it stands against a common (and cosmic) background.

Hence an investigation of the "problem of death" can lead to an outline of a philosophical system, or at least to three basic branches of such a system: an ontology, a metaphysics of organic reality, and a philosophy of the human person. The question of death is not an isolated problem, but rather a cluster of problems—problems about man, Nature, and the structure of reality.

My interest in the subject of death does not arise from morbid feelings. Nor is it linked to the too often talked about Hispanic obsession for the "moment of truth," corpses, funerals, and mourning. If there is such an obsession, I am not responsible for it. As a matter of fact, more is said here about life than about death. The *"problem* of death" is not, or is not only, something to feel anxious about, but rather something to discourse on.

Thus the problem of death does not need to be surrounded by

the somewhat pathetic halo which a number of 'isms,' and in particular Existentialism, have given it in the recent past. No doubt, such 'isms' have helped emphasize the fact that we are confronted with a real problem. Unfortunately, in their frantic attempt to make 'death' synonymous with 'human death,' philosophers subscribing to such 'isms' have soon reached a point of no return: a purely existential treatment of death has ended by severing the links of man with Nature and, ultimately, with reality. To be sure, the heavy emphasis placed on "death" as "human death" by Existentialism—including the anti-Existentialist wing of Existentialism—was understandable enough. A sizable portion of modern philosophers had slighted the problem of death, regarding all attempts to tackle it as an outcome of unreflective anxiety, and hence as a philosophically worthless undertaking. It seemed therefore quite pertinent to arouse the opposite feeling, and to try to convince so-called "philosophical deflationists"—the ones, that is, who denounce all talk except their own as a case of "philosophical inflation"—that the problem of death is a truly significant one. But once existential-minded thinkers had performed their task, it was no longer necessary to aggravate the philosophers' anxieties. For philosophers at least, the age of anxiety is over; the age of critique is here again.

We shall proceed then according to the new times, and treat death as an authentically philosophical problem. We shall do it, however, against a somewhat larger background than that set up by existential or semi-existential philosophers. Furthermore, we shall single out the problem of death as no more, but no less, than a guiding thread for philosophical exploration.

Throughout the centuries, countless human beings have sought and, occasionally, found solutions to the "problem of death" in magic, religion, and myth. Magic is today out of the question. But religious and mythical conceptions are still very much alive. At least with respect to one question—the question of whether there is or is not a survival after human death—

mythical narrations and religious feelings still play a significant role. Nevertheless, although I may at times touch upon them, I will be particularly, if not exclusively, concerned with the philosophical *concept* of death. Hence I will not dwell upon the much talked about question of the "feeling of death," an intriguing problem no doubt, and one that has a long history behind it, but one which, nevertheless, would be of little help in strict philosophical elucidation. Philosophy is not necessarily alien to "feelings," but it should be careful not to be ruled by them. On a philosopher's door, the following sign may not be unwelcome: "Feelings are accepted (sometimes recommended), but only if they help to understand."

Some philosophers stubbornly shun any statements even vaguely hinting at rational analysis or scientific procedure. What can rational analysis and scientific method teach us philosophers, they argue, about such an "irrational," "mysterious," and "unscientific" problem as that of death? I strongly disagree with such quibbling, and what I say throughout this book will, I hope, testify to my disagreement. On the other hand, some philosophers embrace the opposite viewpoint: they scoff at any statement about death which happens to be a more or less mature fruit of human experience or speculative reflection. I disagree no less strongly with the latter contentions, for I do not think that we can so easily dispense with such a rich source of knowledge as human experience and "speculation." In sharp contrast with all these prejudiced and, at bottom, nihilistic attitudes, I have tried to pay heed both to reason and human experience, to analysis and speculation. Only by bringing all of them together shall we be able to cast some light on our subject. As a consequence of this integrating or, as it will soon appear, "integrationist" viewpoint, I have also bypassed two quite similar tendencies. There are those who hold that the problem of death is meaningless. On the other hand, there are those who think that only the problem of death has some meaning. I myself believe that the problem of death has a very definite meaning, but that it is far from being the only philosophical problem enjoying this sinecure. It is one philosophical problem among many, but one which is central enough to make the philosophical wheels turn swiftly.

It has often been said that only in the twentieth century, and in particular after the first World War, have philosophers shown any interest in the problem of death. This is not absolutely true. Death has been a subject for meditation both in "Dark Ages" and in self-styled "Enlightened Ages." Yet, there is some truth in saying that many modern philosophers shunned death as a philosophical problem insofar as they tried to circumvent it. In particular, the so-called "mechanical philosophers," or "mechanists," tried to prove that "death" is more an "appearance" than a "reality." Reacting against "mechanists," and their efforts to eliminate the problem of death, some authors launched systems according to which nothing "mechanical" ever seems to exist, or happen, in the universe. Some of these authors went very far indeed. Not only were they opposed to the idea that the universe is comparable to a clock, but they argued that it is comparable to an organism—or even perhaps to a "Spirit" or a "Soul." Against the thesis that Mind reduces to Nature, they advanced the idea that Nature ultimately reduces to Mind. Thus the door was left open for every variety of uncontrolled speculation. For these "speculative philosophers," it did not seem enough to reject, as Kant did, dogmatic rationalism. They did not stop at anything short of a boisterous irrationalism. Some of these philosophers found it utterly insufficient to point out that, when all is considered, biological organisms or human persons are not inorganic entities. This would be equivalent to yielding to a dualism, which these philosophers staunchly (and rightly) rejected. Thus, they tried to bridge the gap between the world of Nature—with all its "mechanical" properties—and the world of Mind—with all its "spiritual" characteristics, but they based their attempt on one of the following controversial assumptions: either they "constructed" the world of Nature on the basis of the world of Mind, and thus reduced the former to the latter, or else they advanced the idea that there is some kind of entity—"the Absolute," "the Idea"—which underlies both Mind and Nature. To these philosophers death was not an "appearance" but a "reality." Yet, it was a reality that had very little, if anything, to do with Nature—an "unnatural" reality. Thus, whereas some philosophers maintained that, properly speaking, there is no such thing as death, other philosophers intimated that there is nothing "natural" in it.

The above is a rather sweeping description of an embarrassingly complex affair called the "history of modern philosophy." All-encompassing as it is, however, my description serves a purpose, which is to show that, although neither side was completely right, neither side was hopelessly wrong. The present book tries to do justice to both sides without necessarily subscribing to either. Thus, the critique of mechanism contained in chapter 1 is not to be construed as an attack on "materialists" similar to those launched by romantic and postromantic idealists, especially those who have been labeled "spiritualists." It is my belief that mechanism as a philosophy plays no negligible role in the understanding of certain types of reality. It is only fair to add that phenomenalism, organicism, personalism, and other such similar doctrines also play a role in the understanding of at least some aspects of "Being." Each one of these views is, therefore, welcome on the philosophical stage provided that it makes its appearance "on cue." To ascertain the propitious moment is, of course, not an easy matter, but one that no philosopher should consider irrelevant. In some ways, a good philosopher is one who knows when to give (or follow) the right cue.

The view according to which many, but not necessarily all, views can be combined without too much friction is one that I hope to develop in some detail. An intimation of it, however, can be glimpsed in chapter 1. It appears there primarily in the form of an ontology which I have termed "integrationism." It consists roughly in postulating that all absolutes, or all "absolute entities," whether they are called "Nature" or "Spirit," "Object" or "Consciousness," should be given a long, and hopefully permanent, vacation. I am talking about entities, not about names of entities. For I feel confident that the latter can still be used to function as "limiting concepts," so that they may describe, although not refer to, "limiting realities." These "limiting realities," which I will sometimes label "polarities," are, indeed, only limiting; they are not realities at all. What is real is only what exists, lives, and moves "between polarities," without ever being transformed into any of them, that is, without ever being petrified, so to speak, into "absolutes." From this viewpoint it makes sense to say that nothing exists as "pure matter." By the same token, nothing is (philosophically) acceptable as "pure mind." There is no such thing as subject or object. And since it is assumed that nothing exists "absolutely" or, more precisely, that nothing is "an Absolute," the predicates 'is mechanical' and 'is organic' must not be construed as "absolute predicates." Yet, there is a sense in which one could say that these predicates may refer to something actually existing: this is the case when they are used to qualify, in terms of "more" or "less," any entities, or classes of entities. From this viewpoint we can claim that some entities are "more material" or "less material," "more organic" or "less organic," "more conscious" or "less conscious" than other entities.

All this may look surprising, if not downright scandalous; if X is material, certainly it is not conscious, and if X is conscious, it is not, or is not necessarily, material. And if X is both material and conscious, then it *is* material and conscious, but not "more so" or "less so."

I admit that the point is tricky. At any rate, it is not a point that can be adequately elucidated with one stroke of the pen. The present book contains many such strokes, and does not claim to do much more than to try to *see* the point. But, although sweeping formulas do little justice to subtle points, I may be allowed here to put forth a few formulas as an *avant-goût* of more to come.

To begin with, the expressions 'more' and 'less' obviously have no quantitative meaning. To say that X is more material than Y is not to say that X contains "more matter" than Y. It is only to say that X is more of the nature of a material reality than Y. 'More' and 'less' are thus used here as "ontological adverbs," modifying or qualifying reality and making a given reality a "way of being." Therefore, we should not say, even if sometimes we cannot help saying, that X *is* this or that, because, properly speaking, X is never this or that. It merely displays some (ontological) "tendency" to behave the way "this" or "that" would behave if they existed absolutely. Thus to say that X is more material than Y means that X "tends to be" more material than Y. To be sure, the "tendency" I am talking about has nothing to do with any irrepressible urge supposedly felt by X. 'Tending to be material' is not equivalent to 'longing to be material.' It is just "to be" in the way of "being more so." Nor is the tendency in question something like a "becoming." Indeed, I am not talking now about "being" or "becoming," for it happens that "being" and "becoming" are themselves to be construed as "absolutes," and as such they are not allowed to exist or to be exemplified by any given entities. Only because language behaves the way it does must we resign ourselves to saying that X "is" or "becomes" without really meaning it.

Thus, I certainly do not mean to say that, if X happens to be a lump of matter, X is not material because X may partake of consciousness. I am not intimating that matter is mind and mind is matter, or in general that anything is everything. If X is a lump of matter, and this is all that there is to X, then X is obviously not conscious. But denying consciousness to X is still viewing X, or being able to view X, from the point of view of consciousness. X thus falls somewhere *between* two contrasting ontological poles or directions, so that it may be more precisely located in terms of its proximity to one pole and its distance from the other. In fine, X is located at the intersection of two ontological "poles," which are referred to as "matter" and "consciousness" (or "mind"). If such were not the case, then "being material" and "being conscious" would not be possible features of one single world. They would be names of predicates designating two mutually exclusive realms of being. In other words, to say that X is a material entity is, for the moment, to say no more than that it has a place in a real continuum in such a way that 'is material' proves to be the best possible (general) predicate for X.

Since, as suggested earlier, there is more to come, I shall drop the issue here. I would like to add, however, that inherent in the integrationist view just outlined is an integrationist methodology. Roughly, it consists of substituting names of limiting concepts for names of absolute entities. For, although the former names do not in fact name anything, they can "delimit" everything. I use the expression 'names of limiting concepts' and, more briefly, 'concepts,' in the plural form because it is my view that no single concept can ever perform the "integrating" task. Furthermore, concepts cannot perform this task unless they are conjoined *as* opposites—which does not necessarily mean that they are in fact opposites, but only that they should function as such. Thus, 'matter' and 'mind' function here as names of opposite or, at least, contrasting, concepts, and the same may be said about any other concept of similar scope and character. I hold that only by handling opposing limiting concepts can any given reality be "located" ontologically and thus grasped conceptually. As will be seen later (§ 9), any given entity, or class of entities, can be (ontologically) "delimited" by means of two contrasting conceptualizations or, in the language which I will eventually propose, by means of a two-way ontology. And, since a number of relevant philosophical positions have emphasized just one conceptualization, the doctrine of actual integration sketched above may be better understood in the light of a doctrine of conceptual integration. All this is, I assume, quite different from a mere "philosophy of polarity," which is at best a well-meaning eclecticism. "Integrationism," as I understand it, does not limit itself to combining polar concepts or to harmonizing mutually hostile philosophies by arguing, for instance, that only in such a way will each philosophical tendency receive its due. It does not matter to me in the least if any given philosophical tendency can harmoniously combine with any other philosophical tendency. I am not weighing the merits of, say, naturalism and personalism, merely to conclude that both systems have something to say that is true or enlightening, so that some "third system" can then be set up which would be nothing but the sum total of what is borrowed from each one. This type of manipulation of doctrines, which treats doctrines as if they were mere "positions" and looks at them, so to speak, from the outside, never makes much progress. My aim is rather to see whether there is any "third position" or, rather, "conceptual system," which might prove capable of accounting for whatever mutually exclusive—or seemingly mutually exclusive —tendencies may eventually arise. This explains why I do not think it fair to take up, say, a bit of materialism and a bit of personalism, or a bit of mechanism and a bit of organicism, and concoct some sort of philosophical pudding with them. These puddings, made with only the best ingredients, are too good to be true. Even W. H. Sheldon, who, more than any other contemporary philosopher, emphasized "polarity" and "productive dualism," had to acknowledge that what we may call "combinatorial philosophic systems" are satisfactory only because they are "too satisfactory." "They are pervaded," Sheldon rightly noticed, "by an almost saccharine flavour." It is not then a question of "harmony," and least of all a question of harmony among philosophical *tendencies*. It is rather a question of testing to the utmost the adequacy of contrasting explanatory *concepts*. Thus, for instance, if we tackle the problem of whether relations are internal or external, the viewpoint I propose is not based upon the position that relations are both internal and external, or that some are internal and some are external. Rather, it consists in denying that relations can ever be internal or external *in toto*. It makes little difference, although granted it may make some, for an atom to be in this or that point in space (assuming, for the sake of simplification, that there are "spatial points"). Hence an atom is, or rather, tends to be externally related to other atoms. But it makes a great deal of difference, although not all the difference, for a relatively complex organic being to be in this or that point of space, since being in this or that point of space is then definable in terms of organic behavior (such as mating, falling upon a prey, or adjusting to the environment). Thus an organic being is, or rather, tends to be internally related to other organic beings and to the biological milieu. Therefore, in the two-way "direction" of relations, there are points in which the "direction" called "internal relation" almost overcomes the "direction" called "external relation," and vice versa, without the relations ever being, for any given entity, completely internal or completely external. This is, of course, just one example, but I hope it may suffice. If names are still necessary to characterize my philosophical viewpoint, I would then prefer such names as "principle of complementarity" rather than "principle of polarity," provided that 'complementarity' be understood both as conceptual and as real.

It may, of course, be said, that there is nothing really new in an attempt to integrate contrasting concepts, and that an attempt was made by such philosophers as Leibniz and Hegel, not to mention Aristotle. To this I would retort that nothing would please me more than to be able to do what any of these philosophical giants did. But the question is not what kind of an attempt I am proposing, but how it is carried out. Philosophy is not, or should not, be a "program," but the real thing. Thus, I will soon stop talking about what it is that I am trying to do in order to spend more time in actually doing it.

Nevertheless, a few more remarks on the meaning of 'integrationism' may still be in order. And at any rate I would like to add that, although the term 'to integrate' may evoke ideas of "harmony" or "combination," it is a rather unorthodox type of harmony or combination that I have in mind. To begin with, if philosophical tendencies are still considered, I do not propose to string them together but to give each free rein. Let us then, if necessary, carry naturalism, or personalism, or any such philosophical position, to its ultimate consequences. We shall eventually see where it must stop. I was tempted to say that each of them has to stop where the other one starts, but this would still be a one-way ontology of the eclectic type. Thus, I prefer to say that a position does not have to stop but is counteracted all along by some opposite position. The two positions are maintained as opposed. If one comes to the rescue of the other, it is neither to replace the other nor to supplement the other, but to use the other as a brake.

If we now abandon, as I wish we might forever, the language of "philosophical doctrines" and resume the language of "ontological poles," "conceptualizations," "limiting concepts," and so on, I may add that the integrationism I advocate is one in which no given "ontological pole" is even conceivable without the opposing "pole," and also one in which no limiting concept has any great meaning unless it begins by taking the opposite limiting concept into account.

If 'dialectic' had not become a term of abuse, I would have no objection to accepting it as a tentative label for the way of thinking proposed above. In the present state of affairs, however, the term 'dialectic' might seem a misnomer, because it tends to suggest that I am advancing a point of view based upon synthesis rather than one founded on integration. But there is not, in my opinion, any possible synthesis overcoming a so-called "thesis" and a so-called "antithesis." In my "system," theses and antitheses never cease interfering with each other; there is no moment, no point, where one of them is reduced to the other or, in the Hegelian language, "absorbed" by the other. In any given point at issue, there is a "thesis" that is, so to speak, "crossed" by an "antithesis"; any given point at issue is a kind of conceptual crossroads. By now, I hope it is no longer necessary to emphasize that the conceptual crossroads is such only because a real crossroads is constantly underlying it.

I have proposed the term 'integrationism' as an adequate label to describe my way of thinking. I insist on the word 'label' because I am perfectly aware that 'integrationism' does little more than tag a cluster of concepts. Like most philosophers, I am suspicious of 'isms.' They say both too little and too much. Moreover, what they say is usually misleading. I see no reason, however, for abstaining from using a term ending in 'ism' as long as we do not delude ourselves by believing that this is the end of the story. Once this caution has been taken, 'isms' can do no great harm. This is, by the way, the reason why I would like to propose yet another 'ism': "dialectical empiricism." By means of this expression I am trying to suggest that the way of thinking also labeled "integrationism" is one that is faithful both to the structure of reality and to the logic of concepts. But of labels and tags enough has been said.

As to the problem of death, 'integrationism' is meant to designate a point of view according to which we should not be allowed to confine "death" to any privileged area of reality but only to project whatever we can say about this area to the whole of reality. What Aristotle claimed of Being, we can claim of death, namely, that "it can be said in many ways." Thus, I wish to maintain that, although every existing entity ceases to be, and hence in a manner of speaking, "dies," only certain entities actually "die" without ever "ceasing to be." In fine: the continuum of reality includes different types of "mortality." Which specific kind of "mortality" we are facing at a given point depends upon how, and where, two different and opposing ontological "directions" may happen to intersect.

The present book is, I dare to say, both systematic and speculative. It is systematic because the main ideas contained in it are closely knit together within the framework of a conceptual system, and in particular within the framework of a "first philosophy." It is speculative simply because it is philosophical. I am not afraid of being systematic, because I heartily agree with Kant that philosophy should be a system and not a rhapsody. I am not afraid of being speculative, because I see no other way of doing philosophy. I often wonder what other philosophers do who claim that they do not "speculate."

But to be systematic and speculative does not necessarily mean to be reckless. By no means do I want to suggest that all the concepts I use denote a reality. Thus, although I constantly use such expressions as 'inorganic reality,' 'organic reality,' 'being,' 'life,' and so on, I am not assuming that there are such "things." Why then use these and similar expressions? Here is a question that can be answered only by pointing out what happens when one begins to philosophize. All sorts of strange things do indeed occur. For instance, one finds ordinary language most inadequate, and yet one cannot dispense with it. Similarly, one looks around, or perhaps inside, in search of a philosophical language, and finds that there is none. Finally, one begins twisting the meaning of ordinary words while claiming that everyone else, especially other philosophers, have been using these words in the wrong way. No wonder philosophers, even the least rash and adventurous among them, have never had a good press. How could the case be otherwise with people who never say, or for that matter never succeed in saying, what they "really mean," and who, furthermore, constantly claim to have said "something else"? As if that were not enough, philosophers are repeatedly misunderstood by their own colleagues. It would be difficult to find a philosopher who has not been the target of distorted, and often devious, interpretations on the part of other philosophers. Thus let us not waste time complaining. But let us remind the reader that in philosophy there is necessarily more than just one meaning. If there were such a thing as a ready-made philosophical language, misunderstandings could be avoided. But then philosophy would not be what it is: an attempt to create its own language. This attempt usually fails, but in the meantime something is born: let us call it the "philosophical habit." It is a most peculiar habit, since it makes sense only to those who indulge in it, and, furthermore, to those who do indulge in it, it is the only habit that makes sense. So this is philosophy: something that, if done at all, simply cannot be done by halves.

ONE

Death in Inorganic Nature

1
QUAESTIO DE NOMINE

The use of the term 'death' to designate or describe any process in the course of which something is said to pass away, may cause many misunderstandings. Of course, oaks, gazelles, and men die. But can it also be said that civilizations or artistic styles "die"? In one sense, yes; there is nothing which prohibits the use of such terms as 'to die,' 'death,' 'dead,' and so forth in ordinary speech. 'John is dead,' 'A dead squirrel was found this morning,' 'Cubism is dead,' 'It has been discovered that the moon is not a dead satellite,' and other similar expressions are easily grasped by anyone who does not care too much what they "really mean."

But what is obvious in the language of Everybody becomes highly problematical in the more sophisticated language of philosophers. Within the rarefied atmosphere of philosophical discussion commonplace statements become hopelessly muddled utterances. Hence interminable clarifications are as indispensable to philosophers as they are tedious to plain citizens. The examples: "John is dead" and "A dead squirrel was found this morning" illustrate only too plainly the need to clarify the meaning of 'dead' in each instance. We may explain that 'dead' means exactly the same in both cases, because there is no fundamental difference between John and the squirrel; or we may claim that 'dead' means something quite different in each case because John, on the one hand, has or had, something immortal within him, while the squirrel is as mortal as any other soulless creature. In any event we must try to avoid misunderstandings which arise from a too literal interpretation of a casual manner of speaking. Now, misunderstandings can be avoided when we carefully point out what we "really mean" or, still better, when we proceed to translate any given expression into a hopefully more precise language.

The need for "translation" is specially urgent when 'to die,' 'dead,' and so forth are used in ways which might plunge philosophers into perplexities. For example, the sentence 'Cubism is dead' ceases to be a source of philosophical misunderstanding when we translate it into 'Cubism no longed exerts any detectable influence.' 'It has been discovered that the moon is not a dead satellite' is clear enough when we change it into, for instance, 'Phenomena of volcanic origin have been observed on the moon.' Many other, similar examples could be presented which would illustrate the need for clarification or translation so that philosophical misunderstandings would not raise their ugly heads.

Must we then follow in the steps of Wittgenstein, and conclude that there is little in common among the uses of 'to die,' 'death,' 'dead' and other such words? Are there, at best, only vague similarities, mere "family resemblances," in their various uses? No doubt this is so in a number of cases. To equate 'is dead' in 'John is dead' with 'is dead' in 'The moon is dead,' as if such a predicate described some feature common to both John and the moon, would be somewhat far-fetched. Yet, "family resemblances" do not always have to be vague. To emphasize such likenesses we can limit the range of our vocabulary by assuming that words such as 'death,' 'to die,' and so forth can be used properly only within certain clearly specified, or specifiable, conditions.

These conditions can be summarized as follows: the terms 'to die,' 'dead,' 'death,' and so on should be used only to describe the behavior of existent entities. Therefore, they should not be used to describe, or denote, the so-called "death" of political institutions, civilizations, literary genres, and the like, but should only refer to the death of human beings, biological organisms, and inorganic entities. *Death in Nature* would be a fairly adequate title for the present book, provided that the term 'Nature' were understood in an ample sense and provided further that human beings could be exhaustively described as natural beings.

We have thus restricted the range of application of the words in question, but not sufficiently to eradicate all misunderstandings. Although we may speak in the same breath of the death of human beings and the death of biological organisms, it seems less adequate to say that inorganic realities "die." In view of this new risk of misunderstanding, we could do at least one of the following: set up a linguistic convention which would reduce misconceptions to a reasonable minimum, or else rule out inorganic entities altogether.

The first rule is easy enough to follow. Thus, we could use the verb 'to decease' when referring to the "passing away" of human beings; the verb 'to die' when describing the end of organic realities other than human; and possibly the verb 'to dissolve' (or 'to disintegrate') when designating the fact that a given inorganic entity no longer exists. Then, if we wanted to emphasize that nevertheless all these forms of "ceasing" have something in common, we could adopt a somewhat "neutral" expression—such as 'to cease' or 'to terminate'—when describing each and every one of the above processes. Hence the title

Being and Ceasing might be more to the point than *Being and Death*.

Unfortunately, however, adoption of the above rule would defeat one of the purposes I had in mind in writing this book, namely, the attempt to prove that there is one sense of 'death' (or, if preferred, of 'dying') which applies to all existent entities, whether inorganic, organic, or human. I intend to set up a theory which, because of its similarities with Aristotle's doctrine of *analogia entis,* could be called the "doctrine of *analogia mortis"*—a doctrine according to which "death can be said in many (although not too many) ways." Now the proposed analogy would lose its cohesion if we chose a more "neutral" term than 'death,' a term which, moreover, would not intimate much more than the trivial concurrence that everything has an end. Therefore, I have decided in favor of a more controversial, albeit a more incisive general, term to denote the process of the "ceasing" or "passing away" of any existing entity. Thus I will retain the title *Being and Death* even if it is not yet adequately justified.

The above proposed dismissal of all inorganic entities is, I suspect, an error rather than a useful device, for it would irrevocably sever the links of man with Nature in general, or even those of man with reality. Thus the real continuum, of which I spoke earlier, would be split into at least two entirely different and perhaps mutually exclusive realms. It may be argued that no matter how much we proceed to split the real continuum, it will never stop being a continuum of sorts. Thus some philosophers will contend that every conceivable reality, whether existent or not, finite or infinite, is included in or supported by "Being," which is nothing in particular, simply because it is everything insofar as it is. Other philosophers will point out that if A is said to be unrelated to B, this does not dispense with all relations, but produces a most intriguing type of relation: the relation called "unrelated to." I cannot now counter these proposals with the courtesy they deserve, but will claim that the meaning I give to 'real continuum' is somewhat stronger than the meaning of 'Being,' and certainly much stronger than the meaning of 'related by lack of relation.' But the meaning of 'real continuum' has not yet been disclosed, although I have hopes that it will eventually come to light.

The above comments, although mostly linguistic, serve to circumscribe the subject of this book. At any rate, they are not entirely useless, since questions about words often, if not always, lead to questions about things. When one listens to problems of language with a philosophic ear they rarely become merely verbal disputations, for what matters in philosophy is not so much the words as the concepts embodied in them. Philosophers are not lexicographers but rather, if the word is permitted, "conceptographers": they deal with concepts even when they seem to be fascinated only by words.

These comments, however, are insufficient to ascertain the nature of the problem tackled here. This is not at all surprising, since the nature of the problem can only be disclosed in the process of its development. Hurried readers may find it gratifying to learn from the very outset what they are going to read about. Unfortunately, philosophical books are not meant for hurried readers. In any case, only patient readers will be able to put up with a book like the present one which uses a method more "circular" than "linear," and speaks more *in fabrica* than *ex cathedra*.

2
SOME PRELIMINARY DIFFICULTIES

Let us still keep in mind the disputed question of whether or not it is proper to use such terms as 'to die,' 'death,' and so forth when referring to all existing realities, including inorganic realities. I have previously assumed that such usage is adequate, but I am aware that this assumption encounters a number of difficulties.

Experience shows that inorganic entities change and eventually stop being what they once were. A given inorganic entity, E, exhibits a certain structure in virtue of which it is identified as E. But at a given time, it may happen that this structure, and hence E itself, no longer exists. For example, E may have been composed of a certain number of parts which have gradually worn away. We say then that E has ceased to be E, or is in the process of ceasing to be E. At any rate, E no longer performs as it did before, so that there is, in fact, no E. There remains, at most, the idea that E had existed, which may mean various things: that E *was* a subject of causal relations, that E *was* an object of (actual or possible) experience, and so on.

The above statements about E describe what happens, or can happen, or has happened to E in point of fact. Do they also describe what happens, can happen, or has happened to E as a matter of principle? Can't the worn-out parts of E be replaced? Let us consider a machine. The friction among the component parts, the changes in temperature, the erosion produced in some elements by surrounding objects, the molecular arrangements —all these comprise but a few of the many factors which conspire against the possibility that such a machine could last forever. On the other hand, we know that the machine can be repaired, not once but many times. And the case is the same, at least in principle, with all physical objects, whether they are "natural individuals" (such as a mountain, a star), "conventional individuals" (such as a piece of rock, a handful of dust), or man-made objects (such as an engine, a house). All these objects are constantly changing, and in this process of change they will cease to be what they are. The question now arises to what extent such changes, and even the final cessation, can be considered necessary. One way or another, we surmise that these objects could, *in principle,* persist indefinitely.

Let us now suppose that, all things considered, inorganic entities or, as we will also call them, "physical objects," not only change and, in the end, "disappear" *de facto,* but also change and "disappear" *in principio*. Then it would be quite pertinent to ask what the predicates 'change' and 'disappear' mean. The concept of change is not easily grasped but, for the time being at least, it should not present an insurmountable obstacle. Our entity, E, was so-and-so (for example, big, yellow, hard), and it is now so-and-so (for example, small, blue, soft). In brief, E possessed a number of properties which it no longer exhibits; yet it is now exhibiting a different set of properties without ceasing to be E. We may then assume that there have been changes *in* E, and that there is a sufficient reason to account for these changes, so that, although E is no longer how it was, it is still what it was.

Now what about the predicate 'disappears'? To say that E has "disappeared" is tantamount to saying that what we continue to call "E" no longer exists. If E is, as assumed earlier, a physical object, does that mean that instead of E there is nothing? This is scarcely credible, since although E may now be nowhere, somewhere there must be something instead of E. E could very well be replaced by F, or by G, H, or I; the parts that gave E its distinguishing characteristics may now, properly rearranged, be parts of F, and thus constitute F, or they may be distributed among G, H, or I. It would seem then that the predicate 'disappears,' or more exactly, 'has disappeared,' or any such similar predicates as applied to a physical object, should be used with caution, if not eliminated altogether. In fine, we may now wonder whether there is *something* in inorganic reality which never ceases to exist. If such were the case, then there would be *something* in inorganic reality that does not change at all. And if the meaning of the expression 'inorganic reality' is related to the existence of that "something," then such predicates as 'ceases to be,' 'disappears,' and, for that matter, 'changes' should be discarded from our vocabulary. This means, of course, that the expression 'inorganic reality ceases,' let alone the expression 'inorganic reality dies,' would have no meaning at all. If so, then we would do better to throw both of them into a philosophical dungeon and never summon them hither.

3
SCIENCE AND PHILOSOPHY: A DIGRESSION

Before taking any drastic steps in that direction, however, we should clarify the meaning of 'inorganic nature,' as well as the meaning of expressions such as 'inorganic entity,' 'physical object,' 'physical process,' and others used as specifications of the former. This is by no means an easy task. It cannot be undertaken without outlining—or at least presupposing—a "philosophy of Nature," and it is well known that this field of philosophy swarms with pitfalls.

A basic question must be raised: "What formally constitutes inorganic reality?" The term 'formally' is intended to intimate that, even though we may arrive at a formal definition of 'inorganic reality,' we do not claim that such a definition should serve as a starting point for any scientific investigation, for that would not be in keeping with current practice. But then we are obliged to face the problem of what kind of relations, if any, exist between the philosophical approach and the scientific approach.

It is my opinion that in certain areas of knowledge philosophy and science are closely related. How they are related is the point in question. Certainly they are not related in such a way that one is simply the foundation of the other. Scientific statements are not deducible from philosophic statements. Nor does philosophy arise from a generalization of scientific results. Philosophy and science are related in more subtle ways. But before presenting my case, a few words about some contrasting opinions on this issue may be in order.

Kant wrote that "the true method of metaphysics is at bottom identical to the method introduced by Newton in natural science where it has been of such fruitful consequences."[1] Similarly,

Franz Brentano proclaimed that "the true method of philosophy is none other than that of the natural sciences." [2] Both of these statements clearly express the opinion that philosophical reflection should be patterned on the model of scientific inquiry. In this respect, it matters little that neither Kant nor Brentano ever practiced what they preached. For it is well known that their philosophies never even came close to being branches of natural science, either in content or in method. But we are concerned here with an opinion about the relationship between philosophy and science and not with the question of whether certain philosophers ever put into practice the opinions they expressed.

Regarding the above view, Ortega y Gasset wrote that "modern philosophy has been looking in two different directions: it has looked at Reality while casting sidelong glances at what the sciences have to say about Reality. And since it is normal for a science to use an extremely precise language, philosophy has often become envious of science, and has struggled to become a science itself." [3] At first, mathematics was the model for philosophy, while physics later played this role. Still later some other science, or would-be science, from biology to history, exerted a similar fascination for philosophy. It would seem, however, that on account of its enormous impact on the modern mind, physics has been the science most frequently emulated. Opposing this trend, Ortega y Gasset claimed that "the method of philosophy is, in the last analysis, more or less contrary to that of physics." [4] This uncompromising statement cannot be watered down by the remark that Ortega y Gasset probably did not mean what he said. Nor can it be contemptously dismissed by the claim that Ortega y Gasset was, after all, a metaphysician who also happened to be a "Latin philosopher." For one thing, Ortega y Gasset was far from being only a metaphysician. And as for being a "Latin philosopher," this is to say next to nothing. In fact, Oxonians and neo-Wittgensteinians, who are not supposed to be "Latin philosophers," seem to be even bolder than Ortega y Gasset in this respect; at any rate, they actually do what Ortega y Gasset merely suggested should be done.

The opinion that I wish to defend cannot be expressed as simply as any of the preceding statements. What I want to say may seem paradoxical: (1) Philosophy is not necessarily connected with science; (2) philosophy is actually related to science; (3) philosophy must develop its own perspective; (4) philosophy cannot adequately develop its own perspective unless this perspective can somehow be integrated with that of science.

Since the first contention is in conflict with the second, and the third is in conflict with the fourth, I will consider these two sets of conflicting statements separately.

Philosophy is not necessarily connected with science. Its independence is shown by the fact that at one time philosophy flourished although science, at least in the modern sense of the word, did not then exist. On the other hand, philosophy is actually related to science, insofar as we are still deeply immersed in the historical period in which both philosophy and science exist side by side. This coexistence of philosophy with science is a fact. We may deplore this state of affairs, but there is little we can do about it. Since it is improbable that science will become obsolete within the foreseeable future, it seems that philosophers will have to put up with what Kant called the "*factum* of science" for a long time to come.

That philosophy must develop its own perspective should be obvious to anyone who does not believe that "philosophy" is just a bad habit or a well-entrenched illusion. If philosophy cannot develop its own perspective it will be completely destroyed or, what amounts to the same thing, it will become fused with some other way of thinking, scientific or otherwise.

The nature of the philosophical perspective is, of course, difficult to describe. Philosophers have tried unsuccessfully to elucidate it for more than two thousand years. They are still trying. It would be too much, therefore, to ask for a definitive word on the subject. But a few hints may help put things into focus.

1. A philosophical perspective is not meant to produce a special object, or kind of object, and hence it does not have a specific and irreducible "subject matter." Thus, the philosophical perspective is obviously different from any other kind of perspective which in every case is determined by a specific object.

2. Some philosophers have argued that it is their task to work with "orginal data" or to view reality as coexisting with the consciousness of it, whereas it is the task of scientists to operate with "derived data," with "previously constructed (or assumed) entities," and so on.[5] But this argument has two flaws. On the one hand, I find it difficult to admit that "original data" are realities of a kind different from the realities which we acknowledge as such. On the other hand, if there were realities of this special type, sooner or later they would fall within the scope of one of the sciences and would, therefore, cease to be philosophical objects at all.

3. A philosophical perspective must, therefore, be one which does not aim at or focus upon any particular object, no matter how basic that object may seem. A philosophical perspective aims at all objects from a single point of view—a point of view which cannot be compared with any other because it is a point of view on points of view. One of the latter is what is ordinarily called "science." Thus, insofar as science is here to stay, philosophy cannot simply dismiss it. It is in this sense that the philosophical perspective, as suggested earlier, can somehow be integrated with that of science.

4. Philosophical problems in respect to science normally occur when questions about the nature of physical objects, physical processes, and so on, are raised. These questions are raised in the first place when science, or a branch of science, is undergoing the stage often called "a crisis of foundations." When such a crisis is acute enough, it is not even necessary to

inquire whether philosophers are concerned with science, or scientists with philosophy. Scientists themselves are doing philosophy no matter what they think that they are doing, provided, of course, that they are *thinking* about science.[6] We should not assume, however, that once the "crisis" is over, science will be happily purged of philosophy, and will become, at long last, "itself." 'Crisis of foundations' is not an expression designating a particular stage in the development of science; it is an expression designating what science is when it is actually being made.

5. A philosophical perspective is necessarily a universal perspective, and thus instead of relinquishing science it strives to relate science with other ways of looking at, or even acting upon, "what there is." Being universal, the philosophical perspective is not a "subjective view." It is certainly not a collection of subjective impressions and feelings more or less skillfully justified and rationalized. Yet, philosophy is at the same time a personal affair in the sense that a philosopher cannot help committing himself to his own activity as a philosopher. Being personal, the philosophical perspective is not an "objective view." One might now ask how a view can be neither subjective nor objective, and yet at the same time be both universal and personal. There is only one answer: the philosophical activity, and thus the philosophical perspective that it yields is based upon a personal commitment to universality. In his thinking, a philosopher reflects a world which happens to be his own personal world with the hope that this personal world is just *the* world.[7] "*The* world as viewed by *a* person" may be an adequate formula to describe the nature of the philosophical perspective.

The aim of this digression has been to show that mere lack of information does not further philosophy. If it did, things would be wonderful; it would suffice for a philosopher to be as ignorant as possible. When questions, such as those raised in this book, are related to scientific ways of thinking, it would be impertinent to dismiss the latter by claiming not only that philosophy is a world by itself—which is certainly true—but also, and above all, that it is a world completely apart from all others—which is utterly false. Thus, the philosophical reflections which will follow do not claim to be a summary of scientific views. If such were the case, philosophy would not have its own perspective. On the other hand, we will not dismiss as irrelevant for the problems here discussed a reference to, and an eventual analysis of, some scientific concepts, for otherwise we would run the risk of outlining a "philosophy of Nature" which would deal with any reality except the natural reality.

4
SOME THESES ON INORGANIC REALITY

Let us now go back to our question: What formally constitutes inorganic reality? This type of reality can be variously defined. We can assume, for example, that it is made up of "objects" —physical objects which are located in the space-time continuum or which can be, as it has sometimes been suggested, "singularities," "holes," or even "discrete pulsations" in such a continuum. We can also assume that it is made up of "phenomena" of the kind often described as "neutral," and hence never completely physical nor entirely mental, being only "sides" or "aspects" of "the given." These two views have been labeled "physicalism" and "phenomenalism" respectively. Despite some claims to the contrary, neither view is free from ontological commitments. Thus, each one can be taken as a set of theses on the nature of inorganic reality and on the nature of reality in general. Nevertheless, the primary concern of either physicalism or phenomenalism is epistemological. Rather than saying something about what there is, physicalism and phenomenalism say something about how we know, or can know, what there is.

Now, although ontological questions cannot be entirely separated from epistemological queries, I shall temporarily quarantine the latter. At present I am less concerned about "how to know" or about "how to talk about what we know" than about what it is that is supposed to be known. Therefore, I will disregard the concepts framed by both physicalists and phenomenalists, and will consider instead three pairs of concepts whose ontological import overshadows whatever epistemological significance they may still retain.

The three pairs of concepts in question are: matter and form; substance and mode; process and entity. These concepts have been developed primarily by philosophers and occasionally by philosopher-scientists. They are considered to be concepts endowed with a substantial explanatory power, and also concepts summarizing a number of scientific methods or theories prevalent in various historical periods. The concepts of matter and form, as developed mainly by Aristotle, are both "physical" —at least in Aristotle's sense of 'physical'—and "metaphysical." But in either case they are intended to explain the nature and basic behavior of natural objects. The concepts of substance and mode, as they will be treated here, have been developed by a host of philosophers throughout the modern age, mostly in order to clothe some influential physical notions in metaphysical garb, but also to give physical meaning to some metaphysical assumptions. The concepts of process and entity are of more recent date. They have been upheld as a "neutral" way of conceptualizing reality, as well as an expression of a "functionalist" reaction against "substantialism," which has been decried as "too metaphysical," and even "too grammatical," being, as it were, a conceptual leftover from the Indo-European syntax with its emphasis on the "subject-predicate relation."

These three pairs of concepts are germane to three tendencies in natural philosophy: hylomorphism, substantialism, and processualism. As often happens with tendencies of such a scope, each one of them covers a variety of doctrines. Thus, for instance, although processualism can be defined as "a tendency which emphasizes the notion of process and views all entities as processual singularities"—or something along these lines—it varies considerably depending upon how the term 'process' is understood. On the one hand, we can understand 'process' from the point of view of a relational complex, and thus obtain a "relationalism," such as that developed by Ernst Cassirer. On the other hand, we can understand 'process' from the point of view of energy, and thus obtain an "evolutionism," which may follow Bergson's pattern or Whitehead's pattern, to mention only two processualists of the evolutionary type.

Since hylomorphism, substantialism, and processualism are intricate doctrines it may seem arbitrary, not to say unfair, to simplify them in order to take them to task. Unfortunately I do not see how else one could talk about *any* philosophical doctrine. It may comfort the supporters of the doctrines now in question to know, first, that I tend to understand 'to simplify' as synonymous with 'to disentangle' rather than as synonymous with 'to distort'; second, that I am concerned here exclusively with what each one of these doctrines has to say with respect to just *one* problem: the nature of inorganic reality.

Hylomorphism is, no doubt, a memorable intellectual accomplishment. Being memorable, however, does not necessarily make it effective. Many of its supporters seem only too well aware of some of its most flagrant weaknesses, for why else should they take so many pains to surround it with so many qualifications. Most efforts of this kind are superfluous when a doctrine is supposed to carry conviction. To be sure, hylomorphists have tried to show that their doctrine is perfectly capable of explaining (philosophically) the nature of the very same reality as that investigated by contemporary physicists.[8] But their attempts in this respect have been successful—and then only partially—when hylomorphism has been previously purged of much of its traditional content. One of the results of this purge has been the theory called "hylosystemism," but, since adherents of hylomorphism often claim that 'hylomorphism' and 'hylosystemism' are far from being synonymous terms, I will abstain from referring here to the latter.

At any rate, adherents of hylomorphism have come to realize that their doctrine works only (and then only to a limited extent) when the meaning of the expression 'inorganic reality' is equated with the meaning of the expression 'natural objects (and phenomena) as perceived, or perceivable, by the senses, and serving as a starting point for abstraction and, hence, conceptualization.' The second term of this equation may seem too long and involved, but it is, in fact, only a summary of the doctrine according to which there is nothing in natural reality that common sense cannot account for. From this viewpoint, hylomorphism is a philosophical doctrine largely, if not exclusively, based on so-called "common sense." Therefore, we must briefly elucidate the meaning of the latter.

Such an elucidation is far from being easy. There is nothing so elusive as "common sense." If by 'common sense' we understand some kind of "faculty" or "power of the mind," there is no reason why we should consider it as an unchangeable "faculty" or "power." For so-called "common sense" is not common at all, meaning that it is not common to all mankind and at all times. The history of philosophy and of science proves without a shadow of doubt that common sense—or the "faculty" or "power of the mind" thus called—has undergone some fundamental changes. For example, the reasons adduced by Aristotle to explain the nature of "violent motions," and the underlying distinction between "violent motions" and "natural motions," were, even in his own time, considered paradoxical and often very difficult to grasp. Nevertheless, these reasons soon became a matter of plain "common sense"; they seemed to be perfectly obvious to anyone who would not deliberately distort them beyond recognition. Many centuries later, a number of thinkers in Oxford and in Paris paved the way for an understanding of the nature of "violent motions" which ran counter to the old "common sense" conceptions. The new way of physics reached maturity in Galileo's laws, and in particular in the law of inertia. It was, to begin with, a "paradoxical" law, for it seemed difficult for many to understand how any natural body could continue to move indefinitely no matter how "ideal" the conditions of motion might be. Yet again, this new paradox soon became common sense. It is only commonsensical to realize that there is no reason why a natural body should stop moving unless some obstacle hinders it in its path of motion. In more recent times we have been unable to avoid the impression that a great many statements in twentieth-century physics are paradoxical. Such is the case, among others, with the statements concerning the relativity of simultaneity, the negative curvature of space, different directions in time, and so on. In the light of what has happened in the past, however, it may not be farfetched to suppose that such "paradoxes" may eventually be incorporated into the ever-increasing stock of "common sense statements"—while waiting for new "paradoxes," not yet "commonsensical," to be evolved. Therefore, it is only reasonable to conclude that common sense is anything but common, particularly if 'common' means 'universal' and 'unchangeable.'

Now it is the most "traditional" form of common sense that underlies the hylomorphic theory of natural reality. Such a common sense yields a view of physical phenomena as drawn to human scale—which is the favorite, if not the exclusive, scale of common sense. Measured by this scale, microphysical (atomic and subatomic) phenomena appear "exceedingly small," whereas what I shall call "megaphysical phenomena" (astrophysical phenomena) appear "exceedingly large." On the other hand, contemporary physics seems to view things in a completely different manner. The two most significant and enlightening branches of physics nowadays are nuclear physics and astrophysics (sometimes called simply "cosmology"). These two branches of physical theory, which in many ways supplement each other, swarm with problems arising from the sheer "size" of the objects with which they are concerned—

unbelievably small and incredibly large, respectively. One might think that the reasonable thing to do would be to try to reduce such objects to a "human scale"; in other words, it would seem to be commonsensical to try to make them possible objects for "common sense." Yet, this is not done for the simple reason that then they would vanish as the proper subject matter of the corresponding sciences. Subatomic particles and clusters of galaxies *cannot* be drawn to human scale. Yet they seem to be *the* physical realities of our universe, more real, or more basically real, physically speaking, than billiard balls or pieces of rock. Instead of viewing elementary particles and clusters of galaxies as limiting cases of perceptual objects—which may be called "macrophysical objects"—nuclear physicists and astrophysicists tend to view macrophysical objects as limiting cases of elementary particles and clusters of galaxies. Therefore, it seems that macrophysical, or ordinary, objects are not "small enough" or not "big enough" to engage the interest of contemporary physicists.

As a consequence, physicists may conclude that macrophysical reality, if taken as a pattern for the behavior of all inorganic realities, could be truly deceptive. Thus, true physical knowledge—or rather, the true type of physical knowledge—springs primarily, if not exclusively, from the study of microphysical and megaphysical objects, which are anything but objects of common sense.

I have written "the true type of physical knowledge" for a reason which is worth mentioning. A statement may be true and yet belong to the "wrong" type of knowledge. A magician may make a true utterance. Yet, this does not make magic a science. On the other hand, a statement may be false and still belong to the "right" type of knowledge. For example, a physicist may make a false statement, but this does not prove that physics is an inadequate type of knowledge. To be sure, if magic always yielded true statements while physics invariably produced false statements, we would do well to pause for a moment and reconsider our whole attitude concerning knowledge, although even in such an implausible case we should base any definite pronouncements concerning the "right type of knowledge" on reasons less pragmatical than "it just works that way." The eventual failure of a given type of knowledge, therefore, does not make it suspicious, any more than the eventual success of another type of knowledge makes it commendable. The fact that physics—as microphysics and megaphysics—may occasionally fail where common sense succeeds is no reason for hurriedly shifting from the physical view of natural reality to plain common sense.

Since the hylomorphic conception makes ample room for common sense while remaining impermeable to the type of knowledge developed by microphysics and megaphysics, it is only reasonable to hold it in abeyance. Even assuming that hylomorphism plunges deeply into metaphysical depths, the fact is that it scarcely sets foot on physical reality. Philosophers subscribing to the hylomorphic conception of natural reality may argue, of course, that the lack of connection between the hylomorphic conception and physical theory must be blamed on the latter rather than on the former. One can always claim that physics should make room for the hylomorphic conception and not the other way around. I find this claim, however, scarcely persuasive, for, whereas physics does not, and indeed should not, encroach too greatly upon metaphysics, any metaphysics of natural reality which is supposed to make some sense must have some physical significance. It is, therefore, up to metaphysics, insofar as it deals with the problem of inorganic reality, to prove that its statements about this reality are not completely independent of statements made in physics.

I do not propose to make a clean sweep of the hylomorphic conception. The concepts of matter and form so thoroughly elucidated within the framework of this conception may still play a part in the unforeseeable future. But I will certainly quarantine the hylomorphic conception because of its failure to harmonize with the present state of physical theory.

The concepts of substance and mode, as well as those of substance and accident, are less vulnerable to the above reproaches. It is still feasible, even if it is not overwhelmingly instructive, to view a certain number of physical theories as "substantialist-oriented." At any rate, when we refer to "elements," "particles," and so on, we wonder whether they are substances of sorts. Now, it is one thing to use the concept of substance in a rather vague way, as designating some kind of "supporting entity," and another thing to use it as a metaphysical cornerstone for a physical conception of reality. The latter use was widespread when physical theories were patterned on the model of classical mechanics. Newtonian particles and, in general, mass points could be viewed as the physical counterpart of metaphysical substances. To be sure, these substances were supposed to be "hard realities" and not "occult qualities" or "substantial forms." But these "hard realities" could be called "substances" insofar as they were considered the seat of the so-called "primary qualities," and hence insofar as they were the sturdy basis on which "secondary qualities" or "qualities of perception" rested. Curiously enough, even philosophers who sharply criticized the concept of substance, as was the case with some phenomenalists, did little more in this respect than to substitute other kinds of realities such as impressions, perceptions, irreducible qualities, and "phenomena" for the above physical particles. Phenomenalists tended to equate the properties of these "phenomena" with the properties of "physical entities." All these properties were assumed to be invariable elements, which by association yielded all possible "modes." We can thus conclude that the *idea* of substance, regardless of the various ways of viewing the nature of substance itself, has been firmly entrenched both in the physical and in the metaphysical—or, as the case may be, epistemological—conception of natural reality throughout the modern era.

Neither the ideas developed by classical mechanics nor the notions worked out in associationist psychologies and epistemologies have been entirely eliminated from physical theory. They are still used to describe, or even to explain, the behavior of some physical systems. Nevertheless, physical theory nowadays emphasizes a number of concepts in which the idea of substance plays either a very modest role or none at all. Such is the case with concepts like "field," "functional relation," and others. It is only reasonable, therefore, to abstain from insisting too much upon the concept of substance and its correlative concept of mode. To say that physical realities are substances, or that they are to be construed in terms of substances, is to say both too much and too little. In the present stage of physical theory, an elementary particle cannot be said to be a substance in the classical sense of this concept, because it does not fulfill most of the necessary conditions. On the other hand, it displays not a few characteristics for whose understanding the notion of substance offers but little help.

The concepts of process and entity seem to be much closer to many of our present modes of thought. Since the beginnings of the present century theoretical physicists and epistemologists have been concerned with such questions as whether physical realities are, in the last resort, "processes," or, as they are also called, "events." They have directed their attention to such questions as whether a process or an event is composed of an aggregate of entities, or, perhaps more plausibly, whether entities are composed of processes or events. Let us consider the various "models" which have been devised in order to picture the structure of the atomic nucleus. Models such as the "water-drop model," the "shell model," the "optic model," the "collective model," and other such similar patterns describe structures.[9] The question now is whether these structures are made up of entities or whether they should be viewed as processes. To be sure, an answer to this question does not dispel all the difficulties. Epistemologists have long been aware that no single feature of physical reality does justice to its complexity. Thus, they have devised a plurality of features—such as "permanence," "thinghood" and "efficaciousness," [10] or as "concreteness," "acquaintance," "simplicity," "significance," "realism pattern," "process pattern," "model pattern," and so on [11] in an attempt to describe physical reality adequately, or at least effectively. But the concepts of entity and process loom large in any such list of features. Given any physical reality, we may always ask whether it is some "thing" or some "event."

Thus, we might be tempted to pause here, and proceed to utilize the concepts of process and entity with whatever features each concept may entail. But it must be remembered that our original question was not only to ascertain what formally constitutes inorganic reality but also, and above all, what it means to say that such a reality ceases to be whatever it is. From this viewpoint, the concepts of process and entity prove to be insufficient. Let us assume that we can construe physical realities as entities—whether "substantial" or not—and furthermore that we know what it means to say that a physical entity has ceased, namely, that it is no longer *that particular* physical entity. Having made such assumptions, we are still unable to determine *what* it is that ceases to be. If it is said that it is just the entity that has ceased to exist, then we are thrown back upon our "preliminary difficulties," for the entity in question may cease to be, but only in the sense that it has become another entity. Becoming another entity means that either the former entity has sunk into nothingness, or that there is still "something" that persists in being. On the other hand, if we assume that we can construe physical realities as processes, and if we further assume that we know what it means to say that a process has come to an end, namely, that some other process has been initiated, we are still uncertain about what it is that ceases to exist. If it is said that what ceases is just that process, the difficulties encountered will seem less acute than in the former case, for it belongs to the nature of a process to change, and hence to cease to exist. But it is difficult to conceive of a pure process which consists solely of not being what it is. At any rate, it seems that something ceases to be only with respect to something that does not.

We need, therefore, some other set of concepts which will partake of some of the features of each one of those already introduced, but which would be more basic than any of them.

5
ELEMENTS AND STRUCTURES

The sought-after set of concepts are deceptive in their simplicity, for nothing could be more simple than element and structure. They can be defined recursively: "element" designates any component part of any inorganic reality, and "structure" designates the way, or ways, in which elements can be interrelated.

Since elements are supposed to make up structures, and structures are supposed to be made up of elements, it may seem redundant to say that elements are previous to, and independent from, structures, while structures are subsequent to, and dependent upon, elements. It is not so redundant, however, when we consider that such expressions as 'previous to,' 'independent from,' and so on, bear more than one meaning. We may admit that elements are logically prior to structures without necessarily assuming that the former actually precede the latter. Also we may contend that elements precede structures in the order of knowledge without necessarily preceding them in the order of reality. It is then somewhat urgent to clarify in what sense elements are said to make up structures.

It is my view that elements are previous to, and independent of, structures only in the sense that whatever predicates are assigned to structures depend upon predicates assigned to elements, whereas predicates assigned to elements are not dependent upon predicates assigned to structures.

It may now seem that I have strongly committed myself to a doctrine according to which a structure is nothing but the sum of its elements, so that whatever features we may detect in the elements will be detected eventually in the structure. Furthermore, it may seem that I have committed myself to the view according to which no two different structures may be made up of the same elements.

In a way I have committed myself to both tenets, for I maintain that structures of the type I am talking about are concrete entities rather than abstract entities which might be multiplied indefinitely by dint of admitting not only classes, but also classes of classes, and classes of classes of classes, and so on, of elements. If the doctrine maintaining that any given entity is primarily an individual is labeled "nominalism," then I have no objection to this label at least as a characterization of a theory concerning the type of relations between elements and structures.

Yet, I do not think it fair to stop at such a characterization. For I do not see why we cannot admit that different structures can be made up of the same elements without abandoning the assumption that all structures are individuals made up of a certain number of elements. In order to maintain both of these assumptions, we have only to accept the notion that two or more elements can be ordered in a variety of ways, each one of these ways yielding a definite structure. To accept the possibility that a definite number of elements can be arranged in a plurality of structures is not to assert that structures are anything distinct from their constituent elements; nor is it to affirm that structures, as wholes, "transcend," their elements or parts, as is sometimes claimed. I merely maintain that if there is anything in a structure "different" from its constituent elements, this "difference" is not to be construed in the same way as we ascertain "differences" among elements.

To think otherwise is to confuse the following two contentions: (1) A structure is a class of elements; (2) A structure is a certain arrangement or order of elements. The former contention leads, indeed, to the acceptance of abstract entities and, for that matter, to the acceptance of an infinite number of such entities. We reject this contention, and against it we gleefully utilize Occam's razor, no matter how ruthless its gashes may seem. The latter contention leads only to the acceptance of concrete entities. We accept this contention, disregarding Occam's razor for the simple reason that there is no need for it. To accept only concrete entities does not limit us as to the number of these entities. After all, it is not up to us to decide that the universe is best described as a desert rather than a forest. The universe is what it is, and it will not shrink no matter how many razors we may use to make it less luxuriant than some would like it to be.

On the basis of the second contention, then, we must feel no misgivings about the danger of unnecessarily multiplying entities. If entities are multiplied, it will not be unnecessarily. At any rate, the arrangements of elements into structures will be curtailed by very definite possibilities. We can think of many arrangements, but no more than those permitted by the elements which we choose to consider. The number of actualizable arrangements, and only this number, will determine the number of structures which can be made up by the same elements.

Thus, we can still assume that a structure is a sum of elements provided that we add that such a sum is an ordered one. Now the order itself does not exist, or preexist, in the parts. At most we can admit that certain parts, or elements, lend themselves more easily than others to make up, or shape, a given structure so that the structure *as an ordered whole* is possible but has not yet been made real by the constituent parts. To distinguish between "element" and "structure" we need only admit that two different structures can be made up of the same elements.

To be sure, there is one case in which it is somewhat more difficult to distinguish between "element" and "structure." This situation arises when a structure is "composed" of one, and only one, element. Then the distinction in question, if the word 'distinction' still plays a role, will be a conceptual rather than a real distinction. Yet, such cases of strict equivalence between "element" and "structure" can be dismissed here because no problem arises in respect to their eventual cessation. Single-element structures, which we may call "singles," cannot cease. It is only fair to add that, for reasons which will be adduced later, "singles" are not likely to exist. If they did, they would be "absolute beings," and we would have to eliminate them from our universe. Within our ontological framework such entities as "singles" can expect no mercy: if Occam will not suffice, then Dr. Guillotin will take his place.

The foregoing remarks might induce one to suppose that "structures" and "elements" are permanent and unchangeable features of inorganic realities so that whatever is an element will never become a structure, and vice versa. We would then be able to conceive of elements and structures as mutually exclusive aspects of reality which differ from each other just as much as extended substance differs from thinking substance in the dualistic systems of the Cartesian, or assumedly Cartesian, type.

Such, however, is not the case. What is viewed as an element in one inorganic reality may be viewed as a structure in another reality, and vice versa. The concepts of "element" and "structure," in short, are relative concepts—relative, namely, to each other. Molecules, for example, can be considered as elements when described as parts of a chemical compound. These very same molecules can be considered as structures when described as clusters of atoms. Atoms, in turn, can be considered not only as elements but also as structures made up of protons, electrons, neutrons, mesons, and, in general, so-called "elementary particles"—which, by the way, can never be elementary enough to satisfy the condition of being Absolutes in the way described (and criticized) above.

The ideas just outlined immediately present a difficulty. If we admit that the meaning of such expressions as 'to cease,' 'to end,' 'to terminate,' and, *a fortiori,* 'to die,' is not the same when applied to elements as when applied to structures, then we will have to conclude that different meanings of the same term will apply to the same object. By definition, an object is a structure composed of elements, but these elements can also be considered as structures, in which case they themselves are composed of elements. Let us consider a table. If we arbitrarily define it as "an object made up of a smooth, flat slab and a number of legs or supports arranged so as to have a recognizable shape which serves certain purposes," it may be said that the table "ceases to exist" when its constituent elements are taken apart. 'The table ceases to exist' means, of course, that the structure known, or identified, as "a table" ceases to exist. It does not necessarily mean that everything that is, or can be, structural in the table ceases to exist. Since the constituent elements of the table (slab, legs or supports) are, in fact, structures made up of other elements (lumber, nails; or molecules, electrons, and so on), there are in the very same object some structures which cease to exist and others which persist. Similarly, there are in the very same object some elements which cease to exist and others which persist. Thus, the expressions 'to cease to exist,' 'to terminate,' 'to come to an end,' and so on are applied, it would seem, both to structures and to elements in exactly the same way.

The above difficulty is not, however, too serious. In order to avoid it we need only specify in each case which aspects of the object are to be viewed as structures and which as elements. Thus, given an object, O, or class of objects, CO, we can refer to such and such structures or to such and such elements of O or CO. We must, therefore, define O, or CO, by means of a specific set of structures as well as a specific set of elements. A number of conventions may be adopted to that effect. For example, if we "define" 'solar system' as "a structure composed of celestial bodies (a star, several planets, a number of satellites, asteroids, and so on)," we may assert that there are changes which affect the solar system as a whole but which do not necessarily affect each one of its component elements. For this reason, these elements may be assumed to "endure" throughout change. On the other hand, each one of the components of the solar system may also be "defined" as if it were a structure composed of, say, material particles, so that we may assert that any chosen component of the solar system undergoes changes which do not necessarily affect each one of its elements *qua* elements. In short, only by defining any given object as a structure or as an element shall we be able to ascertain what it is that changes in such an object.

Since the proposed definition comes as a "preliminary definition," it may be argued that the above remarks exhibit an air of excessive and overconfident conventionality. Some readers may have scruples about the propriety of introducing conventions when questions about reality and real changes are at stake.

Such scruples could not be ignored if the term 'convention' had the same meaning in the present context as it has in such expressions as 'the conventions of the game.' For although game conventions are less arbitrary than they might seem, they should certainly be avoided as too unmanageable in our case. But I have no great misgivings about the use of conventions when they are meant to stand for assumptions whose choice has been largely determined by previous observations on the behavior of reality. Conventions are to be understood here as points of view, without which we cannot even begin to talk about anything, least of all, reality. Thus, conventions will stand or fall against the test of reality itself.

Since the concepts of element and structure are, as pointed

out earlier, relative to each other, the question now arises whether the notions of ceasing to be, terminating, and so on are also, in some sense, relative. If we say that O ceases to exist, is it not also necessary to add that O ceases to exist only "relatively"?

It seems that such is, indeed, the case. What we call "cessation of an inorganic reality" is, at bottom, not a "real cessation" but a change, a structural change. In other words, 'O ceases to exist' means 'O as a structure ceases to exist, but there is something in O that endures.' In short, something changes only with respect to something that does not. But since what does not change is at the same time a structure, it persists only relatively. When it eventually ceases to exist, there will still be something that for the time being at least is held to be invariable. This process may continue *ad infinitum*. There will always be something remaining that will never cease.

6
THE BASIC ELEMENTS

The pertinent conclusion looks simple enough. In the realm of inorganic reality 'to cease' means only 'to change' and 'to change' means that a particular structure changes. This is tantamount to saying that in inorganic nature only structures exist, and thus what we call "an element" proves in the last analysis to be only "a structure viewed (temporarily or for some well-defined purposes) as an element." Since inorganic nature continuously undergoes changes it may be said that it ceases continuously, but never completely. Death in inorganic nature could be defined as "permanent structural change."

Unfortunately, this simplicity is only apparent; problems soon begin to arise. Some of these problems, although important, are not urgent. If the term 'element' has no denotation, are we justified in using it? Is it legitimate to be a complete conventionalist in respect to elements, while remaining a straightforward realist with regard to structures? I will discard these and similar questions for the simple reason that even if we could answer them the answers would not be very illuminating. There are, however, questions which are both important and urgent. Can we say that nothing remains unchanged in inorganic nature? Are we committed to an embarrassing *regressus in infinitum?* Is the whole of inorganic nature a vast "structural continuum"?

These questions are closely associated with a number of problems which have often aroused philosophers from their dogmatic slumber. Let us now assume that we may practically identify cessation with change in inorganic nature. Does that mean that we fully understand all the implications of the concept of "change"? Are we not almost forced to admit that something is produced and something is destroyed? If we accept the view that, in the last analysis, nothing is either produced or destroyed, do we not then acknowledge the existence of some "basic" (or "ultimate") elements which do not undergo any change?

For centuries human reason has supplied a peremptory answer to these questions: the material world is a never-ending process, or series of processes, in which elements, themselves unaltered and unalterable, unite and separate for no other purpose, it would seem, than to produce an illusion of change. Parmenides formulated this answer in his own radical fashion: only what is, is; and whatever is, never changes or moves. Parmenides' "sphere," as Meyerson has endlessly argued, is the real counterpart of reason, for reason stubbornly refuses to believe that being and change can go hand in hand. If they did, effects could not be explained entirely by their causes. But completely explaining an effect by its causes is the same as identifying the effect with its cause, and this amounts to saying that there is, in fact, no effect, that is to say, no change. Thus we would be forced to acknowledge only a Being which would seem undistinguishable from a non-Being.[12] In the purely rational universe depicted by Parmenides nothing can cease, for ceasing is incompatible with being. Of what is not, nothing can be said, either clearly or obscurely. And of what is, only this much can be said, and this quite clearly: that it is.

It has been claimed that philosophers, scientists, and, for that matter, ordinary citizens have retreated from Parmenides' endless tautology because, although it may fulfill the demands of reason, it certainly does not satisfy the testimony of experience. The fact is, however, that Parmenides' version of human reason does not fulfill all the demands of reason. For reason finds little satisfaction in explaining reality at the expense of reality. Reason acknowledges that there is not the slightest doubt that what is, is. But reason is not yet satisfied; reason still wants to elucidate what "it" is. With Parmenides we have reached the truth concerning what is real; we still have to attain the reality of what is true.

The constant interest elicited by atomistic doctrines, even on the part of those who have done their best to refute them, is due largely to the fact that these doctrines were eminently successful in bridging the gap between the reality of truth and the truth of reality—between reason and "experience." This success has, of course, been doubted by all those who have claimed that atomism has not been "really" able to explain reality, for reality, it is said, changes, whereas atomism ultimately precludes all change. At any rate, it has been pointed out that even if atomistic doctrines were successful in explaining the behavior of inorganic reality, they would fail when they had to explain the behavior of organisms. But when all is said, we must acknowledge a few points.

First, we cannot blithely assume that the behavior of a structure can always be explained by the behavior of each of its constituent elements. "We cannot explain something red by saying that all red things contain red particles. Neither can we explain that something moves by saying that every moving thing contains moving particles." [13] Those who insist on giving such an explanation, or equally, those who reject a theory because it fails to provide similar explanations, subscribe to an extremely naïve doctrine according to which atoms, or elementary particles in general, can be represented intuitively. But even if there were some slim chance of intuitively representing the atoms of Democritus, there is not the slightest possibility of "representing" the elementary particles with which contemporary physics deals.

Secondly, atomism at large is a theory about the structure of inorganic reality. If it is acknowledged that organic substances are also composed of atoms, it is not too often assumed that the properties of the former can be simply derived from the properties of the latter. To be sure, the conceptual structure of atomism, including Democritus' atomism, is far from being simple. Let us confine ourselves for the moment to Democritus. His atomism achieved a remarkable conciliation between two apparently irreconcilable views. He preserved both the rationalistic outlook of the Eleatic school and the phenomenalistic view of reality proposed by, among others, Heraclitus, the "Skeptics," and perhaps most of the early "physiologists." Democritus achieved this reconciliation by accepting a series of possible relations between "phenomena" and "things in themselves." [14] As it is well known, he proceeded to "split" Parmenides' "sphere" into an infinite number of Parmenidean entities, each of them possessing the characteristics of the original "sphere." Thus he followed Melissus' assertion—made in a different context—that "if there were a plurality, each one of the Many would have to be just as I say the One is." In fine, Democritus was able to combine the "highest possible rationality" with "the evidence given by a multiple, changing and diverse reality." From that moment on atomism became truly a "model theory," which nearly achieved perfection when reinforced by the doctrine usually known as "mechanism."

Mechanism is not necessarily atomistic. Noncorpuscular, that is, so-called "continuistic," conceptions of matter have often made use of the notion of mechanical properties. On the other hand, present-day physics, especially nuclear physics, shows an undeniable tendency to distrust "merely mechanical models." In contemporary physics and in some branches of contemporary technology we can detect an increasing tendency toward the construction of "models" which, far from being composed of unchangeable individual elements, are presented as a series of complexly overlapping "primitive groupings." As an example of this tendency we can mention the so-called "functional electronic blocks" consisting of molecular groups arranged in what appear to be "solid structures." These "functional electronic blocks" cannot be easily represented by means of the usual diagrams showing structures composed of supposedly self-subsisting elements. Therefore, it is not necessary to subscribe to the idea that all structures composed of elements are always both purely atomistic and purely mechanical.

All things considered, however, two facts still remain. The first is that throughout modern times atomism and mechanism have been, so to speak, natural allies. Thus, for example, while Descartes developed a theory of the material world as a continuum he also visualized such a world as a structure made of particulars "filling all space." [15] The other and more important fact is that, even if we accept the possibility of talking about "model blocks" of the type referred to above, we are still uncertain about their ultimate composition. In other words, we cannot easily dispense with theories combining a mechanistic view with an atomistic outlook—the so-called "mechanistic-atomistic theories." They seem to be here to stay. We are committed then to an analysis of their ultimate assumptions and basic postulates. In order to perform this task, we shall proceed to a simplification of the "mechanistic-atomistic" solution to the question concerning the nature of inorganic reality.

Roughly speaking, the solution in question consists in maintaining that if, in fact, there is cessation, in principle there is none. Inorganic reality does not *actually* end, cease or "die." 'Cessation' is synonymous with 'disintegration.' Since the component parts of any given structure are supposed to be unchangeable, they can be conceived as elements of any other possible structures. In short, the atoms, with their supposedly permanent properties, mechanical or otherwise, are described as simple elements, that is to say, as the truly indestructible corporeal "substances" of whatever there is.

Atomism and, *a fortiori,* mechanistic atomism tends, therefore, to cast aside any problems raised by notions such as those of "creation" and "novelty." Since nothing new is created or, at least, produced by combinations of simple, indestructible elements, the conclusion is obvious: there *is* nothing really new. What we call "a new thing" is not new at all; it only *appears* to be new. Now when the notion of "novelty" is relinquished, the notions of "discontinuity," "change," and even "temporality" soon go by the board. We can, indeed should, say of each basic element that it is solid, consequently continuous; that it is timeless, therefore not contingent; that it is motionless, thus purely rational. The predicates 'disintegrates' and 'integrates' apply only to structures composed of elements, not to the elements themselves. And since only the latter are "real," nothing really disintegrates and integrates. In fact, of course, everything disintegrates and integrates but in principle and, so to speak, "at bottom," nothing does. Underlying disintegration, temporality, novelty, and change there are permanence, timelessness, rest.

The view of reality described above lacks some consistency. To be truly consistent it would be necessary to dispense with the existence of even separate elements and hence to deny that there can be any combinations of elements. In other words, it would have to abandon the "arbitrary postulate" of Democritus and confine itself to the thesis of Parmenidean unity. Such an "arbitrary postulate," however, has given atomism, especially when supplemented by mechanism, the explanatory power that it possesses. After all, some price must be paid for achieving an explanation of the behavior of reality that is not only rational but reasonable.

Death in Inorganic Nature

Nevertheless, atomism, and in particular mechanistic atomism, fails to provide an adequate conceptual framework for a satisfactory understanding of the role played by cessation in nature in general, and in inorganic reality in particular. It may be argued that we implicitly use the notion of cessation as soon as we proceed to describe or explain how any given structure changes into another structure. Yet, insofar as our description or explanation is based upon the supposedly unchangeable constituent elements of the structure in question, the notion of cessation tends to play a minor role and ends by playing no role at all. It is then assumed, even if it is not always clearly stated, that cessation (and, ultimately, change) affects only what is not "truly" and "completely" real; that is, it affects only, and exclusively, the constitutent elements.

7
BEING "IN PRINCIPLE" AND BEING IN REALITY

As a rule, scientists do not hold opinions such as those outlined above; only philosophers, or more exactly, some philosophers, do. Therefore, we should not expect scientists to worry about whether the term 'cessation' has or has not any definite meaning in their vocabulary. The fact is, however, that scientists, and in particular physicists, carry on their research in a manner philosophically puzzling, namely, as if, on the one hand, things—or, more generally, natural objects—cease to be, and, on the other hand, as if nothing really new is ever produced. It then behooves philosophers, and the so-called "philosopher-scientists," to scrutinize the meaning, and consequences, of the opinions in question.

The first thing to notice is that the opinions summarized by the label "mechanistic atomism" seem to be refractory to any critique. If it is pointed out that atoms in Democritus' sense are no longer unchangeable constituent particles, and that, as a consequence, atomism is no longer a valid or at least universally accepted theory, certainly no one will object. But the fact is that atomism may undergo many transformations without yielding an inch concerning its ultimate philosophical presuppositions. The function formerly ascribed to atoms may be applied to other, more elementary, particles. It may even be ascribed to waves, not to mention the interesting combination of waves and particles which has been given the name 'wavicle.' [16] Suppose now that we go so far as to assume that physical realities are not actually composed of particles, waves, wavicles, and so on, but are describable rather as a series of continuous "fields," or even as a single continuous field, either finite or infinite, which is "modulated" by energy. It would then be difficult to continue to use the term 'atomism.' But what matters philosophically in "atomism," in the sense in which we commonly use this word, is not the fact, or assumed fact, that physical reality is made up of some specific kind of particles, but rather the idea that whatever is supposed to exist "really" is basically "permanent." Under all its forms, atomism is what we may be allowed to call "permanentism."

Now if such is the case then there is indeed no cessation in inorganic nature, and perhaps even in reality at large. This conclusion we are not ready to accept. After all, our purpose is exactly the opposite: to try to show that cessation is precisely "what there is," or, more exactly, that an "analogy of cessation" runs throughout reality. For reasons that I will later try to make clear, I prefer to call this analogy an *analogia mortis*. For the moment it will suffice to say that we can refer to reality by saying that it ceases in various (though not infinitely various) ways. If there is no real cessation in inorganic reality then neither is there any in organic reality insofar as the latter largely depends on, or is largely based upon, the former. Otherwise we must conclude that only realities that are neither inorganic or organic, namely, realities having nothing to do with the natural world, actually cease, or can cease. Such a conclusion would be tantamount to subscribing to a most peculiar kind of dualism—the dualism of two kinds of substances: one, permanent (and "natural"); the other, nonpermanent (and "non-natural"). To be sure, we may plead the cause of dualism by arguing that we are not thereby "bifurcating" Nature, but are simply classifying reality. We are, however, doing far more than that; we are, so to speak, "cutting" reality into two separate and distinct realms without any link between them. Since we refuse, for reasons often stated in the present book, to cut reality into two independent, nay, incommunicable parts, we do not need to plead the cause of the aforementioned dualism, because it is not our cause. Our cause is not an easy one to present and is an extremely arduous one to plead for. It can be stated as follows: "preserve the unity of reality without reducing everything to a single element or to a single type of element." In order to achieve this end we must do more than string arguments together; we must set up the foundations of a new ontology.

The difficulties against which atomism—"philosophical atomism," that is—stumbles are the consequence of having accepted, implicitly or explicitly, a certain ontological principle. This principle can be worded as follows: "To speak of reality is to speak about it as it is, or is supposed to be, 'in principle.'" Now, why we should equate the meaning of 'is real' with the meaning of 'is real in principle' is far from being obvious. To be sure, the ontological principle here in question has not only molded philosophical minds for centuries but has also been remarkably fruitful. After all, most of what has been done in philosophy, and even in science, is indebted to such a principle. Philosophy began only when some thinkers intimated that reality must be viewed from its own "source," *physis,* or from its own "principle," *arkhē.* What is not grasped in its source or in its principle has an air of doubtful or deceitful knowledge, of learning without guarantee or permanence. The senses, as they are employed in everyday life, were held responsible for all untrustworthy knowledge. To be sure, no one proposed the complete abolition of sensory perception, with the possible exception of Parmenides, and then only in his "Way of Truth." Yet, in one way or another, most philosophers, and scientists, have resorted to some criterion of knowledge other than that supplied by "mere sensory perception." In tune with the "Empiricists," Kant maintained that our knowledge begins with experience. It only happens that it cannot be validated by experience alone.

One might well argue that this kind of thinking, from Thales to Kant and beyond, does not always yield an ontology according to which 'is real' is synonymous with 'is real in principle.' But there has always been a tendency, in philosophic thought at least, toward an ideal state of affairs ruled by the ontological principle: to be is to be real in principle. The instrument commonly used to achieve this ideal has been what we normally call "reason." A great many philosophers have been pluralists; a few have been monists. But in either case they have implicitly acknowledged that reality "reduces," so to speak, to some rational principle underlying it and capable of explaining why it is what it is. Meyerson has shown again and again that this "reductionist tendency" is the motive power of human reason. Of course, in this respect not all philosophers have gone as far as Parmenides, who concluded that the real is rational, or as far as Hegel, who claimed not only that the real is rational but also that the rational is real. Some philosophers have even intimated that there is something truly irrational underlying reality. But even in the latter case, we find that reality is "reduced" to its principle. The formula "to be is to be in principle" is, or rather has been, an ontological thesis that no one has seemed able or, for that matter, anxious to discard.

The reluctance felt by most philosophers in this respect is quite understandable. It does not seem reasonable, or even feasible, to abandon an ontological thesis—or, as we have called it, an "ontological principle"—so closely linked with the structure of the human mind and, furthermore, so fruitful. It

Death in Inorganic Nature   55

would seem better to continue using this principle with as many limitations and qualifications as required.

Yet I will brush this principle aside, and contend that what constitutes reality is precisely that it is *not* "in principle." What this contention means is not easy to explain or to understand. If what constitutes reality is what is not "in principle," must we then dismiss the entire history of ontology? Should we then simply adhere to the notion that reality is just as it is given to sensory perception? Must we, in short, retreat, or return, to some kind of prephilosophical and prescientific "metaphysics of appearances"?

Our attempt to "destroy the history of ontology" is very different from Heidegger's. Neither philosophy nor science has evolved in vain. Rather than assume that nothing interesting or instructive has ever happened in philosophy, we shall suppose that everything that has happened in philosophy, and in particular in ontology, is either interesting or instructive. It is, above all, instructive; the failures of preceding ontologies are the *sine qua non* condition for any new, or supposedly new, ontology. A new ontology ought, then, to avoid claiming that the only ontology possible or feasible is a kind of "preontology," which is achieved by simply disregarding any ontological point of view. To understand reality is still to think it, and in thinking it we certainly define it and, to a great extent, make it conform to models or schemes which come either from "outside"—be it a system of categories or a realm of ideas that we assume "preexists" somewhere—or from "within"—be it a system of categories or a realm of ideas which the knowing subject is supposed to carry with him.

Why then say that reality is *not* in principle, except perhaps in the mind? Only because otherwise we would run the risk of confusing reality itself with the schemes used by a knowing subject in order to make reality an object of thought. Such schemes are unavoidable, but they are to the understanding of reality what scaffoldings are to the construction of a building. Schemes—conceptual schemes, that is—are like a temporary framework, always on the point of being removed and replaced by others. The so-called "principles of reality" prove then to be, at most, "principles of the knowledge of reality." In this respect, Kant, at least in the *Critique of Pure Reason,* and more specifically in some sections of the "Transcendental Analytic," understood the nature of our problem as no one else has. Unfortunately, he developed, or helped to develop the notion that the principles of the knowledge of reality can eventually become principles of reality. This development, characteristic of idealistic philosophies, is most unwelcome, for the fact that there are, or that there may be, principles of knowledge does not necessarily entail the idea that there should be some principles of reality distinct from actually existing realities.

The ontological principle "To be is to be in principle" is common both to idealist and to realist philosophies. To refuse to admit the principle is, therefore, to oppose both idealism and realism. On the other hand, we have warned against regressing to a preontological position. Must we then recognize as the only sound ontology the one that has been developed, or presupposed, by empiricism?

The answer to the above question is "yes," to a great extent. There is little doubt that a sizable portion of contemporary philosophers, whether positivist, phenomenologist, or even existentialist, have proceeded in a way similar to that proposed here. At any rate, these philosophers share the belief that reality should not be split into two realms: "reality itself," and "the principle (or principles) of reality." Consequently, they assume that reality is, in the last analysis, what it appears to *be.* Following in Husserl's steps, Jean-Paul Sartre has pointed out that reality is "a phenomenon . . . absolutely indicative of itself." [17] Here we find a clear expression of empiricism as well as of phenomenalism. Now then, to maintain that reality is "phenomenon" does not necessarily mean that it is always as it appears *to us*. Thus empiricism and phenomenalism need not be "naïve." In order to avoid being "naïve," Sartre hastens to add that we should not dismiss the problem of *"the being* of phenomenon," namely, "the being of appearance," or what appearance really *is*. Unlike Sartre, however, I doubt that such a problem can be solved by means of an ontology which begins with a phenomenology rather than with a "critique."

It would seem then that I am advancing some kind of "critical empiricism" and "critical phenomenalism." To the extent that labels are (even if only relatively) harmless, I have no objection to the ones just proposed. But I must point out that an ontology according to which reality is far from being only "in principle" could be expressed in various other ways, just as realism and idealism have displayed multiple forms throughout the history of philosophy while remaining faithful to their common over-all ontological commitments. Whether it is labeled "critical empiricism," "critical phenomenalism," or any other, similar 'ism,' what I propose is, in any case, quite simple: a way of considering reality which, while denying the naïve, pre-philosophical and pre-ontological assumption that reality is exactly as it appears, maintains that there is no "being" or "principle of being" hidden behind reality. Consequently, I shall not inquire what reality is "in the last analysis." Nor will I proceed to investigate the real by presupposing that *nihil est sine ratione*. For, even if we were to lend our support to the latter formula, we would acknowledge it as derivative proposition. The reason for reality is simply reality itself.

Therefore, although there may be a *ratio cognoscendi* there is not necessarily a *ratio essendi*. It may be argued that the *ratio essendi* is precisely the *ratio cognoscendi,* namely, that the reasons that make X what it is, and behave the way it does, are the very same reasons by means of which we can explain that X is what it is, and behaves the way it does. Alternatively, it may be argued that the *ratio cognoscendi* is precisely the *ratio essendi,* namely that the reasons by means of which we can explain that

X is what it is, and behaves the way it does, are the very same reasons that make X be what it is, and behave the way it does. The former argument is typical of idealist philosophies; the latter argument is characteristic of realist philosophies. Both arguments are, at bottom, the same argument; it consists in identifying *esse* with its *ratio*.

We reject this identification because we deny that there is any *ratio essendi,* namely, that there is any principle, or so-called "principle," of reality which is different from, and in all cases previous to, reality itself.

Principles, or *rationes,* of being have usually been described in two ways: as purely logical principles or as ontological principles which are supposed to be in some sense "logical." [18] Purely logical principles raise no problem here. If X is real, then X must be logically possible. But then we say little, if anything, about X *as real.* At any rate, we cannot, or should not, derive the reality of X from the logical possibility of X. Therefore, even if we admitted, as we certainly do, that X would not be real unless it were logically possible, we would still be able to maintain that X is not ontologically preceded, or determined, by some kind of *ratio essendi.* After all, the so-called "logical principles" do not rule the existence and behavior of X; they rule only assertions made about X. On the other hand, ontological principles which are supposed to be, in some sense, "logical" raise a problem which we must face even if only to denounce it as a pseudo-problem. If X is real, then X is real; its reality is not based upon an ontologically previous *ratio.* Therefore, X has no *ratio essendi,* and hence is not "in principle" what it is (or even what it could be). If such a *ratio* existed by itself and were endowed, so to speak, with some kind of metaphysical "density," then it would *ipso facto* make the reality of X unnecessary; only its *ratio essendi* would be real. On the other hand, if such a *ratio* were a more basic reality than X, then X would not be strictly speaking, "real"; it would be only an appearance of a reality.

The ontological principle "To be is to be in reality," which replaces the old assumption "To be is to be in principle," intimates, therefore, that the predicate 'is real' is self-sufficient. However, being self-sufficient, it is also entirely superfluous: X and the reality of X are exactly the same thing. Thus we can assert that there is no difference between reality and appearance, not only because everything that is real is an "appearance" but also, and above all, because what we may call "appearance" is, ontologically speaking, reality. It would be interesting to show that our ontology leads both to the rejection of a *ratio essendi* and to the elimination of *phantasmata,* sense data, and any other such "entities" or "half-entities." Unfortunately, it would also divert our attention from our main point, namely, that being is being in reality and not just "in principle," so that any *ratio* we may introduce is likely to be a *ratio cognoscendi* but will never become a *ratio essendi.* A most important consequence of this conclusion is that, even if for epistemological reasons we had to postulate the existence of a number of permanent ultimate entities, this postulate would not entail the notion that such permanent ultimate entities are real.

8

REALITY AND IDENTITY

If we were to accept the philosophical interpretation usually given to a purely mechanistic, and in particular a purely mechanistic-atomistic, view of reality, we would be compelled to admit that there is something in inorganic nature, namely the "ultimate elements," that never ceases. Furthermore, if in accordance with the above view we maintain that compounds can always be broken down into ultimate elements, then the obvious conclusion is that structures themselves, at bottom, do not cease. Thus every so-called "cessation" will be only an "appearance" of a deeper permanent reality. Hence, if we discard the above view and its consequences we do much more than make a correction of fact; we are actually turning traditional ontology inside out.

According to the ontology outlined in the preceding section, reality is not, and cannot, be determined by its so-called "principles." If any "principles" are still admitted, they must be recognized as abstractions. If these abstractions were only "formal," then we would not have come to grips with reality but only with a type of language which is used to talk about reality. On the other hand, if these abstractions were "material," that is to say, if they were based on experience and observations of reality, then we would be forced to admit that there is a certain mode of behavior in Nature which may be called "cessation."

One might object to these stipulations on the grounds that the ontology proposed here depends in the last analysis on the assumption that the expression 'is real' is synonymous with the expression 'has the possibility of ceasing.'

Have we then, in fact, arbitrarily subordinated the conception of reality to what may be called its "transience"? In any case, is not such an ontology based on the vicious circle which maintains that the concepts of "cessation" and "reality" are interdefinable? And are not vicious circles to be implacably extirpated from philosophic language?

It may indeed happen that some vicious circles are unavoidable. Jaspers has cited an example of such vicious circles: the application of the concepts of the understanding (categories) to reality. Jeanne Hersch has gone so far as to claim that vicious circles are "an inevitable form of philosophic thought," at least in certain extreme cases.[19] Heidegger has pointed out that what is philosophically decisive is not to evade a vicious circle, but to find the right way into it.[20] These remarks are not to be taken lightly; some vicious circles are part and parcel of the philosophical experience. Yet, vicious circles cannot be the sole foundation of metaphysical propositions. It is necessary then to uncover other, less controversial "reasons" to support our contentions.

One of these reasons can be expressed in a conditional form: if we admit the basic assumptions of traditional ontology, then we must conclude that the real is ultimately based on the ideal, and that, insofar as 'ideal' is synonymous with 'universal,' ideal universality constitutes the fabric into which every existence is woven.

Now, we reach this conclusion as soon as we equate the principle *nihil est sine ratione*—nothing exists without a sufficient reason for being what it is—with the principle *ratio est esse essendi*—any reality whatsoever is (metaphysically) reducible to the reason why it is what it is. It goes without saying that these principles are far from being interchangeable. That nothing exists without a sufficient reason to account for its existence is a proposition which may be declared true *quoad nos;* it is, in fact, an epistemological proposition. On the other hand, that the being of an entity is its reason for being what it is, is a proposition which is assumed to be true *per se;* it is, in fact, an ontological proposition. To be sure, although the epistemological principle does not entail the ontological principle, it renders it extremely attractive. It is then easy to invert the relation: since reason is the being of an entity, there must be a sufficient reason to explain why that entity is what it is. Nevertheless, it is difficult, even impossible, to prove the truth of this relation. If the principle that the being of an entity is its reason for being such and such an entity were derived from experience (including in the latter, as phenomenologists intimate, intuitions of "essential relations"), then there would be no objection to accepting it. But the ontological proposition in question is not derivable from any kind of "experience." Nor is it a plausible ontological postulate. It is only a proposition according to which reality consists of some (extremely implausible) principles of its own. As if that were not enough, this proposition commits us to assert, or imply, that these principles are different in nature from the reality of which they are principles. If we now use the term 'existence' as synonymous with the term 'reality,' we may use the term 'essence' as synonymous with the expression 'principles of reality.' The idea that a reality boils down to its principles is then an analogue of the idea that essence is somehow the foundation of existence.

No doubt the term 'essence' is too hot to handle. As soon as we try to give it a meaning, it resolves into a plurality of meanings. None of these meanings is entirely adequate. We cannot claim that essences are merely formal traits which we surreptitiously hypostasize into metaphysical entities. Nor can we maintain that they are logical concepts cleverly disguised as innate ideas. Husserl tried to enlarge the notion of essence by including in it the so-called "material essences." His conception has proved to be very fruitful insofar as it has prevented us from excessively formalizing and idealizing "essence." Unfortunately, Husserl did not succeed in bridging the gap between essences and existences, for, although he claimed that essences, either formal or material, are accessible to the phenomenological intuition, reality remained "between parentheses." Thus phenomenological idealism was not a whim of Husserl's but an extremely plausible consequence of his initial method and of his way of viewing essences. Furthermore, when Max Scheler attempted to "materialize" essences to the greatest possible extent, the result was that 'essences' soon became another name for "values." Neither Husserl nor Scheler succeeded then in turning essences into realities of any kind. Their notions of "essence" remain, therefore, outside the scope of metaphysics. When we refer here to "essences," we need not, therefore, refer to the phenomenological conception; it suffices to refer to what may be called the "traditional" conception. This makes our task easier. From this viewpoint, we can assert now that, since only essences are permanent and indestructible, everything that is assumed to be immutable can be equated with an essence. Hence everything that does not cease can be considered to be "essential," and vice versa.

Needless to say, atomistic mechanism has little, if anything, to do with any traditional metaphysics of essence. The connections between atomistic mechanism and, say, Platonism are, at best, very tenuous. Yet, when we proceed to interpret atomistic mechanism metaphysically, we are allowed to characterize the "ultimate elements" which it postulates in terms of "essences." These "essences" provide, then, the rational framework for any "possible experience." If Kant's well-known postulate is turned inside out, it can be said that, according to the *metaphysics* of atomistic mechanism, "whatever agrees with the formal conditions (of reason) is real." Such formal conditions are fulfilled here by the postulate of a set of basic, ultimate, indestructible particles or elements. And, although these particles or elements are not necessarily "essences," their existence is postulated in the hope that they will behave as such.

The characteristics normally ascribed to the basic and indestructible elements are supposed to be real characteristics: shape, momentum, positive or negative charge, and so on. It would seem to miss the point, then, to say that basic elements have, at bottom, something of the nature of "essences" or "ideal objects." Nevertheless, to claim that there is no real cessation in Nature leads, metaphysically, to an affirmation that "ideality" is of the very essence of reality. The metaphysics of atomistic mechanism seems to neglect the fact that, although "ideas" and "ideal relations" may help to describe reality, they are not supposed to constitute reality. Similarly, the fact that Nature can be described by a mathematical language does not mean that Nature itself is a complex of so-called "mathematical entities."

9
THE TWO "DIRECTIONS"

If it is said that the "basic elements" do not cease, it must be added that they do not exist, and vice versa. Thus, the notion of existence (reality) and the notion of cessation go hand in hand. Now then, although I do not propose to base ontology entirely, and still less exclusively, on the phenomenon called "cessation," I have chosen this phenomenon as a kind of "ontological measure" of existing things. Accordingly, "to be," that is, "to be real" will be put on a par with "to cease" or, better yet, with "to be subject to cessation." If, as will be shown later, the full meaning of cessation is attained only in terms of death, then it can be concluded that 'to be real' and 'to be mortal' are, or can become, synonymous expressions.

Nevertheless, 'to be mortal' is far from being an univocal expression; it is an analogical expression, in a rather broad sense of 'analogical.' Therefore, 'to be mortal' can be said in various ways. How many ways, is a question beset with difficulties. If there were one, and only one, specific way of dying—and, in general, of ceasing—for each particular reality, then there would be an indefinite number of ways in which the predicate 'is mortal' could be used. But the number of ways in which realities can be said to exist and behave is usually definite and limited according to some fundamental *types* of reality. It is only within this limitation that we can subordinate "being real" to "being mortal."

The basic propositions of the ontology underlying the present investigation are the following:

1. To be (to be real) is to be mortal.
2. There are various degrees of mortality, ranging from "minimum mortality" to "maximum mortality."
3. Minimum mortality characterizes the type of reality called "inorganic nature."

4. Maximum mortality characterizes the type of reality called "human beings."

5. Each type of being included in the notion of "reality" can be (ontologically) located within a continuum circumscribed by two contrasting (ontological) tendencies: one that runs from "the least mortal" to "the most mortal" and the other one that runs in the opposite direction.

Propositions 1 and 2 can be understood in the light of the ideas already outlined. Propositions 3 and 4 will be duly clarified later. Proposition 5 requires an immediate elucidation.

Proposition 5 becomes more plausible or, at any rate, more meaningful when related to propositions 1 through 4. According to these propositions, the whole of reality can be depicted by means of an ontological gradation from a more undifferentiated type of being to a more differentiated one, from one less "structural" to one more "structural," from one less "historical" to one more "historical," from one less "existent" to one more "existent," and so on. An example which immediately comes to mind is that type of gradation which goes from pure inorganic reality to the human and personal reality. It must be pointed out that the term 'existent' has been used here in a rather peculiar sense. Generally speaking, inorganic reality exists just as much as organic reality, and the latter exists just as much as human reality. But if 'existent' is qualified so as to be made synonymous with 'differentiated,' 'individual,' 'structured,' 'historical,' and, of course, 'mortal,' then it may be stated that there is a gradation from lesser to greater "existence" in reality. A given reality exists and, in general, "is" more than another in the degree that it is more subject to cessation, and hence ultimately more mortal than another.

It may now be asked if the gradation or "line" of reality of which I have just spoken, is continuous or discontinuous. In other words, it might be asked if the "line" running throughout reality is interrupted and, so to speak, "broken" at various junctures in such a manner that we are left not only with different types of reality but with mutually irreducible and incompatible types of reality as well.

This problem cannot be solved empirically, but it can be elucidated speculatively. Two basically different ontologies confront each other here. According to one ontology, it is necessary to adhere to a complete monism, for otherwise reality would be split into watertight compartments which would require the formulation of sets of entirely different explanatory principles. A monistic ontology of this type is necessarily reductionistic, but reductionism can be understood in two different ways, yielding two entirely different doctrines. The naturalistic, or frequently materialistic, doctrine asserts that everything (wrongly) described as "organic," "spiritual," "personal," and so on, is ultimately explainable in terms of "Nature," namely, "inorganic nature." The other doctrine, which is spiritualistic and often personalistic, asserts that what is described as "natural" happens to be merely something "less personal" or "less spiritual." According to the other basic ontology, it is necessary to maintain at all costs the mutual irreducibility of the various "layers" of reality on the grounds that only in this way are we truly faithful to what is empirically given and, in general, to "experience." For such an ontology, "to reduce" is essentially to abstract and hence to falsify. This ontology also yields two doctrines: one is dualistic, the other is pluralistic. There are, of course, various types of dualism: the dualism of phenomena and noumena, of being and value, of Nature and Spirit, Nature and Culture, Nature and Person, and so on. As to pluralism, it usually holds that even within the realm of the natural (or, as the case may be, the phenomenal) there are different layers—for example, those of the organic and the inorganic—and that their differences are not only epistemological but also, and sometimes above all, ontic and ontological. At any rate, one layer of reality never leads continuously and, so to speak, smoothly to another layer. To acknowledge the presence of "ruptures" between the various layers of reality would then be the only reasonable way to accept the sheer fact of ontological discontinuity.

If we want to be faithful to what is empirically given and, as we suggested, to "experience," it seems that we cannot help adhering to a pluralistic ontology of the type just outlined. Although the behavior of macrophysical reality is founded on the laws which govern microphysical processes, to such an extent that even the so-called "deterministic laws" may be the macrophysical counterpart of microphysical (statistical) laws, nevertheless there are still many forms of behavior displayed by macrophysical reality which are subject to description and explanation by means of a language specifically adapted to them. We can say the same thing, only more emphatically, not only about the relations between the inorganic and the organic but also about the relations between the psychological reality of man and his personal reality. Although both the inorganic and the organic belong to the class of natural objects, they do not behave similarly. If nothing else, then, the different modalities of behavior, when they are sufficiently conspicuous, force us to admit that there must be ontic differences which can be described and analyzed by different languages and different conceptual systems.

Men are made of cells. Men have brains, personalities, financial worries; but it might be no assertion at all to say such things of cells, especially if cell talk were constructed *ab initio* as logically different from man-talk. The two idioms could then never merge. 'It has schizophrenia and an overdrawn account' would express nothing in cell-language. Even though a complex conspiracy of cells could be spoken of in ways analogous to how we speak of a man, this would not conflate the two languages, not even when both idioms characterize the same object, e.g., me. If someone speaks of me as a man but another speaks of me as a collection of cells, although the *denotatum* of both discourses be identical, the two speakers diverge conceptually.[21]

These are pertinent words. They should suffice to convince us that when reason carries its reductionistic tendencies to their ultimate consequences, it ends by demanding that everything be, at bottom, the same. On the other hand, experience, no matter how much its contents may be rationalized, emphasizes a plurality of forms of being and behaving. To the extent that we do not yield to the pragmatic temptation of regarding languages as instruments that are, in principle, indifferent to the uses to which they are assigned, we must recognize that such a plurality is actually founded on the structure of reality.

Since our ontology keeps experience constantly in sight, it would seem that pluralism should take precedent over any form of monism. Such is not the case.

I wish here to express my preference for a particular form of monism, at least with respect to reality, disregarding, for the time being, any contrasts and oppositions between being and value, being and meaning, and so forth. The main reason for my choice is that only when we view reality as a whole—a whole which lies open to transformations and expansions and is not closed by ideal laws or norms laid down beforehand—is it possible to speak of various species of reality without ceasing to speak of the same reality. Only then can we speak of reality—reality at large, and even *the* reality—without assuming that it must always be, at bottom, the same, namely, one and the same type of thing. Our monism is then a monism *sui generis*. The expression 'mono-pluralism' would prove more adequate if it were not for the fact that it might easily lead one to think of an inane eclecticism.

What is the real nature of this "monism" which accepts the label so reluctantly? Above all, it consists of a negative attitude: it definitely repudiates all reductionistic theses of classical monisms. According to the latter, each entity is definable or analyzable in terms of its possible inclusion within a class of entities regarded as the "really existent." If this class happens to be that of material entities, everything nonmaterial—for instance, everything "spiritual"—is said to be matter, reduced to matter, or explained as a transformation or as an epiphenomenon of matter. If spiritual realities, or more precisely spiritual acts, happen to be considered as "what is most real" or at any rate as "what is real *simpliciter,*" then matter is accounted for as the "other side" of spirit, and frequently as a degradation of it, if not as a mere illusion. On the other hand, the monism which I propose does not reduce, or try to reduce, everything to one way of being, no matter how important or basic the latter may seem. On the contrary, it does the best it can to integrate basic ways of being into a reality which is at the same time one and many—or, at any rate, one and more than one. This presupposes a certain tension and conflict between unity and plurality. The nature of such a tension can be understood more clearly when compared with similar tensions and conflicts which occasionally spring forth within the body of scientific theories. It is common practice to recognize not only the existence of "sectors" of physical reality which may be governed by different sets of laws (gravitational laws, electromagnetic laws, and so on) but also the existence of entire bodies of physical theory based on different sets of concepts (generalized Relativity; quantum-mechanical laws, and so on). It is also common practice to recognize that certain phenomena rather than others may be produced depending upon certain conditions of matter (expansion of intragalactic matter caused by the reciprocal repulsion of hydrogen atoms; the permanence of the same matter due to the overwhelming force of gravity, and so on). Yet efforts are constantly being made to achieve a unified, or relatively unified, physical outlook (Einstein's and, more recently, Heisenberg's theory of the unified field; attempts to formulate a single law accounting for the above-mentioned expansion and permanence of intragalactic matter, and so on).

Unity and plurality may then not be entirely incompatible. Once again resuming our ontological language we may assert that reality is one while it is at the same time diverse, provided that this diversity be understood as a peculiar tension rather than as a mere difference. "Spirit" and "matter" may then be neither two mutually exclusive types of reality nor two sides of the same reality; they may be (ontological) "poles" constituting whatever realities there are, so that, again, no given entity can be said, properly speaking, to be "spiritual" or "material," but can be said to be more or less "spiritual" or more or less "material" depending upon its place in the real continuum. To be sure, "spirit" and "matter" should be considered here merely as examples of many other possible ontological "poles" yielding diversity within the frame of unity. As a matter of fact, and for reasons which will soon become apparent, the ontological "poles" which I will call "the external" and "the internal" (and, at the limit, "the intimate") are far more basic than "spirit" and "matter." The former poles help to clarify the peculiar nature of the "monism" here proposed.

It is not easy to define, even sketchily, the expressions "the external" and "the internal" because, among other reasons, the meaning of either one depends upon the meaning of the other. Like the Aristotelian notions of form and matter or act and potency, the concepts of the external and the internal are relative and, as it were, functional concepts. Something is called "external" only in relation with, or by reference to, something else which is called "internal," and vice versa. The external and the internal are, then, not realities in themselves. They only *formally* constitute what is real insofar as nothing real can be grasped (metaphysically) except as a function of both of them. As metaphysical "formalities," the external and the internal are not demonstrable either directly or empirically. They are not even demonstrable in the manner in which a very general natural law can be proved to be true. In some ways, they resemble the Kantian concepts of the understanding. But, unlike the latter, they circumscribe reality instead of merely our knowledge of it. They are given to an "intuition" which emerges as a consequence of a constant and frequent relationship with reality and which does not exclude, but rather attempts to integrate, both the common and the scientific modes of knowledge. Their "demonstration" is, then, extremely indirect, as is that of all metaphysical hypotheses and, to an even greater extent, that of the modes of thinking which give rise to such hypotheses.

In any case, to postulate the external and the internal as metaphysical "formalities" constituting reality does not mean that reality is made up of them in the same manner as it is made up of molecules, or cells, or psychic processes. Nor does it mean that reality can be grasped exclusively on the basis of such "formalities," for in that case they would be transformed into "categories." The external and the internal are limiting principles of reality, in both an ontological and an epistemological sense. No entity can be reduced to either of them, but any entity whatsoever may be ontologically circumscribed and epistemologically explained in terms of both of them.

All this means that nothing is purely external or purely internal—and, as a consequence, that nothing is purely material or purely spiritual, purely inorganic or purely organic, etc. The external and the internal are, again, ontological poles. What we call "realities"—things, phenomena, organic structures, psychic processes, and so on—are to be found between these poles and nowhere else. Thus, each real entity tends to be either more or less external or more or less internal. No doubt some entities look as if they could be characterized by only one polar tendency, but they never succeed in excluding the opposite tendency. According to the conceptual framework outlined in preceding sections, 'the external' and 'the internal' are names of absolute realities, and since the latter do not exist the former do not properly name anything. But by means of them the universe is made intelligible. I have said that every entity *tends to be* more or less external or more or less internal because its being is determined by *both* poles. I am not affirming that reality is primarily something external, for example, something primarily inorganic, so that the ontological measure of each thing would be determined by its orientation toward that exteriority. Nor am I maintaining that reality is primarily something internal, for example, something personal, so that the ontological measure of each thing would be determined by its orientation toward that interiority. I am postulating an ontological succession of entities. *But I assume that this succession cannot be depicted by a single, uninterrupted line having only one direction which, like an arrow, would indicate the direction of being toward "real existence."* It would be more accurate to represent this succession by a line on every point of which two contrary and complementary tendencies or polar directions converge. The corresponding ontology can be variously named: the "ontology of double directions," the "bi-directional ontology," the "two-way ontology," and so on. In any case, it is the "ontology of integrationism." Those metaphysical systems which introduced the notions of process and change clearly recognized that there is something in reality which is explicable primarily in terms of process, but they paid little or no attention to the dual direction of this process. For this reason, reality was often "measured" (ontologically) on the basis of a single direction, particularly that which leads toward "Being," "perfection," "plenitude," and so forth. The further an entity was from one of the "poles" of the ontological line, the less real it was supposed to be. In sum, each entity, or class of entities, was situated or located unilaterally and unequivocally. This was achieved primarily by identifying the other possible "pole" of the line as a signpost of nonexistence. Thus many of these metaphysical systems ended by subscribing to a spiritualistic monism which, although opposite in character, was very similar to the materialistic monism advocated by those who singled out matter as the sole ontological "measure."

The peculiar kind of monism advanced here resembles most other kinds of monism in that it does not intend to chop reality —the so-called "existences"—into watertight compartments.

But it sharply differs from them in that it employs two opposing yet complementary points of view in order to speak about any reality. Thus, every entity can be ontologically situated by virtue of its dual participation in the external and the internal, as well as in the other poles ensuing from them or accompanying them. It can also be said that every entity *tends toward* the external *and* the internal in varying degrees, as long as the expression 'tends toward' is not interpreted either as the sequel of a kind of self-effort or as the result of some kind of basic force which is supposed to be inherent in the very nature of the entity and perhaps even independent from the efficient causes which actually make it what it is. For that reason, the method or methods adopted for the ontological understanding of any reality or type of reality depends on the ontological situation of such an entity or of any type of entity in the real continuum. Methodological pluralism is thus not incompatible with an ontological monism such as the one outlined above. It is, on the contrary, a consequence of this monism. We can therefore choose that mode of viewing which proves the most adequate for grasping the nature and significance of each form of reality. Our choice will be dependent simply upon the *predominance* of either the external or the internal, which each entity, or type of entity, reveals.

It is quite a different matter to ask whether a metaphysical interpretation may later be given to this ontological scheme. In principle there is nothing to prevent us from considering a given ontological "pole" as metaphysically primordial and even as axiologically preferable. But for the moment it behooves us to consider our bidirectional ontology as strictly "neutral." Only insofar as the concepts of the external and the internal are relative and functional are they indispensable for situating reality ontologically.

Which means, of course, that the external and the internal as such, that is to say, as "absolutes" do not exist. Only entities —whether they are things, processes, phenomena, and so on—

exist. Exteriority and interiority, then, can be predicated in varying proportions only of entities. No matter which ontological "pole" we may wish to consider, we must always be careful not to disregard its counterpart, for, if we ignore the latter, then we also ignore the realities which actually fall between the two "poles." Hence, any ontological definition which takes into account only one "pole" is necessarily deficient. But this is by no means the end of the story. Any entity, or type of entity, is ontologically definable in terms of two contrasting ontological "poles" because we understand 'ontological definition' as 'ontological situation.' On the other hand, any "pole" is definable in terms of a contrasting and opposite "pole," but then certainly not because 'ontological definition' can be identified with 'ontological situation.' A "pole" is not situated anywhere, because "poles" are not realities; they simply help to situate, and hence ontologically define, realities. As a consequence, it would seem that if we can never know what any given "pole" is, then we must resign ourselves to complete silence regarding the "poles" themselves.

Such a silence about what, after all, we acknowledge as a basic determination of reality is rather embarrassing. Can we ever dare to say what "matter" is except that it is nothing but the "pole" which contrasts with "spirit"? Can we ever speak of the external and the internal except as conflicting, and, needless to repeat, nonexisting "absolutes"?

Fortunately, lack of a proper definition does not necessarily imply a complete lack of what we may call "orientation." With this limited purpose in mind, I will now attempt to clarify the basic notions of the external and the internal. It just so happens that underlying this clarification is the guiding thread of the present investigation: an examination of the degrees and forms of mortality or, in more general terms, of the capacity of the real to cease.

10
THE EXTERNAL AND THE INTERNAL

A thing is primarily held to be external when, although not entirely reducible to extension or to the geometric properties associated with extension, it behaves as if it were fundamentally composed of extended parts, with only a minimum of "interiority." But that minimum is indispensable, since the complete elimination of every interior aspect would be equivalent to the supression of reality. The interiority of reality which is primarily extended is revealed as spatial interiority. Any portion of this interior "can be made exterior" at a given time. Hegel was not misled when he claimed that exteriority (*Äusserlichkeit*) was the constitutive element of Nature.[22] What I have called "the external" is, in a sense, similar to Sartre's conception of Being-in-itself which he had described as opaque, compact, and dense. For Being-in-itself is that being which is, and which is what it is.[23] But certain significant differences must be established between the conceptions of these philosophers and the one offered here. For Hegel, Nature as exteriority is the being of the Idea outside of itself; it is the Idea insofar as it is alienated. In the latter case, 'exterior' is the name of a metaphysical concept and not of an ontological determination. Furthermore, exteriority for Hegel is not an ontological pole but, to use his own language, a "moment" in a process which exhibits only one direction: the return of being to itself as complete consciousness of itself. For Sartre, the "In-itself" is absolutely opposed to the "for-itself." Accordingly, he states that "the In-itself does not have an *inside* which could be opposed to an *outside* and which would be analogous to a judgment, a law, a consciousness of itself." Thus, while an absolute monism of process is paramount in Hegel, we find in Sartre a sharp dualism between being and consciousness. Unlike these conceptions, I maintain that the external is neither a "moment" in a process of interiorization, nor is it in absolute opposition to the internal. It is, rather, a tendency that all entities exhibit in varying degrees.

Inorganic matter is an example of a reality with a strong "tendency" toward exteriority. I am not referring to the composition of such matter for that is the subject of physical science. I am referring to its "ontological situation." I have already surmised (§ 3) that the mode of knowledge of natural science and the results which it has achieved are not indifferent to philosophical reflection. Nevertheless, philosophy is not exclusively conditioned by scientific information. Hence, no matter what the composition of inorganic matter may be from the point of view of natural science, it is still ontologically plausible to consider it in terms of its exteriority. Inorganic structures are aggregates which can be composed and recomposed. In such structures nothing, properly speaking, is produced or destroyed. To be sure, the exteriority of inorganic structures is not identical with the exteriority of some of the objects that have been called "ideal objects," such as geometric figures. In the inorganic realm we find fields and forces irreducible to any structure consisting of a mere juxtaposition of parts which are completely exterior to each other, and hence definable as a set of *partes extra partes*. Inorganic entities can never be made absolutely exterior; after all, they are real, not ideal objects. But any exteriorization which they may possess is of a spatial nature and follows either quantitative or topological spatial models. For that reason, mechanical descriptions and explanations of reality are better adapted to inorganic nature than to any other type of entities. To be sure, the mechanical or, as it is sometimes called, the "mechanic-mathematical" view of inorganic reality is not the only one possible. But it is often adequate. In a number of ways, this form of the real resembles the ideal.

By no means am I intimating that inorganic reality is composed of, and thus, so to speak, tinged with idealities, that is, "something" like geometrical figures, quantities, essences, principles. It has already been shown that an ontology of what is actually real does not, or should not, depend upon an ontology of what is real "in principle." But in regard to its ontological situation, inorganic reality exhibits characteristics very close to those displayed by what is real only "in principle," namely by the so-called "ideal objects," characteristics such as timelessness, reversibility, perdurability. 'Very close to' is, of course, not synonymous with 'exactly the same as.' Thus, for example, inorganic reality and inorganic processes are not timeless. But they are less time-determined than organic reality and organic processes, even allowing for the extremely important role played by whatever stands for 'time' in physical equations, including equations in classical mechanics, and, hence, needless to say, equations in Relativity, in at least one of Heisenberg's uncertainty relations, etc.[24] In any case, time in inorganic reality is, as it were, "minimal time," because it implies a "minimum of history," unless we define 'historical time' as a "simple succession of events." Nevertheless, "minimal time" is not timelessness; it is simply one of the two possible ontological directions of time. Now then, since any ontological "direction" is correlative to any other opposite ontological "direction," what we call an (ontological) tendency toward "minimal time" does not exclude the participation, though of course "minimumly," in the opposite, and complementary "direction" toward "maximal time," which is understood primarily as "historical time." If we consider timelessness as one of the possible characteristics of ideality and the latter as the best example of pure exteriority, then we can assert that, without being purely exterior, inorganic reality tends to be more exterior (or external) than interior (or internal) without, of course, ceasing to be the latter. All things considered, the exteriority of inorganic reality is truly real, and not ideal.

Until now we have spoken of "inorganic reality" as a whole, as if there were no possible differences among various types of inorganic reality. It is reasonable, however, to assume that 'inorganic reality' is just a handy name to designate a number of forms of such a reality, each one of these forms being "situated" at a given "place" in the real continuum. What these forms may be, and how many of them there are is something about which little or nothing can be said without some aid from the natural sciences. It is possible, for example, that even within the relatively well-unified realm of physical reality, there are forms of being which prove to be more or less "external," in the sense of 'external' outlined above. The form of physical reality which is primarily, although not, let us insist, exclusively composed of "exteriority," might well be certain simple elements which, at least in appearance, are indestructible, perdurable, and interchangeable. I have frequently referred to these elements as "ultimate particles" without, however, suggesting that they exhibit the same characteristics as the "mass points" described by classical mechanics. Discoveries in modern physics such as the rapid disintegration of a number of particles (certain mesons), the absence of mass in other particles (photons, which acquire mass only through velocity), the mutual annihilation of particles and antiparticles, and so on—all these results tend to belie the idea that "ultimate particles" are, so to speak, "simple entities." But if a less specific meaning is given to the expression 'ultimate particles'—such as "what is ultimately permanent, whatever it may be (material points, elemental vibrations, energy quanta, etc.)"—then it can readily be admitted that "they are what they are," which is merely another way of saying that "they are always what they are," with only a minimum of "interiority" capable of modifying its ontological structure. Such particles are the "indiscernibles" in nature, or at any rate what most closely approximates them.

In a universe consisting solely of an aggregate of such indiscernible elements or particles, 'to cease' simply means "to separate that which had formerly been united." Cessation does not affect such particles themselves, but it can be predicated of the aggregates composed of them. In this sense, it can be said that inorganic reality as such neither ceases nor, of course, "dies." In the composition and recomposition of these aggregates the principle *ex nihilo nihil fit* (nothing comes from nothing) is rigorously exemplified. It is, let us remember, one of the underlying principles of classical atomism.[25] Of course, one runs into trouble either when qualities which are not reducible to purely mechanical models are introduced or when mechanical models themselves no longer function as relatively simple and entirely closed systems. From the microphysical point of view there may not be any cessation but there certainly is from the macrophysical point of view. And since the macrophysical realm is not unrelated to the microphysical realm, what happens in the former may not be indifferent to what occurs in the latter. Only in the case of a system which is both closed and reversible can the absence of cessation be predicated without any risk of being impugned. In such a case, we can even assert that 'cessation' is a name applying to those phenomena which, in principle, are not likely to have taken place at all, and which seem to be made of the same "stuff" as the ideal entities—for example, the mathematical representations—used to describe them. Yet since such a system is not real but is, rather, an ideal limit, the conclusion that there is, indeed, cessation in inorganic reality and in inorganic processes seems plausible enough.

I am not claiming, then, that there is not any cessation in inorganic reality regardless of whether the latter could be exhaustively described by means of purely mechanical models. But I do maintain that inorganic reality tends not to cease, or more precisely that any so-called "cessation" in such a reality tends to be obscured by the possibility of a continual combining and recombining of the same supposedly unchangeable elements. In any case, cessation in inorganic reality is predominantly "external" to it. It appears, so to speak, "from the outside," interrupting a process or altering a structure. It never comes "from within" as an internal phase in a being's development or as the final point in a being's history. Indeed, there is some doubt whether we should use the word 'history' in reference to inorganic reality, for nothing that we can call "history" resembles that kind of "intimate process" which, according to Whitehead, is part and parcel of the "actual occasions." The latter concept was introduced to account for inorganic reality from the point of view of a "philosophy of organism"; no wonder then that it should emphasize the "other ontological direction" and not any "bidirectional ontology" of the type here proposed.

It might be tempting to conclude that if there are types of inorganic reality which are subjects of cessation in varying degrees, then they must begin with such "entities" as atomic nuclei. Atomic nuclei would then cease, or tend to cease, to a lesser degree than atoms at large; atoms at large would cease, or tend to cease, to a lesser degree than molecules, and so on. Now then, although we have frequently spoken of "ultimate particles" as "elementary particles," and although there is little doubt that such particles can often be identified with atomic nuclei (or, in any case, with atomic components), it would be too expeditious to assume that the degree of cessation in inorganic reality is strictly correlative to the "degree" of "simplicity" ascribed to its various elements. After all, it may well be the case that an atom, or even an atomic nucleus, proves to be more complex, and more subject to cessation, than a molar or macroscopic structure. Therefore, once again we do not claim that minimum cessation—or, more precisely, the possibility of cessation—should be ascribed to what we call today "basic particles" and to "basic particles" alone. We assert only that, whatever the so-called "ultimate particles" are, or prove to be, they will tend to cease to a lesser degree than nonultimate particles. If it is demonstrated beyond any reasonable doubt that elementary particles, as they are understood (or half-understood) today, are *grosso modo* indiscernibles, then, and only then, will we be allowed to conclude that they are what minimumly ceases in inorganic reality. Nevertheless, we can say with a reasonable degree of certainty that some types of inorganic reality cease to a greater extent, and more often, than others. An example of this type of inorganic reality is crystals. Crystals exhibit certain structures which are, to be sure, causally conditioned, but which are explainable nonetheless in terms of some "internal" plan or scheme. It has sometimes been contended that crystals are a form of reality intermediate between the inorganic and the organic. Yet, it is not necessary to advance such a hypothesis in order to recognize their high degree of self-organization and their minimal amount of combination and recombination of constituent, basic elements. Utilizing our terminology, it may be said that crystals can be "situated" in that section of the ontological line where the tendency to endure and not to cease prevails over the tendency to cease. But to state that a crystalline structure "ceases" still makes more sense than to say that an aggregate of elementary particles "ceases," particularly in view of the fact that the composition of such an aggregate is usually explained in terms of the behavior of its constituent particles. If we are momentarily allowed to use a somewhat anthropomorphic vocabulary, we could say that crystals "vacillate" in their being, for on the one hand they "tend" to behave as mechanistic-atomistic structures, while on the other hand they "tend" to behave as amputated stumps of biological organisms. Nothing could be farther from my plans than outlining an "ontology of crystals." Such an endeavor would be foolish, if not altogether grotesque. But I wanted to show by means of a particularly striking example that even within a certain realm of reality—inorganic reality at large—there seem to be various possible modes of cessation.

Chapter 2 deals with death in the organic realm. The complex relationship between organic and inorganic nature is thoroughly elucidated there. At this point, I will only state that, even if there were a clear-cut difference between them, it could still be held that organic reality is more "interior," ontologically speaking, than is inorganic reality. The term 'interior' says, of course, very little by itself; like most terms which are both common and abstruse, it needs to be filled with meaning. Part of this meaning can be ascertained when we take into account some traits exhibited by biological organisms, traits such as the greater irreversibility of organic processes; the increased importance of the role played by time (which accounts not only for development but also, and above all, for maturation); and, in particular, the possibility inherent in biological organisms to "hide," in a sense of 'hide' that will be clarified later, that is, to appear in ways different from the ways they "are" while at the same time revealing what they are by "exteriorizing" themselves. These and other traits are closely related to the production of some kind of "internal being" which is not exhausted by spatial relations. To all these characteristics must be added one which is particularly noteworthy: what may be called the "specificity" of organic substances, that is, the fact that an organic substance undergoes inorganic changes which operate in the service of configurations and behavior patterns specific to organic beings. It is true that some degree of "specificity" can also be detected in nonorganic compounds, for example, in chemical mixtures. But this only proves that, even if we consider an entity, or type of entity, which seems to be situated primarily in terms of one of the two ontological "directions"—or, more precisely, in terms of one of the two sets of ontological "directions"—so often described, it is still subject, however slightly, to the other "direction" or set of "directions." Thus, the characteristic here called "specificity" is particularly conspicuous in organic beings, but it runs continuously, in varying degrees, throughout reality. It just so happens that in organic beings "specificity," which is a clear manifestation of "interiority," not only exists, but even prevails over the tendency to a mere juxtaposition of elements.

It has occasionally been pointed out that one of the most characteristic features of organic substances is what we call "individuality." This is certainly true of most, if not all, of the organic realities with which we are acquainted. Yet we must not overlook the possibility that organic structures might have existed or might exist which are very different from the ones we know. For example, organic structures might exist, or have existed, as "shapeless" aggregates organized neither into species nor into individuals within species. In such a case, could we still speak of "specificity"? I think we could, for the predicate 'specific' is previous to, and in some sense more basic than, the predicate 'individual.' In fact, although all organic substances are, in the sense described, "specific," not all of them have attained a sufficient degree of individuality to deserve being called "individuals." Furthermore, if the degree of individuality closely corresponds to the degree of complexity in organic reality, then it is reasonable to suppose that there is some kind of parallelism between the degree of "interiorization" and the degree of individualization. Organic reality as fully developed, then, could be used as a point of reference to clarify the meaning of the term 'internal' (as well as the meaning of the term 'interior'). In an individual the "interior" is not constituted, or not exclusively constituted, by spatial relations between its various parts or even by the relations between its different functions. The "interior" of an inorganic reality is always, in some manner, present. On the other hand, that of an organic reality is essentially latent. The latter characteristic of organic reality is caused not only by the fact that its being is manifested beneath its appearance but also, and more significantly, because its appearance forms part of its being. Hence, we must relate the behavior of organic realities not only to their exterior, but also to their interior. In inorganic realities, cessation is minimal because it is, in the last analysis, external; it comes, so to speak, from the outside, as an interruption, disjunction, or disintegration. In organic realities, cessation constitutes a basic, although by no means absolute, predicate of their existence. For this reason we can now, at last, without danger of equivocation, change the vocabulary used to designate, or describe, the termination of an entity. In reference to the inorganic we shall continue to speak of cessation, but with respect to the organic we may already speak of "death." In this sense, though only in this sense, will we be able to assert that cessation in the form of death is part and parcel of organic reality.

Human life is both biological reality and inorganic structure. After all, what we call "a human being" comes into existence only when certain elements, organic and inorganic, are combined in definite ways.[26] But the fact that human life might be determined by such elements, and even be predictable in terms of their combination, does not necessarily mean that it can be *reduced* to them. Three features, or qualities, in human existence cannot be derived automatically from the elements which materially constitute this existence. These features we shall name "the historical," "the dramatic," and "the intimate." I will examine them at length later (§§ 23–24). For the present, let it suffice to say that the ingredient called "historical" in an organic being *qua* organic is, or rather tends to be, a cyclical process, a repetition of forms and patterns of behavior. In a human being, on the other hand, the ingredient in question is fundamentally irretrievable. To be sure, there is also something of a cyclical nature in human life. On the one hand, a relatively unalterable linear succession of organic stages determines a substantial portion of human behavior. On the other hand, human beings display psychological and sociological cycles, phases, and patterns which resemble those exhibited by biological organisms. Yet none of these factors constitutes what is "truly historical" in a human being. There are ontological reasons to account for this basic difference. To begin with, human life is not, properly speaking, human unless it is endowed with "meaning," in a sense of 'meaning' which would take too long to elucidate here. In other words, whereas inorganic and organic realities are what they are—or, as the case may be, what they become—human life, which *also* is what it is—and, of course, what it becomes—embodies a kind of "residuum" which is exhausted neither in its being nor even in its becoming. Hence the "dramatic character" of human life. Hence, also, its "intimate" and, so to speak, "innermost" character, the crowning point in a tendency toward "interiority" which such terms as 'is' and 'becomes' seem utterly unable to describe or ontologically circumscribe. In the transition from the "most exterior" to the "most interior," we seem suddenly to have stumbled upon a realm where even the very "anology of being" breaks down. It does not, in fact, break down, for in our ontology the idea of continuity—some kind of pluralistic continuity, let us hasten to add—still prevails over any ideas of "rupture" or "chasm," not to say of "jump."

11
BEING AND MEANING

This realm, which the very concept of being—even if supplemented by the concept of becoming—barely succeeds in grasping, I shall call the realm of "meaning." It could also be called the realm of "significance" or of "sense." In any case, the aforementioned tendency of reality toward "interiority" is culminated here. The same thing happens with "meaning" as with "interiority"; just as "interiority" and "exteriority" oppose and yet complement each other, so "meaning" and "being" also oppose and complement each other. Therefore, just as (if we take one of the ontological directions) meaning is a way of expressing being, so (if we take the opposite ontological direction) being is one of the ways of expressing meaning. In short, any entity, or type of entity, is (exists) only insofar as it has some meaning or sense, and it has some meaning or sense only insofar as it is (exists).

The analogy of being and what may be called the "analogy of meaning" are, therefore, concordant, or more precisely, parallel, except for the fact that each takes a different (and, of course, opposite) pole as a point of departure. Pure and simple being, which is equivalent to pure and naked fact, has hardly any meaning and yet it is not completely devoid of, or unrelated to, meaning, for if it were it would cease to be a reality and would become "an absolute." Pure meaning, or significance, or sense, is hardly a fact and yet it is not completely detached or isolated from fact, for if it were it would also cease to be a reality and would become "an absolute," the opposite kind of "absolute." Since "absolutes" have been admitted here only as limiting concepts describing limiting, but nonexistent, realities, pure being and pure meaning can only be limiting realities which the concepts "being" and "meaning" are apt to describe but cannot possibly denote.

The meaning given here to the terms 'being' and 'meaning' does not correspond to their meaning in ordinary language. It would be preposterous to maintain that "inorganic nature has no meaning" or, as it could also be said, "inorganic nature has no significance," "inorganic nature has no sense," if by this we understood that such a nature lacks ontological justification. For analogous reasons, it would be nonsensical to say that "spirit has no being" or "spirit has nothing to do with facts" if we understood by this that it had no reality. To state that inorganic entities "tend" more toward being than toward meaning is equivalent to saying that they are definable primarily by what they are. Thus the predicates which ontologically circumscribe inorganic entities are as close to their subject as predicates can possibly be. These entities display only a minimal ontological "doubleness." Their being makes itself apparent *almost* as it really is. It is being in itself and not being for another. The subject is never, of course, identical with its predicates, for if such were the case then we would not have "being" but rather nothingness. Something is predicated of a certain subject which, in some way, is not the subject itself, but which tends—at least in the knowing mind, and hence, on a conceptual level—to be reduced to it. On the other hand, to affirm that the realities designated by the terms 'spirit,' 'consciousness,' and so on, and, in the last analysis, 'the internal,' "tend" more toward meaning than toward being is equivalent to saying that they are primarily definable by what they mean. In this case, the predicates used are separated to the greatest extent possible from the subject which they (onotologically) define, or circumscribe. But, they are never completely dissociated from it. Here the ontological "doubleness," or "dissociation," reaches a maximum. Such a reality manifests itself *almost* as "the other" of what it is. It is a "being for . . ." and, as it were, a "being by reference." [27]

The nature of this "being" and "meaning" poses a problem that can only be touched upon here. Even when it is acknowledged that they are only limiting concepts apt to ontologically circumscribe realities rather than concepts which would denote so-called "absolute realities," we must still ask ourselves whether it is proper to talk about them or whether it would be more sensible to limit ourselves to using them as *fictiones mentis*. After all, neither "being" nor "meaning" as such exist, and, therefore, they cannot be said to have any "nature."

If we were to choose the first alternative, the resultant philosophy could be called, to a great extent, "traditional." We would then assume that philosophic thought, even the most cautious and least speculative can, if only indirectly, by means of a language which is acknowledged to be inadequate, attempt to talk about reality *qua* reality. If, on the other hand, we were to choose the second alternative, the resultant philosophy would deserve to be called "linguistic," at least in the sense that it would be primarily concerned with use rather than with meaning or, of course, reality. Now then, while I find linguistic philosophy both useful and interesting, the type of thinking I have adopted here is somewhat more "traditional" than "linguistic." At any rate, I believe that it is legitimate, not to say instructive, to elucidate the concepts of "being" and "meaning" within the framework of ontology. I do not mean to suggest that any ontological talk about "being" and "meaning" can ever succeed in completely clarifying the nature of the corresponding concepts. After all, neither being nor meaning *per se* are, or can ever be, accessible to any kind of experience. Only entities which can be said "to be" and "to mean" in varying degrees can be the objects of experience. Yet, some characteristics of being (as embodied in things that "are") and of meaning (as embodied in things insofar as they have some significance or sense) can be, so to speak, "represented" by means of any set of ontological polarities which we choose to use.

The concepts of "being" and "meaning" can also, and above all, be represented in terms of the notion of cessation. Pure being not only does not cease but cannot cease: it is what it is, and it always is what it is. Pure meaning is that which essentially can cease, so that it might be designated as "dying as such." Can we say then, that reality insofar as it is, does not cease, but that insofar as it means, does not even attain being? It would be tempting to embrace such a conclusion were it not for the purely limiting character of the concepts of "total absence of cessation" and "total presence of cessation." Thus, nothing really existing is completely "immortal," and nothing is completely "mortal": inorganic reality ceases to be, no matter how slightly, while human reality, again no matter how slightly, endures. Human reality, as personal reality, is indeed the most mortal of all realities to the extent that it might even be said that it exists in terms of its dying, although never completely, or exclusively, in terms of its dying. Only what transcends both the inorganic and the personal, such as ideas, values, and so on, can remain eternally. But then it can no longer be said that it exists, since its reality, like the reality of everything that is not, properly speaking, real but only ideal, consists in being incorporated, or embodied, into some existing reality. Ideas and values could not even *be,* if they did not eventually emerge within the context of personal life. The latter, in turn, is made possible within the context of organic existence. It is only in this manner that a certain continuity can be ascertained between what is real and what is ideal, and in particular between the personal and the so-called "transpersonal" realm.

12
CONCLUSION

The problem of cessation has forced us to find our way through the labyrinth of general ontology, and in particular through that of one of the so-called "regional ontologies": the ontology of inorganic nature. I hope I have provided justification for believing that such a problem is a central one in philosophical elucidation. As soon as we so much as touch upon the concept of cessation, we stir up a hornet's nest: philosophic concepts such as "being," "meaning," "existence," "essence," "reality," "nature," "person," "value," and so on, swarm around our heads demanding to be explored as thoroughly as possible. In any case, there is little doubt that a philosophical examination of the problems of cessation and death has a strong bearing on how the foregoing ontological concepts are to be understood.

"Death," similar to the reality (being) of which Aristotle spoke, can be said in many ways: ὅ θάνατος λέγεται πολλαχῶς. But one can say in many ways only what one can also say in one fundamental way. We would be reluctant to emphasize the diversity of reality if it were detrimental to its unity and continuity. On the other hand, the idea of continuity has been grounded not on a type of reality which would easily and almost automatically extend, and expand, to any other remaining types of reality, but on a dialectical contrast of ontological "poles" whose interweaving circumscribes the type of reality we may choose to consider. From this point of view, we can speak of a progression of the capacity to cease until the level of death is attained. Everything that ceases participates in death, while at the same time death is not entirely comprehensible unless we keep in mind the general and universal phenomenon of cessation to which it is indissolubly attached. We could thus assert that the philosophy proposed here rejects not only all dualisms but also all monisms of the purely reductionist type. The monism and continuism *sui generis* which I postulate are, so to speak, made up of tensions. The nature of these tensions is such that they are never likely to be resolved into a "third term" which would absorb and, as it were, "pacify" the contrasting "poles." Thus, it does not seem necessary to repudiate completely two doctrines which are unacceptable only when approached in isolation, namely, atomistic mechanism and some kind of "spiritualism." Each of these doctrines has a role to play. It is up to the philosopher to explore the possibilities which each one has to offer.

We can thus say that it is necessary to see how far any given doctrine can go. But this is not enough, for the task remains of finding out where any given doctrine cannot go. Hence every metaphysical doctrine, provided it is sufficiently comprehensive and at the same time kept within reasonable bounds, may prove useful. But every metaphysical doctrine, particularly if taken in isolation, will prove defective because everything will then be seen in terms of the particular hue of its spectacles. Thus, for instance, to see matter from the point of view of spirit is just as prejudiced and one-sided as to see spiritual realities, personal realities, and so on, from the point of view of matter. It is a distortion of reality and, to be sure, a fundamental philosophic mistake. The root of such a mistake is always the same; it consists in using a basic metaphysical concept as if it actually designated some sort of absolute reality and, even worse, as if there was one, and only one, type of reality. The two-way ontology proposed in the present book is meant to prevent just such confusions. It is meant, above all, to throw every kind of "absolute" overboard.

Although cessation is coextensive with the real, it does not affect all forms of reality equally. Just as we have assumed that "reality" can be said in various ways, so we can also admit that some of them are more adequate, or, at any rate, more enlightening, than others. It might be noted in passing that Aristotle gave "substance" some sort of ontological precedence over other ways of being. Similarly, we can also admit that certain modes of cessation are more prominent and, of course, more significant than others. More precisely, we can say that certain realities cease "more than others," so that we may be allowed to speak, metaphorically at least, of a "progression" in cessation until it culminates in what will be called "death."

The modes of cessation in organic nature typify a decisive stage in this "progression." Hence, the time has come to make them a subject of inquiry.

TWO

Death in Organic Nature

13
MATTER AND ORGANISM

I have assumed that the process called "death" is more internal to reality than is the process called "cessation." At the same time, I have surmised that, although biological organisms are made up of inorganic substances, they are situated ontologically on a more "advanced" stage of the real continuum, namely, that stage in which the ontological tendency toward interiority prevails, or at any rate begins to prevail over the opposite—and, needless to say, complementary—tendency toward exteriority. It would seem plausible to conclude, then, that biological organisms, henceforth often called "organisms," cease to be for reasons which are not, or are not entirely, "accidental"—for reasons which are in any case far less "accidental" than the ones accounting for cessation in purely inorganic compounds. In short, it would seem that cessation, viewed as death, is essentially, or at least quasi-essentially, inherent in the organic world.

Plausible as they may seem to be, these conclusions give rise to embarrassing problems. In the first place, there is also something "interior" in inorganic realities, at least insofar as they are made up of structures whose properties include that of being subject to cessation. In the second place, organic realities are, to some extent, "exterior," at least insofar as they are composed of, and determined by, physico-chemical elements and processes. The inorganic modes of cessation have already been described as (predominantly) external, and consequently, to the extent that organic realities can be said to be (ontologically) exterior, their mode of cessation can be similarly characterized. Is the conclusion, then, that death is inherent in organisms, only an illusion prompted by the difficulties that often follow any attempts to "reduce" organisms completely to their inorganic components?

I cannot agree, for the close association of organisms with death has solid ontological foundations. Now then, since the ontology of organic reality, which we shall soon outline, has much to do with a number of tenets concerning the nature of organisms and their relation to inorganic reality, it will be necessary to break ground with a succinct examination of such tenets. I refer, of course, to the tenets known as "mechanism," "vitalism," "organicism," and so on, and in particular to the various polemics which they have originated: "mechanism versus vitalism," "mechanism versus organicism," "organicism versus vitalism," and so on.

The tenets in question are in the main the following ones: 1. There are basic and irreducible differences between organisms and inorganic reality. 2. Organic phenomena can, and should, be "reduced" to purely material processes. 3. Organisms are ontologically prior to material processes, so that all matter is, fundamentally, "organic."

The first tenet completely separates the living (animate) from the inert (inanimate) without, however, considering the latter as being devoid of energy. The second tenet considers the living in terms of the inert. The third tenet holds that the inert can be thoroughly understood only in terms of, and by analogy with, the living. Tenets first and third are usually regarded as expressing the point of view of "vitalism," although in point of fact only the third tenet actually deserves the name 'vitalism.' The first tenet can be, and usually is, identified with "organicism" (or with "biologism"). The second tenet expresses the point of view of "mechanism." In order to simplify matters, I shall associate the third tenet with the so-called "radical (or extreme) vitalism." As to the first tenet, I shall consider it as exhibiting two forms: "vitalism in the strict sense" and "organicism." We are then in the presence of four philosophies of organic nature: "radical (or extreme) vitalism," "vitalism in the strict sense," "organicism" (or "biologism"), and "mechanism."

It should be pointed out that the expressions 'reducible to' and 'irreducible to' can be understood in two ways. Let us consider for the moment only the expression 'reducible to.' On the one hand, we can speak of A as being reducible to B in a real sense, in which case we assume that A is, at bottom, B, that phenomena associated with A are, at bottom, phenomena associated with B, etc. On the other hand, we can speak of A as being reducible to B in a conceptual sense, or in a linguistic sense; then we assume that whatever we can say of A we can say of B, or more precisely that A is thoroughly explicable in terms of B, or that the set of concepts—or the "language"—by means of which we describe A can be, and indeed should be, reduced to the set of concepts—or the "language"—by means of which we describe B. The same goes, of course, for the expression 'irreducible to,' with the pertinent modifications. Now then, it is possible to maintain a reductionist attitude on the conceptual, or the linguistic, level without necessarily adhering to a reductionist attitude on the real level. It is also possible to maintain that a conceptual, or linguistic, reductionism would prove indefensible unless it were supported by a real reductionism. It is, of course, impossible, or at least quite implausible, to hold a real reductionism without adhering at the same time to a conceptual, or linguistic, reductionism—or without constantly trying to develop the latter type of reductionism as thoroughly as possible.

It is not always easy to ascertain what type of reductionism (or anti-reductionism, as the case may be) a given philosopher or biologist has in mind. As a rule, almost all the "organicists" (or "biologists") and a number of "mechanists" are careful enough to distinguish between real reductionism and conceptual, or linguistic, reductionism. Radical (or extreme) vitalists, nearly all the vitalists in the strict sense, and a number of mechanists, on the other hand, exhibit a strong tendency to put the two types of reductionism (or anti-reductionism) on a par. It will suffice for the moment to keep in mind the possibility of the aforementioned types of reductionism (or anti-reductionism) and the general tendencies displayed by philosophers and biologists in this respect.

A few words are in order before we proceed to what we shall call an "examination of doctrines" (§ 14). To begin with, and in order to avoid unnecessary confusions, I will abstain from any reflections of an axiological character. I am aware of the fact that in philosophy, and even in science, basic judgments of value are often disguised under the cover of "objectivity." But to discuss this aspect of the question would take us too far afield. For this reason, I do not think it would be pertinent to consider those forms of vitalism which are found in the writings of Nietzsche and Dilthey. Nietzsche in particular held that the so-called "primacy of life" is basically an axiological primacy; "life" for Nietzsche was a value rather than a fact. Something similar is true of authors like Max Scheler and Simmel. Thus, when Scheler points out that the "organ" is superior to the "instrument," that "spontaneous life" is superior to "inert (and merely useful) matter," and so on,[1] he is obviously making judgments of value. When Simmel writes that "life has two definitions which mutually complement each other: it is 'more life' and 'more than life,' "[2] he is outlining an axiology rather than an ontology, not to say an epistemology. As a matter of fact, some materialists and mechanists proceed along the same lines, although they maintain the opposite opinion, namely, that since the living is based on the inert, the latter is more "important" and even more "significant" than the former. Yet authors like Scheler and Simmel and, of course, a number of materialists and mechanists have evolved philosophical biologies which can be studied independently from any underlying judgments of value. In this sense we will include these authors in our examination.

I shall consider the radical (or extreme) vitalist, the strict vitalist, the organicist (or biologist), and the mechanistic doctrines in that order. The first says that the inanimate (often identified with the inert) is, at best, only a form of the animate (of the living). The second holds that the animate can be distinguished, essentially and, as it is often expressed nowadays, ontically, from the inanimate. The third states that, although there are marked differences between the animate and the inanimate, they are neither essential nor ontic but merely structural differences. The fourth doctrine asserts that the animate is only a form, or mode, of the inanimate. Let us then proceed to their examination.

14

EXAMINATION OF DOCTRINES

1. Radical vitalism is not, strictly speaking, a philosophy of Nature. Neither is it a metaphysics. It is a world view, a *Weltanschauung,* from which a metaphysics and a philosophy of Nature are *frequently* derived. Basically, it consists in emphasizing the "living," the "animated," and the "spontaneous" sides of reality. It views Nature as a conglomeration of organisms pulsating in diverse rhythms and yet throbbing in unison with

the great organism of Nature, which some ancient philosophers had visualized as a gigantic animal. In this sense, many Greek and Hellenistic philosophers adhered to "radical vitalism." The reality of a thing was, for them, a kind of living wellspring. Such a view of (natural) reality was held even by Aristotle, although with the restraint and moderation so typical of him. For in no way did Aristotle neglect the role played by mechanical processes and least of all by efficient causes. Yet he often took organisms as models of natural reality, and in this sense at least he can be considered as a fair representative of radical vitalism.

The vitalistic *Weltanschauung* outlined above is mostly, if not entirely, teleological; efficient causes, although necessary, are held to be secondary. It should be pointed out that such a *Weltanschauung* has found favor in some modern philosophers. Thus, thinkers such as Leibniz and Lotze, who were quite different from Aristotle in many respects, followed in his footsteps in this particular respect. To be sure, both Leibniz and Lotze, but especially Leibniz, were straight "mechanists" in regard to physics. But at the same time they were out-and-out "vitalists" in regard to metaphysics. And since they held that metaphysical explanations are, in the last analysis, more basic than physical explanations, they ended by subordinating the mechanical order to the teleological order, and, in consequence, the inanimate realm to the animate realm. To some extent the same goes for Bergson. It is true that inanimate "material" systems are, for Bergson, fundamentally different from animate "organic" systems. But it is no less obvious that, when Bergson speaks of the entire universe, he cannot resist the temptation of imagining it as some kind of "huge organism." In all these philosophers, therefore, "the living" is viewed as *the* reality and as the starting point for the understanding, and even the production, of all realities. Thus, we can claim that all of them are, to a greater or lesser degree, "radical vitalists."

The vitalistic *Weltanschauung* has often been vindicated by an abundance of subtle arguments and by some thought-provoking facts. Yet facts, or rather interpretation of facts, and arguments in vitalistic *Weltanschauungen* are always based on a previous view or, as the case may be, "vision" of natural reality. Bergson's vitalism is, in this respect, particularly enlightening, precisely because he was so insistent upon the need for argument and analysis of natural facts before making any pronouncements on the nature of the basic structure of reality. Thus, inorganic matter and organic matter are equally "material" for Bergson. It would seem then that the predicates 'is inorganic' and 'is organic' merely express two different points of view on Nature: one appears when a "mechanics of translation" is developed; the other is manifested when a "mechanics of transformation" is promoted.[3] The physico-chemical explanation of organic reality may be compared to the analysis of a curve into its differentials; the understanding of the ultimate nature of such a reality is comparable to the intuition of the never-broken continuity of the curve. Thus, the various natural systems are like points of view on the totality of the cosmos. Yet the cosmos is not the sum total of these points of view but rather a unique and indivisible continuity that grows larger with the indivisible movement of "duration," which is none other than "duration itself" in the process of growing. For this reason, Bergson could not maintain that there is an essential difference between the animate and the inanimate. Nor did he advance the idea, so characteristic of the philosophers and biologists whom we shall name "strict vitalists," that organic processes are conditioned by some specific "vital substance." In this respect, Bergson was less "vitalist-minded" than the "strict vitalists," so that it would seem we are completely misunderstanding his thought; how can a "vitalist" who is not even a "strict vitalist" be counted among the defenders of a radically vitalistic *Weltanschauung?* But in another, more important, respect, Bergson was truly a radical vitalist, for he viewed the entire cosmos as a basically "vital" reality.

Although I could not help mentioning radical or extreme vitalism, I consider its tenets to be less significant for the problem under discussion than any of the other doctrines considered here. Radical vitalism says little, if anything at all, on the problem of death. Let us now assume that radical vitalism is a "true doctrine." What sense would it make to say that the phenomenon called "death" is more characteristic of organisms than of so-called "inorganic systems"? What sense would it make to claim that organisms die while inorganic realities merely cease to be? Above all, what sense would it make to maintain that there is a continuity between the two orders of reality—the inorganic and the organic—if such a continuity turned out to be based upon the "reduction" of one order to the other? If we could prove, or at least be reasonably convinced, that radical vitalism is a "true doctrine," there would be no fundamental difficulty, but only because there would be no problem. But it is far from proved that radical vitalism is a true doctrine, whereas we are still convinced that our contentions do make some sense. At any rate, they raise problems which radical vitalists are unable to recognize as such.

2. Strict vitalism—which henceforth I shall simply call "vitalism" or, as the case may be, "neovitalism"—maintains, as does organicism, that there are notorious differences between the animate and the inanimate. But while organicism accounts for these in terms of "structural differences" and often in terms of "modes of conceptualization" and/or "modes of speech," vitalism ordinarily assumes that there are actually different "realities," or rather, different "principles of reality" which condition not only the structure and behavior of the two types of "substances" (the organic and the inorganic) but also their specific and irreducible "nature."

As a rule, 'radical vitalism' is the name of a *Weltanschauung*. More modestly, 'strict vitalism' is the name of a doctrine (or, more properly put, of a hypothesis or a series of hypotheses) concerning the ultimate constitution of organic reality. To be sure, strict vitalism is a variegated doctrine. Furthermore, some radical vitalists have also been strict vitalists. Nevertheless, strict vitalism, as we understand it, has been developed mostly by philosophers and biologists during the first quarter of the present century, so that there is a family resemblance among most strict vitalists or neovitalists. Among the more or less philosophically minded biologists who have been outstanding neovitalists are Johannes Reinke, Jacob von Uexküll, and Hans Driesch. Now then, since neovitalism as a full-fledged philosophical doctrine has been elaborated principally by Driesch, I shall single him out as the main representative of this trend.

All neovitalists in the sense described above agree that every organism possesses a ruling principle, a so-called "dominant element" (Reinke) or "entelechy" (Driesch). The embryology of the "mechanics of evolution" (*Entwicklungsmechanik*) worked out by Wilhelm Roux opened up a new field of research which, according to Driesch, helped to support the idea of the "autonomy of life." [4] A number of experiments seemed to give solid empirical foundations to some neovitalist tenets. For example, in a famous experiment performed by Gustav Wolff, it was discovered that a new cornea could be generated around the rim of the original cornea extracted from the eye of a water lizard (*Triton taniatus*).[5] Driesch's own experiments with the eggs of a sea urchin looked particularly impressive to the eyes of neovitalists. Driesch found that embryos which were complete, although smaller, could be developed out of sections of sea urchin eggs. To this empirical foundation Driesch hastened to add a conceptual one, both metaphysical and epistemological. He was soon led to believe that there are organic totalities which are entirely irreducible to inorganic processes. According to Driesch, the concepts of "prospective value," "prospective potency," and, above all, "equipotential ontogenetic system" could not be derived from notions belonging to the language in which purely chemical processes are ordinarily described. Consequently, it seemed inevitable to him to postulate the existence of some "vital principle," particularly in view of the fact that various experiments in the physiology of movements happened to confirm those already performed in morphology.

Driesch called this "vital principle" an "entelechy." But unlike the "vital principles" conjectured by a number of Renaissance natural philosophers and some modern "antimechanical philosophers," the "principles" postulated by neovitalists, and especially Driesch's "entelechies," lacked energy of their own. He wrote:

> An entelechy is something that is not physico-chemical; and the only positive character that we are allowed to attribute to it, so far, is that it is an actual elementary agent or factor of *Nature,* the word 'entelechy' being not merely a name to describe a formal point of view. It is important to grasp the *provisional negativeness* of entelechy, because we will then avoid a mistake often committed by vitalists, namely, the mistake of regarding the vital agent as something "psychical" without further consideration. But the contrary of *mechanical* is merely *non-mechanical,* and not "psychical." [6]

In other words, the vital principle referred to here is not a formal element, and yet it is not a completely positive element. It is an agent of direction and suspension, a principle of order and organization that makes the development and individuality of "harmonious equipotential systems" possible.[7] Thus the entelechy—or, more precisely, the various entelechies, morphogenetic, psychoid, and so on—does no more than activate or halt organic functions without violating the physico-chemical laws and, needless to say, without running counter to the law of conservation of energy. Driesch chose the term 'entelechy' because it entailed the idea of "finality," a finality that was supposed to be static as well as dynamic. The entelechy, then, is not a producer or maker of biological organisms, but a regulator of them.

Neovitalism seems to be the most adequate doctrine for supporting the thesis that biological organisms die "more" than inorganic structures. Neovitalists do not feel any need to subscribe to a metaphysics of the Bergsonian type. Furthermore, neovitalism, especially as elaborated by Driesch, does not even assert that death is metaphysically inherent in biological organisms. Driesch confines himself to maintaining that death neither results from mechanical causes nor is it a consequence of specific chemical processes. Rather, it ensues from a "direction" given by the entelechy leading to the suspension or interruption of all possible processes.[8] The activity of the entelechy depends on differences in potential, since an organism is *also* an inorganic system. But within the limits set up by physico-chemical processes and the laws ruling them, the entelechy has the possibility of bringing about adjustments capable of explaining why organisms decay and die.[9]

Despite neovitalists' efforts to avoid metaphysical "extremism," their contentions do not carry much conviction. First and foremost, neovitalism has become a doctrine that has found little support in the developments of contemporary biology. It may be argued that new developments in biology may change the picture; after all, what we call "biological philosophy" is, and probably will be for a long time, in a fluid state. We are reasonably convinced, however, that the picture will not change, and this for a very simple reason: because the "principles" postulated by neovitalists will always remain unverifiable (and hence, also unfalsifiable) unless they are so drastically changed as to be no longer what neovitalists want them to be. The "dominant elements" in Reinke's sense and the "entelechies" in Driesch's sense are not genuine biological entities. Nor are they metaphysical principles. Thus, neovitalist doctrines wander in a no man's land without much opportunity to extricate themselves from this rather uncomfortable position.

Secondly, neovitalism has failed to provide a convincing explanation of why death occurs in biological organisms. Driesch's entelechies, for instance, are not supposed to change or alter any process; they confine themselves to "halting" a given process. If this were not enough, Driesch makes it clear that entelechies possess no specific energy. But then it is difficult to understand how such entelechies are able even to initiate a process. A force that does not possess a force remains a mystery, or at least a puzzle. Nor is it too clear how entelechies are able to perform any function without following orientations or directions other than those emerging from their own "nature." How does it happen that entelechies tend toward this or that particular organic form? Only one answer is tenable: "finality." But unless neovitalism throws all caution to the winds and transforms itself into radical vitalism, biological finality will remain incomprehensible. Either finality cannot explain itself or else it must be based on the tautology that there is finality just because there is finality.

3. Neovitalists are far from neglecting the problems raised by the conceptual analysis of the predicate 'is irreducible to.' Indeed, they often claim that 'A is irreducible to B' is synonymous with 'A is conceptually irreducible to B.' Yet the neovitalists' contention that the animate is conceptually irreducible to the inanimate is almost invariably based on the belief that the animate is, in fact (or "really"), irreducible to the inanimate. Hence, neovitalism affirms, or at least presupposes, that there is an "essential and ontic difference" between the animate and the inanimate. On the other hand, organicism may conclude that the irreducibility in question is, at bottom, real, but it tends to buttress it by means of the notion of "conceptual irreducibility." In this respect, organicism looks both plausible and promising. At any rate, it is a fact that the conceptual system—often called "the language"—of a science cannot easily be reduced to that of another. Such a reduction proves difficult even within different areas of the same science. Hence when a reduction of this type is achieved it is hailed as a great accomplishment. Now, how can we expect a conceptual reduction to be easy, and even feasible, when it is a question of the relation between a conceptual system such as that of biology in general and another such as that of physics in general? To be sure, many fruitful

points of contact are constantly being emphasized (for example, those between certain biological functions and the laws which govern the behavior of electrical charges). Nevertheless, conceptual reductions cannot be extended indefinitely without running the risk of sliding into conceptual confusions.

A number of biologists display, or have displayed, organicistic tendencies (Ludwig von Bertalanffy, Oscar Hertwig, J. S. Haldane, E. S. Russell, etc.). Next to them we find a few authors proclaiming that a pure phenomenology of organic reality can reveal an "essential and ontic difference," if not an "essential and ontological difference," between the animate and the inanimate.[10] The latter authors (whom I shall call "phenomenologists" in a rather loose sense of this word) argue that all that is needed to prove such an "essential and ontic (or, as the case may be, ontological) difference" is a careful *description* of the nature and behavior of organic entities. In a sense, they are right: there is always some danger involved in completely dismissing description for the sake of explanation. This danger we may call the "Cartesian danger" and also the "Cartesian mirage." It is exemplified in the famous paragraph of the *Second Meditation,* in which Descartes points out that as soon as a piece of wax is placed near the fire it loses all its qualities: the taste vanishes, the odor evaporates, the color changes, the form disappears. To all this we may answer, with the Argentine philosopher Francisco Romero, that "present-day philosophy has learned, and slowly continues to learn, that there is much to see and consider in the wax before it is placed near the fire." [11] Now, philosophers such as Nicolai Hartmann, Günther Jacobi, and Max Scheler have been, in the above sense, "phenomenologists" and have helped to spread the idea that some kind of "descriptive ontology" should precede any theory or doctrine. All these philosophers believe that a "pure phenomenology" of the nature and behavior of organisms will reveal a number of properties which cannot be detected in purely inorganic entities. A common characteristic of these properties is, in Scheler's words, "the essential spontaneity of organisms."[12] Thus, a phenomenological description of organic nature tends to confirm the organicist theses and give them an ontological foundation.

Organicists and "phenomenologists" seem to agree with sheer common sense: is it not perfectly obvious that a description of organisms yields different results than a description of inorganic entities? It would seem, then, that we must acknowledge that the organic is conceptually (if not "really") irreducible to the inorganic. Yet, things are not as simple as they might seem. Ernest Nagel has rightly pointed out that, if one "views the reduction of one science to another in terms of the logical connections between certain empirically confirmed statements of the two sciences,"[13] it may be concluded that the fact that one science appears to be reducible (or, we can add, irreducible) to another depends, to a great extent, on the (historical) state of the science in question and, in no small measure, on the "linguistic" conventions (in a very broad sense of 'linguistic') adopted. Thus, it has often been claimed that mechanism "has failed" in its chimerical attempt to explain fully the behavior of inorganic—and *a fortiori,* of organic—reality. But doesn't this happen only when mechanism is understood as "classical mechanism"? Doesn't the explanatory power of mechanistic theories increase when we enlarge their conceptual resources? These points raise the question of whether the terms 'mechanism' and 'mechanistic theory' are still adequate. If we contend that they are adequate in one sense but not in another, we run the risk of turning our discussion into a mere *quaestio de nominibus.* Wouldn't the so-called "organicism" be nothing more than a refined mechanism? And if such were the case, why dismiss mechanism in the name of organicism?

Many organicists and all "phenomenologists" will argue that there is, and always will be, a "residue" in the language of biology which is, and will be, in principle irreducible to the language of chemistry and physics. The reasons adduced to support this argument are numerous and subtle; it is most improbable that neither rival will win the dispute once and for all. Nevertheless, there are reasons to suspect that when a suitably amplified and refined mechanistic theory goes to the heart of the problem concerning the nature of biological processes, its explanatory power becomes extremely impressive. Nagel emphasized this point when he maintained that the two most significant points—definability and derivability—involved in the explanation of one scientific language in terms of another, are still unable to disclose sufficient reasons to prove that in principle the language of mechanism is *not* capable of accounting for many phenomena described by biologists. If it is argued, for example, that mechanism does not take into account the notion of "totality" so typical of organisms, we can answer by pointing out that (1) such a "totality" is usually defined in a very vague manner, and that (2) if a more precise definition of 'totality' were provided, it might also apply to inorganic structures. Thus, Nagel writes,

the distinction between wholes which are and those which are not sums of parts is clearly *relative to some assumed body of theory T;* and, accordingly, though a given whole may not be the sum of its parts relative to one theory, it may indeed be such a sum relative to another. Thus, though the thermal behavior of solids is not the sum of the behavior of its parts relative to the classical kinetic theory of matter, it is such a sum relative to modern quantum mechanics. To say, therefore, that the behavior of an organism is not the sum of the behavior of its parts, and that its total behavior cannot be understood adequately in physico-chemical terms even though the behavior of each of its parts is explicable mechanistically, can only mean that no body of general theory is now available from which statements about the total behavior of the organism are derivable. The assertion, even if true, does *not* mean that it is *in principle* impossible to explain such total behavior mechanistically, and it supplies no competent evidence for such a claim.[14]

In support of the above statements we may point out that some experiments (Paul Weiss, A. C. Taylor) have conclusively shown that every cell or group of cells possesses "specific internal directions," so that, once isolated, they develop their own characteristics independently of a biological complex "externally" given. But in no case do these "specific internal directions" justify the postulate of some kind of "Drieschian entelechy" which could govern specific processes. Nor do they justify an organicistic view according to which a conceptual and/or real reduction proves to be a hopeless undertaking. For it has been shown that the "direction" of these processes can always be broken down into a series of factors which represent specific codes, analogous to those which rule genetic processes.

4. Having rejected vitalism of all kinds, and having warned against what we may call the "appeal" of organicism, are we to conclude that mechanism is the only fitting solution, at least as a very general principle, for the explanation of the nature and behavior of organisms? Such a conclusion would be rash. In the first place, we should avoid practicing what Nagel himself has called "the black magic of extracting one set of phenomena from others incommensurably different from the first." [15] A radical mechanism can be as deceptive and arbitrary as any type of vitalism, including the very moderate brand of vitalism called "organicism." To be sure, it may be argued that we need not deal with "radical mechanism," and that we may content ourselves with some kind of refined and at the same time enlarged conceptual mechanism, which is endowed with a reasonably sufficient explanatory power without yet really claiming to be able to extract "sets of phenomena" from other "sets of phenomena." Will such a "conceptual mechanism" provide a way out?

Let us make our point as clear as possible. If the term 'mechanism' designates any "classical" type of straightforward reductionist theories, we may as well do away with it. But what if 'mechanism' is a name designating the vast theoretical body of contemporary physics with its seemingly infinite possibilities? What if "mechanism" were to include the study of servomechanisms and of the well-known similarities between the latter and nervous systems? Would not our perspectives change, and, of course, enlarge if we considered from this "mechanistic" point of view such processes as the feedback in the self-regulation of organisms (Van R. Potter, James A. Bain)? "The obvious inability of present-day physics and chemistry to account for such events," Schrödinger wrote in 1947, "is no reason at all for doubting that they can be accounted for by these sciences." [16] The construction of organic models (of which Ashby's "homeostat" is now a "primitive" but still "classical" example), the investigation of the feedback processes in automatically controlled mechanisms and in groups of nerve cells, the successful attempts to describe organisms as open systems endowed with the property of equifinality (Ludwig von Bertalanffy), and so on, clearly show that cybernetics and the theory (or theories) of information, which are often treated "mechanistically," can contribute much to our understanding of the behavior of organisms, especially those endowed with neural systems. Thus, although it would be risky to proceed to hasty analogies, it is still plausible to conclude that there are no well-defined borderlines between the behavior (or at least the explanation of the behavior) of complex mechanisms and the behavior (or at least the explanation of the behavior) of biological organisms. And, paradoxical as it may seem, it is the very uncertainty and blurred character of borderlines—real, or conceptual, or both—that leads biologists and neurophysiologists to find mechanistic explanations quite enlightening when such explanations are given by contemporary physicists and cyberneticians.

The success achieved with the application of physical models or, as the case may be, physico-chemical and biochemical models to the study of the behavior of organisms when such models have been sufficiently complex, has been confirmed in the course of numerous investigations into the organic catalysts known as "enzymes." An outstanding example of this successful application is the epoch-making investigations made by Severo Ochoa and Arthur Kornberg in their attempts to synthesize ribonucleic acid. The discovery of an enzyme capable of catalyzing the polymerization of nucleotides in order to form ribonucleic acid (composed of chains of mononucleotide molecules) has led scientists to a better understanding of the mechanism of the biological formation of polynucleotides.

The data collected by Ochoa indicate that the ribonucleic acid produced by enzymatic synthesis has a structure identical to that of natural ribonucleic acid, including the polynucleotide chains of certain vegetal viruses. In view of the fact that ribonucleic acids are able to serve as molds for the synthesis of specific proteins, the synthesis of specific ribonucleic acids is of considerable significance. It is a well-known fact that different species of viruses contain ribonucleic acids with diverse compositions and that, inversely, different viruses of the same species contain ribonucleic acids with identical compositions. The capability of biosynthetic ribonucleic acid to bring about the synthesis of proteins was demonstrated by Ochoa when he succeeded in producing streptolysin by means of a synthetic ribonucleic acid, in a manner analogous to that which occurs in natural ribonucleic acid.[17]

Here we have a startling example not only of a "conceptual reduction" but of a "real reduction" as well. It is far from being the only example to prove our case. Other equally significant examples can be discerned in contemporary genetic research. The so-called "genetic code" can be found in the nucleus of reproductive cells. This code has, or rather consists of, "instructions" in the form of chains of large molecules of deoxyribonucleic acid for complex organisms, and in the form of chains of molecules of ribonucleic acid for certain viruses. These chains of molecules can be viewed as genetic models capable of being "translated" into a physico-chemical language. Furthermore, the more complex models—those consisting of deoxyribonucleic acid molecules—seem to be understandable in terms of the simpler models—those consisting of chains of ribonucleic acid molecules. Thus, the basis for the so-called "induced mutations" seems to be definitely established, and few would deny the importance of these "mutations" for a deeper comprehension of the nature of organic reality.

It may be argued that we ought not to rely too much on the aforementioned types of "reduction," since what is discovered in one field of biology, however important, may not necessarily be conclusive for the whole of biological science. After all, experience has taught us again and again to be extremely cautious in this respect; Jacques Loeb's "tropism theory" is only one among the many examples of failures that were produced by overconfidence in results obtained in only one limited area of biology. But there is little doubt that every positive result gained in the explanation of biological processes in physicochemical terms is an improvement on explanations based on notions which are held to be completely independent from, and hence entirely irreducible to, any others. More sensible than making biology independent of physics is making physics—the conceptual system called "physics," that is—flexible and subtle enough to "embrace" as much of biology as possible.

Yet when all is said, there remains something basically unsatisfactory in any mechanistic approach, no matter how "enlarged." Let us now imagine that there are no limits to the application of physical models to an understanding of the nature of biological processes, and that, moreover, each one of the basic characteristics used to describe organic systems is coextensive with each one of the basic characteristics employed to describe inorganic systems. In fact, the two sets of characteristics seem often to coincide. Isn't irritability, as the common property of all responses to stimuli, something that can also be detected in many inorganic substances? Don't some inorganic systems exhibit "growing processes" which are formally analogous to those observed in living beings? Can we not affirm that there are "metabolic processes" in inorganic substances when we take into account phenomena such as the so-called "autocatalysis"? Now then, even if we were able to give an affirmative answer to all these questions, doubts would subsist about whether we have, with the excuse of enlarging the scope of our conceptual models, not just simplified them beyond recognition. That biological laws are, so to speak, encased in physicochemical laws is one thing; that biological laws are the same as physico-chemical laws is quite another. Schrödinger has surmised that there are two different "mechanisms" by means of which natural processes arise. These two "mechanisms" include a "statistical mechanism" which produces "order from disorder," and a "new mechanism" which produces "order from order." He wrote,

> To the unprejudiced mind the second principle appears to be much simpler, much more plausible. No doubt it is. That is why physicists were so proud to have fallen in with the other one, the "order-from-disorder" principle, which is actually followed in Nature and which alone conveys an understanding of the great line of natural events, in the first place of their irreversibility. But we cannot expect that the "laws of physics" derived from it suffice straightaway to explain the behavior of living matter, whose most striking features are visibly based to a large extent on the "order-from-order" principle. You would not expect two entirely different mechanisms to bring about the same type of law—you would not expect your latch-key to open your neighbour's door as well. [18]

Schrödinger's words must be taken here only as a warning against the frequent temptation to conclude that, because physical explanations of biological processes are possible and even desirable, a physical explanation of an inorganic system is *toto caelo* identical with a physical explanation of an organic system. The same adjective 'physical' may cover two different, although not necessarily incompatible, types of explanation. In other words, even if we admit the possibility of applying physical models to the understanding of biological processes, we must acknowledge that their application yields different "principles" in each case. It is, therefore, a question of "principles," but, of course, not of "specifically vital principles" as opposed to those of a "merely" physical and physico-chemical character. By no means am I now rejecting the possibility of physicochemical explanations of biological processes in favor of "purely vitalistic" explanations; I am just suggesting that if vitalism, including organicism, proves inadequate—in view of the explanatory power of mechanical models—mechanism, including "enlarged mechanism," fares no better—in view of the difficulty, if not sheer impossibility, of reducing all biological laws to physical laws. "Vitalism" fails where "mechanism" succeeds, and "mechanism" fails where "vitalism" succeeds.

Must we then conclude that organic systems are both reducible and irreducible to inorganic ones, so that what we most urgently need is some sort of "principle of complementarity" similar to that proposed by Niels Bohr in a more restricted area? Or should we abandon the "dogmatic method," in which an affirmation excludes its negation, for some kind of "dialectical method," in which an affirmation includes its negation? In some respects the answer to the second question is "yes," but for the moment I beg the reader to forget this answer and to believe me if I say that my aim has been rather modest. I have tried to find some justification for at least three, in particular, two (organicism and "enlarged mechanism"), of the doctrines outlined above. I have also tried to emphasize the shortcomings of these doctrines. If we turn now to those I hold most adequate (or rather, least inadequate), namely, again, organicism and "enlarged mechanism," it should be obvious that neither is acceptable in its entirety but both are acceptable insofar as each is restricted by the other. "Organicism" is, then, a "true doctrine" when, and only when, it is not proved inadequate or insufficient by "mechanism," and "mechanism" is a "true doctrine" when, and only when, it is not proved inadequate or insufficient by "organicism."

Philosophically speaking, the consequence is that within our context the expressions 'reducible to' and 'irreducible to' are both meaningful. How, and why, this is possible we will try to find out by means of the ontological scheme that follows.

15
THE NATURE OF ORGANIC REALITY

What does it mean to maintain that organic systems are both reducible and irreducible to inorganic ones? It means simply this: that in each case we emphasize just one of the two ontological "directions" of which we have spoken (§ 9). Both the expressions 'reducible to' and 'irreducible to' can have meaning within our context because we do not take only one point of view, and least of all do we take a definitive and never-changing point of view, on organic reality. We merely approach (conceptually) such a reality by viewing it as a point of convergence of two ontological directions which are both opposite and complementary.

We can thus affirm that organic reality is continuous with, and indeed supported by, inorganic reality without claiming that the former is reducible to the latter.[19] Ontologically speaking, the nature of organic reality can be equated with the nature of a certain segment of the two intercrossing ontological directions. Keeping this approach in mind we can single out a certain number of characteristics of organic reality—characteristics which may be more properly called "tendencies" or "inclinations to exhibit certain properties."

These characteristics are five in number. They include: (1) "indecisiveness" (or "oscillation"), (2) "being for itself" (understood as "usefulness" or "utility"), (3) "spontaneity," (4) "specificity," and (5) "individuality." All these characteristics, tendencies, or "dispositions" result from a way of looking at organic reality which consists in emphasizing behavioral patterns not absolutely peculiar to that reality but sufficiently distinctive to make it possible to distinguish between organic and nonorganic entities. Thus, the characteristics of organic reality which we shall sketch are not to be considered as "essential differences," but only as what we may be allowed to call "tendential differences."

1. The characteristic called "indecisiveness" or "oscillation" results from the difficulties encountered in most of the attempts made to "situate" (ontologically) organic reality in a hopefully definitive manner. Organic reality, on the one hand, consists of much that is inorganic—there is, indeed, no difference between "organic matter" and "inorganic matter"—and, on the other hand, of much that can be called "psychical." Hence we often run the risk of making organic reality coextensive either with inorganic reality or with psychic reality. The risk would become a boon if the properties of organic reality could be deduced without any significant residue from the properties of either inorganic or psychic reality. Since such a deduction does not prove feasible, however, we must admit that organic reality is related to inorganic and psychic processes without ever being entirely coextensive with the latter. All this means that the organic realm unfolds, so to speak, between two "extremes," and thus shares in both of them, in varying degrees according to whether we are dealing with more or less "inferior" or "superior" types of organisms. In other words, organic reality is more or less inorganic and more or less psychical depending upon what "segment" of it we choose to consider, but it is never either entirely inorganic or entirely psychical. Indeed, the predicates 'is inorganic' and 'is psychical' are, from the viewpoint of organic systems, two limiting concepts describing two limiting realities never completely attained by any organism.

The "oscillating" character of organic reality is considerably more marked than the "oscillating" character of any other types of reality. After all, inorganic reality is, ontologically speaking, quite "stable": in a way, it is precisely what it is. As to psychical processes, they are, as a rule, properties of organic systems. On the other hand, organic systems can be viewed alternatively as inorganic realities or a psychical processes just because they are never reducible to either. As a consequence, we are confronted with a most paradoxical situation: whereas we need to use concepts designating properties which belong to inorganic systems and concepts designating properties which belong to psychical processes in order to "situate" ontologically organic reality, the latter can never be described as being inorganic or as being psychical.

A problem arises now: is the "oscillating" structure of organic systems itself "real" or only "conceptual"? We cannot tackle the problem here; let it suffice to say that, in our opinion, the structure of organic reality is clearly manifested only when we conceptually emphasize some types of behavior which would make little sense unless they were, in fact, real. Thus, in order to define ontologically organic reality we must adopt a point of view which emphasizes its "oscillating" character. Yet, this point of view would never work if it did not have some *fundamentum in re*. In some respects the conceptualization of a reality is both cause and effect of the structure of such a reality.

2. "Being for itself," even in ontology, is a concept so vague as to become plainly irritating. Yet we can make it somewhat less vague by referring to that "tendency toward interiority" discussed earlier (§ 10). Seen from this angle, organic reality can be defined as a "tendency to turn toward itself." It may be said that in a most general way this tendency is characteristic of all types of reality insofar as all realities "tend" to be what they are. Nevertheless, it is notoriously manifested in organic beings. Furthermore, it appears in these beings in a relatively well-defined manner: as what may be called "a utilitarian orientation."

If the behavior of organic beings can be described as "useful," it is certainly in the sense of being useful to themselves. To be sure, the notion of "usefulness" (or of "utility") is vague enough. But in the present context it is also precise enough here: "to be useful to itself" means "to be interested in itself" primarily as a member of an organic species, and secondarily, although in many respects quite fundamentally, as an individual within a species. The processes called "assimilation" and "generation" exemplify the basic "utilitarian tendency" exhibited by living beings. Most, if not all, of the activities of organisms are directed toward a kind of self-satisfaction: satisfaction of their inclinations, appetites, instincts. It is in this sense, and only in this sense, that the expression 'being for itself' must be understood here.

3. "Spontaneity" does not seem to be compatible with "utility." The former concept emphasizes dispersion of energy; the latter emphasizes concentration of energy. After having mentioned "utility" as one of the basic characteristics of organic beings, how can we add now "spontaneity" without contradicting ourselves? And yet we not only can but should refer to "spontaneity," provided that, as with "utility," we consider "spontaneity" as a tendency or disposition of organic systems.

Every living being exists, acts within its species, and tries to adapt to its world. But the manner in which an organic being exists and adapts itself cannot be described as "economical." We can now combine "utility" with "spontaneity": the former concept refers to the (conscious or unconscious) purposive actions performed by a living being; the latter refers to the ways in which these actions are performed. From the "economical point of view," namely from the point of view of adaptation of means to an end, the actions in question appear, indeed, to be wasteful. The abundance of means employed for the reproduction of many animal species seems to be totally out of proportion with the "end" pursued. For this reason, some authors have reached the conclusion that organic processes are always "spontaneous" and never "economical," that is to say, strictly "useful." In my opinion, these authors are wrong, for the characteristic called "utility" is never completely absent in the behavior of organic beings; otherwise, much in this behavior would remain incomprehensible. Yet there is no denying the fact that spontaneity, as a tendency to continual dispersion of energy, also plays a fundamental role in organic nature.

To say that one of the characteristics of organic nature is spontaneity does not necessarily mean that all organic beings, or even all organic species, are spontaneous in the same way and to the same degree. It is possible that organic nature displays varying degrees of spontaneity, and hence of "vitality." It is also possible that in some cases an organic being can reflectively direct its spontaneity. In the latter case we have an instance of an organic being which could be capable of resuming a tendency toward "utility." But this "utility" now has a different character: it is "objective" and no longer "purely subjective." I will not deal with this question now, for it will be discussed later (§ 21), in reference to the organic basis of human behavior. Let it suffice to say that, far from being mutually incompatible, spontaneity and utility can easily complement each other.

4. Specificity, also considered as a tendency, is so pronounced in organic beings that it seems to belong to them alone. Actually, a kind of elementary specificity can also be detected in entities currently described as inorganic or, at least, as "oscillating" between the inorganic and the organic. For example, consider some processes of autocatalysis as they have been found to take place in bacteria and possibly even in some proteins. Now, the specificity characteristic of living beings transcends the aforementioned elementary type: it consists in the fact that most of the transformations which a substance undergoes help to sustain the specific and, above all, the structural character of a living being. It is not, then, a question only of the assimilation of external ingredients for the constitution and maintenance of the cells; it is a matter of the conservation (and change, according to evolutionary laws) of the very structure of a living being. To be sure, all existing beings have a structure, and in this sense they can be said to be "specific," but living beings have a structure to an almost essential degree. We could go so far as to say that, whereas all existing beings are "structured," living beings

are "over-structured." It is as if a living being had only the following "purpose": to develop a structure, its own structure, and maintain itself in this structure by reproducing it. No doubt, cases of abnormal development are possible in Nature. But even if such cases were frequent, they would still be "abnormal." On the other hand, it is normal for an organism to be, or rather to become, a self-completed structure. The same materials can constitute very different organic structures; the structural diversity of organisms, then, is not due, or at least not entirely, to the diversity of materials. Expressing this thought in plain language, we may say that although a horse feeds on hay it does not turn into hay, nor does a man become a lamb because he eats lamb.

It should be pointed out that adoption of the notion of specificity, as structural specificity, does not entail acceptance of final causality. Efficient causes may offer quite adequate explanations of structural specificity. The results obtained by current biological research corroborate the trait of specificity which is intimately associated with that of individuality.

5. Ontologically speaking, individuality is the crowning point of specificity. Only because organic beings have the tendency to be, or become, specific can they be made, or tend to be made, into individuals and groups of individuals.

To be sure, every existing being is an individual or, more precisely, a "particular." Thus, any adequate ontological explanation of what 'to exist' means entails, explicitly or implicitly, an answer to the question: "What makes an individual an individual?" It is the question known as "the problem of the principle of individuation." This name is, indeed, ill-chosen, for the so-called "problem of the principle of individuation" is really the "problem of the *principles* of individuation." Not all existing beings can be individuated in the same way. In fact, not all individuals are individuated to the same degree. Let us consider for a moment the "elementary particles" of which all material bodies are supposedly made. In these particles there is a certain indifference in respect to their individuality to such an extent that they seem to be, for many purposes at least, "indiscernibles." Of course, they are not completely indiscernible. But their indiscernibility and, hence, their individuality is minimal: each elementary particle is an individual only insofar as it is not the same as another elementary particle. It may happen, therefore, that space, time, and perhaps quantity of a sort suffice to explain the individuality of elementary particles and, in general, the individuality of inorganic systems. It would be naïve, however, to claim that these factors are sufficient to individuate organic beings.

As if this were not enough, the plurality of principles of individuation operates not only in respect to the differences between inorganic and organic systems, but also within the realm of organic systems. It may be assumed that not all organic beings, or types of organic beings, are individuated in the same manner and to the same degree: some organic beings may be "more individual," and, therefore more strongly individuated, than others. This assumption yields interesting results. Let us imagine that there are degrees of individuality in the whole of reality, and that such degrees of individuality are particularly marked in the realm of organic reality. This means that the tendency to be more strongly individuated would be more or less salient according to the organic beings considered. In this case, we could picture the organic realm as a continuous line going from "mere particularity" to "full individuality," without, however, achieving the latter completely, since if such were the case we could not speak of "organic species," but only of individuals. Then, organic reality could be defined as "oscillating" between the particular and the individual. The problem would then arise concerning the principles of individuality for organic realities, or groups of organic realities. It is obvious that neither space nor time nor quantity would suffice as principles of organic individuation. But no principle or sets of principles would, indeed, suffice. In some cases, the principle, or principles, chosen would work only if they were, so to speak, "external"—although never completely "external"—to the entity or group of entities discussed. Such is the case with organic beings whose individuality exhausts itself, or nearly so, in their being members of an organic species. In some other cases, the principle, or principles, chosen would work only insofar as they were "internal"—although never completely "internal"—to the entity or group of entities discussed. Such is the case with organic beings whose individuality is so strongly marked as to be (partly) irreducible to a given set of principles, such as space, time, quantity, and so on. When an organic being develops primarily as an individual, its individuality seems to reside within its depths: the entity in question is then practically identical with the intrinsic principles constituting *this* particular entity. Nevertheless, being an individual is never an absolutely internal property, so that no organic being, however individualized, is an individual and only an individual. In short: the degree of individuality of any given organism depends upon its "situation" on a line picturing a growing tendency toward individuality. Therefore, all organic beings can be said to be individuals, but "in different ways."

16
FROM CEASING TO DYING

I have outlined some features of organic reality, and have insisted on the property called "oscillation" (in the ontological sense of this term) because I wanted to emphasize two basic points. The first point concerns the fact that the organic realm, although linked by its inorganic foundation to the processes of cessation described in the previous chapter, has its own particular mode of ceasing or, at the very least, a "tendency" toward its own mode of ceasing. The second point concerns the fact that organic beings die more or less—which means "more or less inevitably"—in accord with the greater or lesser amount of the aforementioned features that they exhibit. Not all of them are mortal to the same degree. Above all, not all of them are mortal in a manner equally "essential" and, so to speak, "their own." Some of them can be characterized as immortal, in the sense, of course, of "potentially immortal." As examples of potentially immortal organic beings we may mention a large number of unicellular organisms, many organic tissues composed of relatively undifferentiated cells, and various organic systems which reproduce agamically. Others may be characterized as almost essentially (or quasi-essentially) mortal. As examples of the latter we may mention all the rest of the organisms, especially those enjoying a high degree of individuality. I have used such expressions as *potentially* immortal' and *almost* essentially mortal' because neither complete immortality nor absolute mortality could be admitted within the framework of an ontology dismissing all "absolutes" and emphasizing "tendencies." I will then confine myself to affirming that the first group of organic beings referred to above—which I shall conventionally call "primary organisms," or simply "primaries"—exhibit "minimum mortality," while those in the second group—which I shall qualify, also conventionally, as "superior organisms," or often simply as "organisms"—reveal "maximum mortality." While we can, and must, admit that there is a continuity between the two groups, it so happens that methodologically it proves to be more befitting to admit a division between "primaries" and "organisms."

Only after taking into account the distinctions already noted can it be said that death in living beings is not purely and simply what we have called "cessation." 'To die' describes a process more inherent in the very nature of the being considered than the process described by the verb 'to cease.' From this, and only from this, point of view can we assent to the idea that organic life is characterized by the phenomenon of death. "Life," Bichat once wrote, "is the sum total of the functions which resist death." [20] It is highly probable that death is not an absolute necessity for living beings of any kind whatsoever. After all, there are always some causes—hence, a series of "external events"—which seem to bring death in its train. But such causes would not operate if living beings were not in some ways "ready" to die. Even if we admit, in agreement with Weismann, that organic beings have had to "invent" death so that "life"— the life of the species, as well as "life at large"—could continue, we must realize that there was some deep reason for such an "invention," and hence that death is not completely accidental to organic life.

In the light of a purely mechanistic interpretation of death there is no such thing as death, if by 'death' we understand a phenomenon somehow inherent in the very nature of at least some organic beings; viewed mechanistically, death is a purely accidental event. As far as we know, organisms do die, but they might not die at all. In the light of a purely vitalistic interpretation of death, on the other hand, organisms not only die in fact, but they die, so to speak, as a matter of principle; viewed vitalistically, death is an essential ingredient of organic life, to the point that organic life is not even conceivable without death. In short, mechanists describe death as an external, and always accidental, event; vitalists describe it as an internal, and always essential, phenomenon. In this respect mechanism and vitalism are irreconcilable doctrines, for death cannot be both external and internal, accidental and essential, at the same time. If death were an accident, organic beings could, in principle, live indefinitely; and if organic beings cannot live indefinitely, then it is because death is a necessity for them.

In accordance with the ontology underlying the present work, I do not believe that either of these two doctrines are entirely plausible. Nevertheless, each emphasizes a most enlightening side of living beings. Insofar as living beings are structures which in principle can be constantly and indefinitely "repaired," death occurs in them as an accident which could be endlessly retarded. On the other hand, insofar as living beings are organic structures whose simplest elements are subordinated to more complex forms, they exhibit a gradually increasing tendency to some kind of "self-limitation." Thus, although death almost always comes about by an accident explicable in terms of a succession of "external causes," it also appears as a "natural phenomenon."

We can say, then, that the "advance" of death which is revealed in the whole realm of existents is accelerated, so to speak, in organic beings. They are neither completely immortal nor entirely mortal. Depending largely on the place that they occupy in the so often described "ontological directions," organic beings *tend* either to survive indefinitely or to die necessarily. Yet neither tendency is entirely carried to an end, nor is it ever converted into a definitive state of affairs.

17
DEATH IN PRIMARY ORGANISMS

A tendency to what we have called "indefinite survival" can be detected in the organisms named "primaries." It has been said of them, and in particular of many one-celled organisms, that they are, at least potentially, immortal. Before I examine the accuracy of this claim I wish to anticipate my conclusions: (1) If there are any organic beings which deserve to be called "potentially immortal," then they are the "primaries." (2) Even the notion of "potential immortality" is not definitive because biologists who have made the most important contributions to the problem discussed here have been apt to disregard —quite understandably, from their own point of view—a number of ontological presuppositions. These presuppositions we will try to unearth in the following pages.

There has been much research on the processes of aging and dying in primaries. I will mention here only the best-known or most significant investigations in this respect. Maupas, Jennings, Calkins, Woodruff, Conklin, and Metalnikov, among others, have studied unicellular organisms, particularly certain kinds of paramecia. Spencer, Vieweger, Beers, Jollos, Carrel, Ebeling, Fischer, Hartmann, Hämmerling, and others have worked with unicellular organisms as well as with organic tissues and organisms such as hydras, annelids, and so on.[21] To call all these organic systems "primaries" is not to say that they are necessarily more "primitive" than all other organisms in terms of the evolutionary scale. "Primitiveness" in such systems refers, above all, to factors such as the relatively slight differentiation of their constituent parts, the minimum centralization of some leading biological functions, and the low level of organization as compared with other organisms.

The research on "immortality" of unicellular organisms, beginning with Maupas, has consisted, *grosso modo,* in determining how long a one-celled organism (such as Woodruff's *Paramecium caudatum* or Metalnikov's *Paramecium aurelia)* can survive in a culture from which have been removed all "external causes" normally responsible for bringing about the processes of aging and the final conditions of senility and death. In this manner, not only the effects of changes in the environment can be ascertained but also the number of generations produced in a given time.

The results of these investigations have led to the idea, proposed and developed primarily by Weismann, of the potential immortality of unicellular organisms. Maupas maintained that such organisms can survive indefinitely only when they conjugate periodically. According to him, conjugation renews the constantly depleting strength of the cell, whose process is then arrested and perhaps even indefinitely postponed, but never completely canceled. Calkins postulated the existence of a *quantum vitale* which could be maintained, and even occasionally increased, but which is finally and definitively exhausted. None of these more or less "vitalistic" hypotheses were held for long. Woodruff was able to prove that conjugation is not necessary for the survival of unicellular organisms, since the latter can indefinitely endure by means of parthenogenesis. Later Woodruff himself, along with others, demonstrated that not even parthenogenesis is necessary. In fact, these biologists succeeded in maintaining the life of a cell without reproduction of any kind, by periodically sectioning off portions of protoplasm in order to preserve the original size. In this respect, variations of temperature also constitute an important factor. It has been possible to prolong considerably the life of both unicellular organisms and tissues at low temperatures, especially when a method was found to avoid the formation of ice crystals. The various experiments performed in view of the revivification of dehydrated bacteria which were alive millions of years ago (by Heinz J. Dombrowski and others) have confirmed the thesis that some unicellular organisms can in principle live forever.

Although different techniques were employed, the investigations concerning tissues and some organic systems which reproduce asexually have given similar results. The classical example is that of Carrel's fibroblast, which continued living *in vitro* long after the chicken from which it had been extracted died. Similar experiments were performed on hydras and on some annelids. These organic systems seemed to be able to survive indefinitely, at least in the stage known as "gemmation," which constantly produces new generations. All these experiments led to the conclusion that there are certain organic beings which are potentially immortal, in the biological sense of 'immortal.' Many cells, once they are placed in a culture, exhibit the same property.

These experiments, and above all the way they have been interpreted, have brought forth heated discussions among biologists. As a rule, vitalistic hypotheses (Maupas, Calkins) have been discarded. But many questions still remain unsolved. Let us put aside a difficulty which in other contexts might prove to be serious but which is only of minor importance here. I refer to the fact that most conclusions regarding the immortality of primaries were reached through inductive generalization and thus cannot be held in complete certainty. For our purposes, it suffices to qualify the immortality in question as "potential." Other difficulties, however, are formidable enough to retain our attention. For instance, it would seem that potential immortality can be attained only, or at least considerably more easily, in experiments using undifferentiated cells. Weismann's theory of the "continuity of the germinative plasma," entailing the "discontinuity," and hence the mortality, of purely somatic cells (if any), explains why only experiments with undifferentiated, or relatively undifferentiated, cells are or appear to be successful. But Weismann's theory fails in various respects. As a matter of fact, tissues composed of basically differentiated cells have been preserved indefinitely without altering their specific properties. "Epithelia," observes Hämmerling, "grow [and, therefore, survive] epithelially, conjunctive tissues conjunctively, etc." [22] Furthermore, ". . . intestinal epithelia . . . have been cultivated . . . which produce ferments which flow into the culture plasma, a function they continue to perform. As another example, let us point out that, according to Ebeling, an epithelium from an iris produced pigments constantly during an eighteen-month culture. A cell from the iris, a producer of pigments, is a highly differentiated tissue." [23] Thus, the differentiation of cells does not seem to be a decisive factor. Let us now consider the so-called "rejuvenation." No theory seems to provide a satisfactory explanation of this phenomenon. Does the immortality of the cell depend on the fact that it is rejuvenated either by conjugation, division, or simply by the conservation of the original system? It is not an easy problem to solve, for, as Hämmerling points out, we are confronted here with an inextricable causal relation. "Of course, we observe the close association between youth and the capacity to divide, but the relation of cause and effect has not been adequately investigated: does the cell age because it does not divide or does it fail to divide because it ages?" [24] Problems of a similar character arise when we try to produce the same effect by means of certain manipulations of an organic system, such as regulating its nutrition or changing the temperature of its environment. It may well happen that a cell ages until the very moment of its rejuvenation so that in such a case the potential immortality of the cell would be equivalent to the rejuvenation of an organic system—rejuvenation produced by causes somewhat "external" to the so-called "pure natural processes."

Even from the strictly biological point of view, the whole situation is far from clear. Nevertheless, let us suppose that all the problems in the field of biology have been solved, and that the thesis of the potential immortality of a large number of unicellular organisms is definitively established. Since many-celled organisms are composed of cells, could we not claim that all organic systems are potentially immortal? Are not aging, senility, and death merely accidental? Is not death, inevitable in fact, "unnecessary" in principle?

It seems sensible to admit that if there are potentially immortal organic entities, then they are the primaries, and in particular certain unicellular organisms. As of now, no one has been able to discover any factors, processes, or principles inherent in an organism and leading inevitably to aging and death. There is certainly no entelechy, of the type proposed by Driesch, which has the ability, if not the power, to "suspend" and "interrupt" organic processes. In fact, there is not even such a thing as organic matter per se, namely, a type of "matter" peculiar only to biological organisms and not found anywhere else. Thus, the constant recomposition of at least some organic systems seems not only possible but even more intelligible and "natural" than their degeneration due to supposedly inherent causes or principles.

From the ontological point of view, things do not proceed so smoothly. Although there is no specifically organic matter, there are, as I have endeavored to show (§ 15), properties which tend to be peculiar to organisms. If such is the case, can it be said that organisms are potentially immortal? Is an organism potentially immortal in its "being for itself," in its spontaneity, in its specificity, and, above all, in its individuality?

I very seriously doubt it. Unless the term 'memory' is given a very broad meaning which includes the notion of the sum total of typical responses to typical stimuli, it can be asserted that primaries do not have any memory. Lack of memory enables the primaries to live with what we may call "a minimum degree of temporality." Time, and all that 'time' means here—the existence of, and predominant influence exerted by, "phases of development," "vital rhythms," etc.—is relatively unimportant in the life of primaries. What we may call "history," understood as a basically temporally conditioned process, is imperceptible in primaries. Now, is time, and hence "history," totally absent in such organic systems? I do not think so; time influences the behavior of all organic systems capable of specific reactions provided that such systems are considered *in concreto* and not, or not only, *in abstracto*. To be sure, if we viewed time, by analogy with space, as a *compositum* consisting of *partes extra partes*, it would not affect the existence of any being, either organic or inorganic. But how can time be viewed as such a *compositum* if even space itself, insofar as it is concrete, cannot be defined by its pure exteriority? It may be argued that time and space should be viewed as subjective or quasi-subjective (transcendental) systems of relations. But then we would have to subscribe to some form of idealism, a doctrine which finds no place within our ontological framework. It is more plausible to conclude, then, that time, as a reality, fundamentally affects all existing beings. Above all, it affects organic beings, whether they are "primaries" or organisms, because the ontological features which define them are closely bound to temporality.

It is highly probable that the concrete temporality of organic beings is closely linked to the predominance of interiority in the sense of 'interiority' already discussed (§ 10). Now then, since an organic being is not purely and exclusively an "internal reality," that is to say, an entity whose behavior is determined by, and only by, its internal structure, we cannot conclude that organic beings are completely and necessarily mortal. We may still agree with the results of biological research described earlier, and affirm that certain organic systems are potentially immortal. But we need not equate the predicate 'is immortal' with the predicate 'is necessarily immortal,' even in the sense of 'is in fact necessarily immortal.' If we hold mortality to be a "tendency" in organic beings, then we must also hold immortality to be another similar, although opposite, "tendency." The degree of mortality of an organic being will depend upon its degree of "interiority." If the term 'interiority' is considered to be too vague, and hence misleading, we may translate it into a more precise, and undoubtedly less metaphysical, vocabulary. We may say that an organic being A is more "internal" than another organic being B when A depends more upon its own organization than does B. Since primaries depend upon their own organization less than do organisms, we may conclude that primaries are less internal, and hence less mortal, than organisms. Primaries are still, however slightly, "internal"; therefore, they are not absolutely immortal. They are nonetheless the most immortal entities in the organic realm. They are, for all practical purposes, immortal, or rather, potentially immortal. Paradoxically we could add that they are also, for all theoretical purposes, immortal.

I have denied complete and absolute immortality to primaries on the basis of the notion of interiority. I will now argue in favor of the same denial on the basis of the notion of individuality.

Let us consider a paramecium. It divides into two; each one of the two resulting paramecia divides into two others, and so on successively. Let us now suppose that the generations resulting from the consecutive divisions are eliminated so as to preserve a single paramecium, which I shall call the "original paramecium" or the "mother cell." Since this cell continues to live limitlessly, its immortality seems to be assured. But what does the demonstrative pronoun 'this' in the expression 'this cell' mean? Does it always and unequivocally refer to *"the same entity"*? Ludwig von Bertalanffy has made this point very clear: ". . . in unicellular organisms the notion of the individual becomes muddled . . . Individual means something 'indivisible'; how can we call these creatures individuals when they are in fact 'dividua' and their multiplication arises precisely from division?" [25] In order to be sure that a paramecium dies, it would be necessary to be able to associate the phenomenon of death with the presence of a dead body. But does death always and necessarily entail the presence of such a body? Might we not conjecture that, at least in some organic systems, death is associated not so much with the presence of a dead body as with reproduction? In order to answer these questions satisfactorily, it would be necessary to be able to define an organic system by means of some completely stable and absolutely definitive feature, and then determine whether that feature disappeared when division took place. Now, it just so happens that the required definition is unattainable. To be sure, for any given organic *definiendum* we have in principle a most plausible property, the one called "individuality." But while this property is suitable and sufficient in some cases, it becomes vague and blurred in other cases. The fact that organic beings are individuals is beyond discussion. Therefore, an isolated cell is also an individual. But "being an individual" is, as we have pointed out, a property admitting of degrees. An isolated cell is an individual only to a degree, and certainly not a very high degree. It is an individual *minime*. Hence a very disconcerting paradox arises. On the one hand, the isolated cell dies in some manner, even if its death is less definitive and demonstrable than that of other organic systems, particularly that of complex organisms. On the other hand, the isolated cell persists in some manner, even if its persistence is difficult to ascertain. All this means, of course, that primaries die while being the least mortal among all organic beings. If the notion of individuality becomes uncertain, the notion of death follows in its footsteps; the death of the primaries is mostly the de-individualization of organic systems which are already only minimumly individualized.

The above arguments are applicable even to those primaries that are apt to survive without parthenogenesis; in the course of the manipulations to which we submit them, their slight amount of individuality is constantly modified. As to other more complex systems, if they can be said to be potentially immortal, the meaning of 'potentially immortal' becomes less and less well defined. Let us again quote von Bertalanffy:

> The same holds good for asexual reproduction by fission and budding, as it is found in many of the lower metazoa . . . Can we insist on calling a hydra or a turbellarian worm an individual, when these animals can be cut into as many pieces as we like, each capable of growing into a complete system? Other experiments with freshwater polyps also demonstrate the extreme vagueness of the notion of the "individual." It is easy to produce a double-headed polyp by making an incision at the anterior end. Afterwards the two heads compete: if a water flea is caught, both heads quarrel about the booty, although it does not matter at all which one takes it—in any case it goes down into the common gut, where it is digested and so benefits all parts. [26]

The impossibility of reaching definitive conclusions on the question discussed here, and the "oscillating" character of our contentions (primaries are potentially immortal; they are not, however, completely immortal; they are what is least mortal within the organic realm, etc.) should not astonish anyone. There is a complete agreement between the "vacillating" nature of our theses and the vacillating nature of the reality to which they apply. The primaries represent a kind of bridge linking complex inorganic systems to more highly developed organic beings. Thus we find in them much that is characteristic of the phenomenon called "cessation" in inorganic matter. But we also find in them some degree of death in the sense of "biological death." We can detect in the organic realm what we have referred to as the "advance of death," from a minimum mortality to a maximum—but never absolute—mortality.

18
DEATH IN SUPERIOR ORGANISMS

The degree of mortality can be taken as a criterion of the type of organic being to which we may refer. We have elucidated the degree of mortality in primaries, and have concluded that primaries are potentially immortal, which in our vocabulary means 'minimumly mortal.' Since most primaries are unicellular systems, and such systems constitute the so-called "superior organisms," henceforth often simply called "organisms," it may be concluded that there is no basic difference between the degree of mortality in primaries and that in organisms.

This conclusion would prove wrong. Biologists and philosophers of Nature understood this point quite clearly when they evolved theories accounting for death in organisms which were substantially different from the theories developed to explain how, and why, primaries die. We may well hold the view that many cells and tissues are potentially immortal; this view will fail when applied to systems composed of highly differentiated parts.

All this does not mean that the processes of senility are always irreversible in organisms. Many interesting results obtained from experiments in rejuvenation would contradict such an idea. But the possibility of rejuvenation does not, whether empirically or logically, lead to the idea of potential immortality in organisms. The very same biologists who have emphasized the potential immortality of many cells and tissues admit that there must be some other causes, no matter how often postponed or suspended, of aging, and, therefore, of death. Where it is a question of an organism as complex as a human being, the existence of such causes seems obvious. Jean Rostand clearly expressed this idea when he wrote that aging in human beings —and in many highly developed organisms—is an "entirely natural phenomenon" which is manifested in such processes as puberty and menopause.[27] The "stages" in the development of certain organisms are not external to the latter; it would be otiose to try to understand the nature of such organisms without taking these "stages" into account.

It may be argued that the above is the case only with warm-blooded animals, especially those whose body temperature is regularly uniform. The life cycle of these animals passes through definite phases, whose duration, although variable within limits, is never indefinite. Nor, except to a very slight degree, does the duration of these phases depend, or depend entirely, upon the conditions of the environment. These animals, then, are the best examples that can be found of a "natural mortality." Hence I shall primarily refer to them as I proceed to view various doctrines concerning the causes of their death. Nevertheless, even if cold-blooded animals seem to be able to evade passing through relatively well-defined phases of growth and maturity, they are not in this respect comparable to primary organisms. Cold-blooded animals continue to grow throughout the course of their existence, although they show no traces of the senile involutions so characteristic of warm-blooded animals. As a consequence, the longevity of cold-blooded animals is not only greater but also more indefinite—as is their size—than that of warm-blooded animals. Which is not to say that there are no "natural causes" capable of accounting for the death of cold-blooded animals. After all, the aforementioned "phases of development" are not, properly speaking, causes, but ways in which the mortality of warm-blooded animals is manifested.

Let us now ask the question: why do organisms, especially warm-blooded animals, which represent a more complex stage of organic development, die? It goes without saying that I do not claim to be able to give the question a convincing answer, but only a series of more or less plausible answers. "There is scarcely a cause," Hämmerling wrote, "which has not been held responsible for the old age and death of organisms. Biologists have spoken of metabolic collapse, of arteriosclerosis." [28] Indeed, biologists have spoken of many other things: autointoxication, colloidal dehydration, glandular atrophy, basic malnutrition, loss of mechanisms which produce antibodies, and so forth. They have evolved hypotheses based on statistics, on data provided by the theory of information, and so on. "We are not, at the moment," a biologist writes, "short of hypotheses—only of facts and experiments to support them. A satisfactory theory of aging must account for the known range of specific ages and the relation of these ages to body size, cell number, mutation rate, and so on." [29]

When all is said, however, thanatological hypotheses can be classified into two basic types: the type that emphasizes biochemical and physico-chemical factors, and the type that relies on structural-organic factors. I will examine briefly a few examples of each type.

The best-known example of the first type of hypotheses is Metchnikov's theory of the autointoxication of organisms. Metchnikov blamed the process of organic degeneration on the accumulation of toxic substances which destroy the so-called "noble tissues." According to this theory, death ensues as the inevitable consequence of the struggle—in itself harmful to the organism—between the "noble elements" and the "simple (or primitive) elements." [30] The macrophagi end up by atrophying and finally devouring the living cells. It is as if the organism became progressively petrified. This process can sometimes be retarded for a long period of time (Metchnikov thought, or rather hoped, that it could be retarded indefinitely). But this means only, in our opinion, that certain involutions are normal in organic development. After all, organisms can often recover from some degenerative processes, provided that the latter have not reached too advanced a stage. Thus, for instance, arteriosclerosis can be retarded by means of drugs, changes in temperature (dilatation of arteries in mild climates), and so on. These involutions do not provide sufficient evidence against the idea that rejuvenation has its limits. No matter how often, and how successfully, organisms can be rejuvenated, they continue to age and, finally, to die.

Another example of the first type of thanatological hypothesis is the theory of colloidal dehydration. This theory is, in important respects, less controversial than Metchnikov's, but it eventually stumbles against similar difficulties. In fact, all "biochemical" and "physico-chemical" theories suffer from severe limitations. They explain a great deal, but they leave a great deal more unexplained. Their explanatory power is noticeably increased when other factors—statistical factors, for instance—are taken into account, but then they cease to be theories of a purely "biochemical" and "physico-chemical" character.

The second type of thanatological theories I shall call "structural" because they are mostly, if not exclusively, based upon factors involving the organization of a system. The most general and well-known example is provided by the hypothesis that the aging and death of any (higher) organism is a function of the so-called "soma." Individual cells—in particular "germ cells," insofar as they differ from "somatic cells"—do not die. Neither do most of the tissues die. But the whole organism, conceived as a complex system of functions, cannot escape death.

The word 'complex' is itself complex, and, to be sure, ambiguous. A higher organism is complex; a cell is complex; molecules and atoms are complex. If we were to associate complexity with the number and variety of component parts, we would have to admit that the complexity of an organism hardly exceeds that of an atom. It is necessary then to make the meaning of 'complex' and 'complexity' more precise. To this effect we shall resort to a number of auxiliary concepts, such as "differentiation," "specialization," and "centralization."

A higher biological organism becomes increasingly complex

the more its component parts (the tissues) are differentiated and, at the same time, the more effectively they are subordinated to a central system. An adequate example of the latter is man's neurovegetative system. This sytem does not need to be differentiated—"internally differentiated"—because "it represents the basic unity in which all specialized activities converge," [31] that is, because it is the organ which directs all specializations. Incidentally, the proposed meaning of 'differentiation' explains why we do not need to be unduly worried by the fact that some "potentially immortal tissues" in primaries (§ 17) can also be described as differentiated. For differentiation does not have the same function in those tissues as it has in the tissues of a complex organism. As the biologist Raymond Pearl rightly pointed out long ago,

whether the protozoan *cell* is as highly differentiated as a metazoan cell, is not the point at all. For, to have any pertinence so far as the present issue is concerned, the comparision must be between the differentiated protozoan cell, *and the whole metazoan soma,* not one of its constituent cells. In the protozoan, all the differentiations are in and a part of one single cell operating as one metabolic unit, of small absolute size, and consequently easier and more labile internal physico-chemical regulation. In the metazoan soma we have organ differentiation, with the constituent cells in each organ highly specialized functionally, and dependent upon the normal functional activity of wholly other organs in order that they may keep going at all.[32]

Furthermore, it happens that differentiated cells composing tissues preserved in a culture are not directly subservient to a system of functions within which they are more or less harmoniously integrated. If the differentiation were simple, there would be no reason to deny that it is manifested not only in a given type of cell in a tissue but also within each individual cell. As a matter of fact, Daniel Mazia has demonstrated that mitotic cell division is achieved by means of a special mechanism, called a "mitotic apparatus," which occupies only one-tenth of the area of the cell. On the other hand, the differentiation to which I have referred appears as a series of integrated functions within a system: here the integration of tissues within an organism corresponds to its growing specialization.

Therefore, to say that aging and death in an organism is due to the latter's complexity is equivalent to saying that such an organism can be greatly affected through the growing centralization of its functions. In this case, aging is not a process that extends uniformly throughout the entire organism. Certain tissues renew themselves, while others, such as the nervous tissues, not only are not rejuvenated but even become "rarefied." Similarly, death does not equally or simultaneously affect all the parts of an organism. This is the reason why it is often so difficult, not to say impossible, to determine the exact moment when an organism dies. Hence the well-known problem of the determination and recognition of so-called "clinical death"; there would certainly be no problem if it were always possible to know the "exact moment" of death. Organisms which were apparently dead have been "revived." [33] We need only mention here the "miracles" produced by cardiac massages. All this means that determining the "exact time of death" is, to a great extent, a "practical matter" for, in fact, certain organs have died while others continue to live. Furthermore, certain organs can, within limits, be "revived." No wonder that several kinds of death have been distinguished: apparent death, clinical death, absolute death.[34] Only in the case of absolute death can it be said that there is absolutely nothing to be done; no really vital organ remains alive.

It is for this reason that some authors have spoken of a "social bond" which breaks down completely as soon as one of the vital organs becomes basically affected, even though many other organs continue, or could have continued, to live. André Lalande has described this state of affairs in philosophical terms.

> Consider the same being a few minutes before and after death. The same material atoms, the same shape, the same physical and chemical compositions (insofar as we are able to judge). But life is

no longer there, because the parts have suddenly become strange to one another, without unity, without solidarity, and, instead of strongly resisting the disintegrating effect of the incidental forces, they are ready to yield to them docilely, each in its own way, gradually and imperceptibly merging into the whole from which they had been previously separated—an indefinite mass, incapable of being recognized, which *has no name in any language,* because it can no longer be the logical subject of any proposition.[35]

To be sure, the idea of death as the "rupture of a social bond" is derived from an image of death which is both mechanistic and, as it were, "sociological." This idea is far from being obvious; yet it casts vivid light on the process of organic death, provided we are ready to acknowledge that the "bond" in question is not a mere *compositum* of static elements but a system of functions integrated into one *function* called "an organism." The idea is, moreover, interesting insofar as it emphasizes the importance of the phenomena of centralization and individualization. There seems to be little doubt that the senility and mortality of a complex organism are functions of its degree of systematization. As one biologist has put it, it is "the degree of solidarity among the parts that leads some of them toward the catastrophe experienced by others, just as in a delicate mechanism the disturbance of one small disk gradually produces the total decomposition."[36] But we must be careful not to interpret too literally expressions that have strong metaphorical overtones. Therefore, we suggest that notions more complex than those derived from predominantly mechanical models and images should be introduced. For example, it might be useful to take into account the notion of "adaptability of organisms," a notion which, by the way, can be easily related to that of complexity. This notion was introduced by Oscar Hertwig, who wrote, "We can assert that the very processes by means of which the cells of multicellular organisms, in virtue of their differentiation and division of work, prepare themselves for the highest functions of life, involve circumstances which in turn bring about senile death due to wear and exhaustion."[37]

Are we to conclude then, that the complexity—centralization, systematization, individualization, adaptability, and so on—of higher organisms is the *causa vera* of their aging and death? Such a conclusion would be premature. If the aforementioned characteristics make aging and death possible, they also make life, as highly developed biological life, possible; if they are causes, they are causes of opposite effects. Furthermore, and in particular, it is not yet known whether aging and death may not be the product of a gradual accumulation of injuries, imperfections, disorders. It is not easy to find out what kind of causal relations exist (if any) between the process of aging and the injuries suffered by some vital organs. We are confronted here with a problem similar to the time-honored discussion about the nature of human rationality. Just as philosophers once asked, "Is man rational because he is endowed with hands, or is he endowed with hands because he is rational?" so we could now ask, "Does an organism die because it has suffered injuries, or has it suffered injuries because it has grown old and cannot any longer fight effectively against death?" In short, although structural-organic theories are sometimes more satisfactory than biochemical and physico-chemical theories, they are still not adequate enough. On the other hand, since we are reluctant to rekindle the platitude, disguised as a profound metaphysics, that death is absolutely essential to all organisms—which ultimately is equivalent to saying that death is the cause of death—then it would seem that we have reached a blind alley, and that our only alternative is to suspend our judgment, in tune with the skeptics' way.

19
IN SEARCH OF A WAY OUT

A complete suspension of judgment on the problem is, however, not strictly necessary. Some conceptual resources are still left at our disposal.

In the first place, we might resort to the solution of the problem which Max Scheler developed on the basis of Husserlian phenomenology. Basically, it consists of relinquishing the notion of cause as the principal, or sole, means of explanation. From the point of view of the cause-effect relation—the so-called "causal relation"—we cannot conclude once and for all that a higher organism dies inevitably and necessarily. Let us now substitute what we may call the "foundational relation"— the relation between a *fundamentum* and the *fundatum*—for the causal relation. Whereas the causal relation refers to natural facts, which are the subject matter of natural sciences, the foundational relation is supposed to refer to so-called "pure facts," which are the subject matter of phenomenology. Needless to say, we must then admit that there are such things as pure ("phenomenological") facts [38]—a contention which Scheler and most phenomenologists would rebuke as extremely inaccurate, first because pure facts are not supposed to be "things" at all, and second because we are not supposed to "admit" (in the sense of 'assume') pure facts but confine ourselves to intuiting (and hence "immediately seeing") them.

We have intimated that foundational relations refer to "pure facts." Strictly speaking, foundational relations refer to pure facts as *fundamenta* and to other facts (such as "natural facts") as *fundata*. Since the *fundamenta* are, in the phenomenological sense of the term, "essences," we may be allowed to use the expression 'essential relations' in lieu of the expression 'foundational relations.' It goes without saying that, in Scheler's opinion, essential relations are more basic than any other relations; they are fundamental because they are, as it were, "foundational." Thus, essential relations are the foundation of any other types of relations, including, of course, causal relations.

The problem poses now, Is there any clear criterion for determining whether we are dealing with an essential relation rather than with a causal relation? According to Scheler, the answer is "yes":

In the sphere of real objects, the way I know when I am dealing with an essential relation is to determine whether, as I try to provide a *causal explanation,* I move constantly in a circle so that I find it necessary to consider, on the one hand, that A is the cause of B and, on the other hand, that B is the cause of A—in which case it is obvious that I am concerned with, and only with, functional relations, to the extent that I must then assume that either A or B is the independent variable. It is in the course of unsuccessful attempts of the type described that the nature of essential relations is revealed to my intuition. [39]

We might now wonder whether most of the obstacles we have encountered (§ 17–18) could not be removed if we simply subscribed to Scheler's doctrine of essential relations. Will not death prove to be a "pure fact," directly given to an essential intuition often by means of a single, and simple, example? Isn't our deep-rooted conviction that we all must die, and that all organic beings die, based upon an intuitive grasp of the mortal nature of all living beings? Why try to discover a cause when we can seize "something" more basic than a cause, namely, an "essence"?

Scheler had no qualms about the possibility of finding "death as an essence"—which is the same as disclosing the "essence of death." According to him, the idea of death is rooted not only in our consciousness but in all vital consciousness as well. We need only unearth it. Then we will obtain the following results: (1) The "extension of the present" becomes progressively "compressed," as it were, between the future and the past. (2) What is left to be lived, namely, the possibility of continuing to live, decreases in proportion with the amount of time already lived and the experiences had during this time. (3) No matter where and when we have the experience of the progressive "compression of life," and even when such an experience results from a comparison between various phases in the vital development, the fact is that such an experience "is always there waiting." The "continual variations in differences among various phases of the vital development" are clearly indicative of the "fundamental phenomenon of aging" and hence of the essence called "aging"—an essence which is presupposed in all questions about the causes of decay in organisms. (4) Death is not simply the final limit of senescence, because the reverse is the case: the process of aging becomes meaningful only because it appears within the context of death as a "pure fact," which remains inexplicable only because it is "evident." Thus, the essence of death can give a meaning to the so-called "causes of death," and not the other way around.[40]

Scheler's ideas on the problem of aging and death have a virtue: bringing to light the limitations of causal explanations. Unfortunately, Scheler's ideas are based on a most controversial ontology, which in its turn is based on a most controversial assumption about the "existence" of "pure facts" and the possibility of intuiting them directly. Much more to the point, in my opinion, are the solutions to our problem suggested by our anti-absolutist ontology (§§ 7–11). In the light of this ontology I contend that it is not necessary to hunt for the essential character of aging and death in organic nature for the simple reason that there is no such essential character. Death cannot be equated to, or even compared with, an "essence": it is a fact, and certainly not a "pure fact." Nevertheless, death is not a mere accident or set of accidents without which living beings would be able to persist indefinitely. 'Death'—'organic death' that is—is the name of a process toward which all living beings tend by virtue of their basic constitution. When this constitution is particularly oscillating, in the sense of 'oscillation' described above (§ 15), the accidental factors clearly overpower any essential, or rather quasi-essential, factors; death is then a process closely resembling that of cessation in inorganic systems. The less differentiated, less centralized, and less individualized living beings tend to endure and hence postpone the moment of organic annihilation. The obstacles which threaten their biological persistence are more external than internal to the beings considered, in a sense of 'external' and 'internal' which should be clear enough by now. Some of these living beings can survive for very long periods of time, and in principle, indefinitely, but only insofar as a number of "external conditions" are maintained. On the other hand, the more highly differentiated, centralized, and individualized living beings exhibit a complex structure which easily yields, as it were, to mortality. Moreover, as these complex beings develop according to certain phases (puberty and so on), without which they would cease to be what they actually are, their aging and death become more and more "natural," and hence more and more "inevitable." Plainly, aging and death seem to be inevitable, and thus almost "essential" in those beings which, as is the case with human beings, exhibit emotional tensions closely intertwined with physiological processes.[41]

Just as there is an "advance" of, and in, death from the inorganic to the organic realm, so also there is an "advance" of, and in, death within the organic realm itself. In other words, organic systems "cease more" than inorganic ones, and some organic systems are "more mortal" than others. Some organic systems seem to be, but are never, "essentially mortal." At any rate, death does not appear as an absolute or as an absolutely necessary fact. Rather than saying that organic systems die inevitably or necessarily by virtue of their own constitution, we should state that they gradually develop as mortal beings—constituting themselves, as it were, as mortal beings. In sum, mortality is not a constitutive, but rather a constituting, property in such beings. Therefore, throughout the scale of organic beings, including man, insofar as he is a biological organism, death is a process or an event which is neither completely alien to organisms nor completely peculiar to them. Mortality then is not a "property" of biological organisms in a sense of 'property' which will be eventually elucidated (§ 23).

The mortality of a higher organism is primarily that of an individual. An individual dies, but the species endures. Although many species become extinct, biological life in general endures, at least as long as the pertinent physical conditions are given. Organic death operates, then, within some kind of circle: in fact, death occurs only, or mostly, because, far from definitively disrupting the "circle of life," it tends to renew it. In the case of higher organisms, death plays an ever more important and creative role: it elicits certain possibilities without which some organic forms could never come to life. The organic form in which the above possibilities achieve their highest fulfillment is called "a human being." Thus, in this respect, as in many others, the existence of human beings raises problems which cannot be tackled adequately by appealing only to a general ontology or even to a metaphysics of organic nature. To these problems I shall now turn.

THREE

Human Death

20
MAN AND HIS BODY

For many centuries it has been assumed that man possesses, as a defining characteristic, some "element" or "principle" substantially different from his body. This "element" or "principle" has been given various names: 'mind,' 'reason,' 'spirit,' 'soul,' and so on. A few daring thinkers have even gone so far as to conclude that, if the element in question is the defining characteristic of man, and if it does not necessarily entail the existence of the body, then the body does not belong to the essence of a human being. More cautious philosophers have claimed that the body is still a significant element in man, but since it is, so they believe, an element substantially different from the rational or spiritual part, then there must be some way of explaining the undeniable interactions between soul, spirit, or reason, on the one hand, and the body, on the other hand. A host of metaphysicians, particularly since the time of Descartes, have spent much time and ingenuity in providing elaborate explanations of such interactions.

The numerous blind alleys up which all these philosophers —both daring and cautious—have stumbled, have led some thinkers to hoist the flag of naturalistic, even materialistic, reductionism. Since man, they argue, is at bottom a natural being, and since natural beings are material entities, man's nature and activities must be thoroughly accounted for in terms of material organization. We may, if we wish, talk about mind, soul, spirit, and so on, but these are only epiphenomena of the material body. Naturalistic and materialistic reductionism explains away the so-called "spiritual manifestations," "mental events," and, it goes without saying, "spiritual substances," as mere appearances, if not plain forgeries.

The above account of the philosophical controversies on the mind–body problem is, of course, a deplorable oversimplification. But it may help us to understand the nature of the difficulties encountered when man has been defined either as only a soul (or a mind, a spirit, etc.), or as only a body, or as some uneasy combination of both. In contrast to the doctrines sketched above, some thinkers have tried to view man's body in a different light, for instance, as man's inalienable property and at the same time as a reality which cannot be accounted for only as a material system. Curiously enough, some efforts in this direction were made by thinkers who are customarily described as throughgoing spiritualists. Such is the case with Thomas Aquinas, who followed here in the footsteps of Aristotle, and subscribed, *mutatis mutandis,* to the Aristotelian definition of the soul as "the form of the organic body having the power of life." [1] To be sure, Thomas Aquinas concluded that the human soul is a spiritual substance, not just an "organic form," but nevertheless his philosophical starting point was a conception of the soul which seemed to entail an idea of a certain way of being a body. Such is also the case with St. Augustine, at least when he declared that "the way in which the body attaches to the soul . . . is man himself" (*hoc tamen homo est*).[2] These opinions—or rather, a certain (no doubt, somewhat biased) interpretation, of these opinions—are quite similar to some of my own. Unfortunately, the former have been expressed at times obscurely, and often, as it were, half-heartedly, for practically all the thinkers I praised as my possible predecessors have ended by defending the doctrine that there is in man some principle substantially different from the body.

The first point I wish to put forward is this: man does not have a body, but *is his* body—his *own* body. Another way of expressing it is: *Man is a way of being a body.* Thus, I seem to subscribe now to naturalistic or materialistic reductionism. I hope to be able to prove that I am not so rash. If my philosophical anthropology has some analogues, they can be detected in a number of contemporary philosophical elucidations.[3] This does not mean that my ideas are derived from such elucidations, and the ensuing contentions; it only means that they are often in tune with some of them. Like a certain number of contemporary philosophers, but with vastly different assumptions, I try to shun both classical monism (spiritualistic or materialistic) and classical dualism, such as that exemplified in the Cartesian, or Cartesian–Augustinian, idea of an entirely spiritual substance more or less uncomfortably lodged in the body. Basically, what I contend is that nothing can be detected *in* man that absolutely transcends his body; *and* that man is not reducible to a material substance. A human being is not a reality, or a cluster of realities, unified by a certain element or principle existing "beyond" or "beneath" it. Man can be defined tentatively as *his* living. If man is formally defined as a set, he is a set whose only subset is himself.

21

BIOLOGICAL LIFE AND HUMAN LIFE

Let me put it this way: living beings—"organisms"—*live;* man, on the other hand (or rather, besides) *makes his own life.* This distinction looks overly subtle, or perhaps merely verbal. Could it not be asserted that organic systems, and in particular higher organisms, also make their own life? After all, organisms behave, as pointed out earlier, "spontaneously." This does not necessarily mean that their behavior is uncaused; it only means that it springs forth from them and yet is reflected upon them. This latter meaning is not to be dismissed lightly, for it conveys the interesting idea that organisms possess an "inside" as well as an "outside."[4] To be sure, 'inside' and 'outside' are also names of attributes of inorganic systems. However, whereas in the latter 'inside' and 'outside' primarily designate spatial attributes, in the former they principally designate behavioral characteristics. Organisms are capable of revealing, and of concealing, attitudes, purposes, impulses, emotions. Furthermore, they do that, not just accidentally, but constitutively. Rather than *having* an "outside" and an "inside," organisms *are* an "outside" and an "inside."

The terms 'outside' and 'inside' designate here, so to speak, ultimate behavioral attributes of organisms. Organisms reveal and conceal *themselves* instead of being "revealed" and "concealed" to a knowing subject, as is the case with inorganic realities. Organisms express "what they are" no less than "what they are not." They are capable of deceit and of dissimulation. They express themselves not only impulsively, but also cunningly. In *this* sense, organisms also make their own life. But the expression 'to make one's own life' must have a stronger meaning than the one surmised above if it is to serve as a feature capable of distinguishing human life from biological life *in genere*. Should we say that the expression 'to make one's own life' easily acquires such a meaning when it is made synonymous with 'to behave rationally' or 'deliberately'? I do not think so. We have experimental proof that some higher animals display an impressive amount of intelligence in their behavior. Not even tool-using and tool-making are exclusive attributes of human beings; some prehuman primates discovered that certain stones, sticks, and bones could be used as tools and even as tool-making tools.[5] The same may be said, even if less confidently, with respect to language. If the term 'language' designates a set of signals, expressed by means of bodily behavior, to impart information, then the bees use language. If, however, 'language' has a stronger meaning than the one just indicated, then its existence can be very intimately tied up with the human meaning of 'making one's own life.' [6]

The difference between "to live" and "to make one's own life" must be based, therefore, on less controversial features. One of them I consider noteworthy: it is the one revealed through a study of the type of relationship existing between living beings and their world, both the inanimate and the animate world.

All organisms develop within the frame of a more or less definite biological species. Each one of the species is adapted, or becomes adapted, to a certain "world" by means of a fixed system of challenges and responses. The behavior of each individual organism fits almost perfectly into the structure of its world, to the extent that the latter can be defined conversely by the set of operations which each individual organism can perform within it.

The dependence of each individual organism on its species is practically complete. The individual organism limits itself to performing those actions which become biologically possible within the species to which it belongs. When an individual organism attempts to perform actions of a quite different character, its survival as an individual is gravely impaired. If I may be permitted to use a formula infected with Platonic realism, "the species prevents the individual from acting otherwise." The well-known expression 'the genius of the species' summarizes metaphorically this almost consummate adaptability. Without such a "genius" the species would fade away or would change so drastically as to become a different species. Far from making its own life, each individual organism is "making" a part of the life of the relevant species. This I call "to live" *simpliciter.* In order to make, or be able to make, its own life it would be necessary for an individual organism to deviate from the perpetual cyclical movement of the species. If the individual organism succeeded without perishing, and if enough individual organisms followed suit, then the species would no longer be a species: it would be a community.[7] An essentially different type of relation between the individual organism and the species would then emerge. For such an event to happen, two basic conditions are required: on the one hand, the subordination of a certain number of primary impulses, among them the sexual impulse, to communal needs;[8] and on the other hand, and quite paradoxically, the possibility of a further inadaptability to, and even revolt against, communal patterns. Yet these conditions would still prove insufficient for the emergence of a full-fledged society. For such an emergence it would be necessary for the individual organism to invent and put forward new ways of life capable of transforming the behavioral structure of the community. Then, and only then, would the individual organism make its own life or have the possibility of making it. This happens, however, only with human beings. They belong to their community in a sense different from the one in which even prehuman primates belonged to their species. Human beings can, as a consequence, have a history, and not merely a temporal development. And in the course of history, behavioral changes occur which are, to be sure, based on biological processes, but which are not exclusively subservient to them. To make one's own life requires, thus, the transcendence of biological conditions. On the other hand, to live *simpliciter* looks more like sinking into life.

Individual organisms not only adapt to the conditions imposed by their biological species; they are also subordinated to the specific biological world corresponding to the species. This world is not an "objective world"; it is a biologically conditioned world. If we are ready to make 'reality' synonymous with 'objective reality,' then the world in question is not a "real world." The reality peculiar to the biological world is determined by the sum of biological needs and impulses shaped by a definite physical environment. The various biological worlds can be intertwined, and together can constitute one world, the so-called "biosphere." But there is no world transcending these various worlds, that is, no objectively transbiological world. For an organic world to trespass beyond its own limits it would be necessary for the individual organisms belonging to it to stop, at least intermittently, acting according to a definite challenge-and-response pattern. They would have to be capable of refusing to fulfill biological demands for the sake of values of a more objective character.

That is what the human beings do, at times. They repress their biological drives in the name of possible actions having some end in themselves, for instance, in the name of knowing for knowing's sake. We may call the result of these actions "cultural achievements." Now, although such achievements must draw their energy out of the sublimation of biological processes, they cannot be measured solely in terms of this sublimation. Max Scheler wrote that man is the only animal capable of saying "No," or, as he put it, he is "the ascetic of life." [9] He was right but only up to a point, because refusal is not enough; otherwise what we call "culture" would become a rather uncomfortable display of asceticism. In point of fact, "culture" can also mean fostering life, including biological life. But in such a case, this is not to be done in the name of biological life (if it can be said that it should be done "in the name of" anything); it is to be done in the name of vital *values*. What, therefore, ultimately counts, is not what the individual does, but the purpose with which he does it. A nonascetic life permeated by values—for instance, beauty—is as cultured as any other, and sometimes even more so. Thus, we must not hastily conclude that cultural values are solely obtainable by the repression and sublimation of biological drives, for in such a case they would not possess values of their own. Yet without some transformation of biological impulses there would be no possibility of an "objective world"; there would only be what we may call a "subjective-biological world": the world of the species.

To make one's own life can now be defined as follows: as the possibility of making the biological-subjective interests of the species, and of each one of its members, serve as the energetic basis for the final recognition of objects as objects. This may in principle seem to lead to a type of existence in which the subjective drives of individual organisms are stifled so as never to recur. Nevertheless, the subservience of subjective-biological drives to objective realities and/or values need not be love's labor lost. The transformation of the self-enclosed biological world into an open objective world may be—it has, indeed, been—the necessary condition for a later much more effective fulfillment of biological impulses. The demands imposed upon men by the recognition of reality as objective reality have, in fact, led them to a mastery of the same biological world in which they were originally confined. Thus, to recognize reality as it is, and not as our whim takes us, has become—through science, for example—the most efficient means of mastering it. One of the many paradoxes of the human condition is that men may have to emphasize reality to the utmost in order to fulfill more completely the demands of their subjectivity.

22
BEING, BECOMING, EXISTING

The concepts thus far introduced can now be translated into an ontological vocabulary. Inorganic matter I understand as "being in itself," namely, being what it is. Organic reality I understand as "being for itself," namely being for the sake of its own fulfillment—the development and survival of biological species. Inorganic matter I conceive as "something that already is"; organic reality, as "something that is in the process of being."

In some sense, organic reality can also be conceived as "that which is not yet what it is."

The term 'being' must not be construed here as designating something forbidding or recondite. In the present context 'being' means 'way of behaving,' in the general sense of 'way of being actualized.' To say that inorganic matter is already given is tantamount to saying that it is actual, or nearly so. The expression 'nearly so' I cannot adequately clarify here; suffice it to say that I am assuming the following ontological postulate: no reality is absolutely actual; and its counterpart, no reality is absolutely potential. In my ontological scheme there is no room for absolute attributes (or entities) of any kind; there is, at most, room for some concepts—which then become limiting concepts—of (equally limiting) absolute attributes or realities. Inorganic reality is, from this viewpoint, the most actual of all types of reality. If it is not purely actual, it "behaves"—or rather, it appears—*as if* it were so. Whenever there is something determinate, and determinable, that is the inorganic world. This is, by the way, the reason why it lends itself so easily to description in that language in which, according to Galileo, the "Book of Nature" is written: the language of mathematics.

Inorganic realities undergo a number of stages. Organic realities, and in particular higher organisms, undergo a number of phases. The former endure a series of processes; the latter, a series of developments. Terms such as 'state,' 'phase,' 'process,' and 'development,' are, of course, utterly inadequate. Furthermore, the distinctions which these terms are meant to convey do not in any way presuppose that organic realities cease to behave in the way inorganic realities behave. After all, there is only one species of matter: the so-called "physical matter." But organic realities, or, as I have also called them, "organisms," do something that inorganic realities do not: they realize, and constitute, themselves in the course of their development. They bring themselves, successfully or not, to an issue. They appear, much more than inorganic realities, as a set of potentialities which may or may not become actual. In principle, an organism could be expressed (ontologically) as a τὸ τί ἦν εἶναι—the well-known Aristotelian expression, sometimes translated, rather hastily, as 'essence.' But, of course, organisms are not essences. They are existences developing according to certain forms and patterns which, no doubt, change in the course of evolution. In *this* sense, organisms are even more "determined" than inorganic realities, if the semantics of 'determined' is duly clarified. They possess, as it has been put, a "determined future," and abide by a "certain generic and specific cycle." [10] Organic life, and in particular complex organic life, has, thus, a "direction." Which, of course, does not mean, even if it seems to mean, that life always and necessarily follows a preconceived plan, or develops according to a preestablished finality. We need not presuppose the existence of immanent final causes in the evolution of the organic world as a whole. We need only presuppose that organisms become what they are within a certain temporal-cyclical pattern, and according to certain laws of structural transformation.

When all is said, however, one thing remains certain: that both types of reality tally (ontologically) with the concept of "being." To be sure, one of these two types of reality is more aptly describable (ontologically, again) as "becoming" than as "being." Yet the concept of becoming is still indebted to the concept of being. At any rate, both inorganic and organic realities can be understood as "things" of some sort—things which move and change; and things which, besides moving and changing, grow, develop, and reproduce themselves.

The most striking characteristic of human life, as we view it ontologically, is that it can scarcely be called a "being," namely, a "thing." Following, deliberately or not, in Fichte's footsteps, some contemporary philosophers have emphasized that human life as *human* life is not a thing, not even a "thing that becomes." In the sense in which I have employed such terms as 'to be,' 'being,' 'it is,' 'they are,' and so on, it can be said then that human life, properly speaking, "is not." It is not what it is. But neither is it what it becomes. Can we then talk about it at all? If we were very particular about language, we would conclude that we obviously cannot. Happily enough, language is a somewhat pliable tool; we can make its terms mean, if not all that we wish, at least some things that we very much want. In consequence, we can also say that human life "is." But we must hasten to add that it is not a "something," but rather a "someone." A few philosophers have even gone so far as to define it as some sort of absolute in which everything that is or becomes remains, as it were, "enclosed"—at least insofar as it is, or becomes, perceivable, knowable, and so on. I cannot go along with them. But I am ready to admit that if human life is some sort of thing, it is a very unusual thing indeed. This thing which is not a thing, may be called "an existent," not, however, in the simple sense of "something that exists," but rather in the sense partly uncovered by some traditional metaphysicians when they coined, for another purpose, the expression 'the pure actuality of existing.'

The natural sciences and the social sciences contribute valuable information about human life. It would be unwise to dismiss all these sciences with a stroke of the pen, claiming that they touch only the "ontic" realm while in no sense reaching the "ontologic" realm, as Heidegger puts it.[11] For these two realms are not incommunicable. It has been said that, after all, we are quite uncertain about where one such realm ends and where the other begins.[12] I heartily subscribe to this view. Translated into a somewhat less esoteric vocabulary, it simply means that metaphysical speculation and ontological analysis, while they do not need to follow scientific research blindly, should never proceed stubbornly against scientific results. If for no other reason than that science is here to stay (§ 3), philosophers would do well to resign themselves to the fact that it may set certain bounds and exert certain controls on metaphysics (the converse may, of course, also be the case). The frontiers between metaphysics and science will eventually change; after all, neither one nor the other is a ready-made system of knowledge. Now, setting bounds to metaphysical speculation is far from equivalent to determining the direction such speculation must take. Metaphysical speculation and, *a fortiori,* ontological analysis use concepts wrought by science and by common sense, but do not meekly conform to all the meanings established by them. That this is so we will verify at once. I will introduce a few terms whose ontological meanings will prove to be quite different from, albeit somehow related to, their usual meanings. Among such terms, one is notably singled out for distinction: it is the term 'property,' considered here as designating the positive and concrete aspect of a yet undefined concept: the concept "selfhood," a rather clumsy translation of the German *Selbstheit* and of the Spanish *mismidad.*

23

MAN AS SELFHOOD AND AS PROPERTY

To begin with, I will distinguish between "ipseity" (*ipseitas*) and "selfhood." The term 'ipseity' is meant to designate the fact that any given thing is what it is, namely, the identity of any given thing with itself. Since such an identity is accomplished only when we arbitrarily disregard the temporal element in a thing, pure "ipseity" is an attribute only of the so-called "ideal objects"—mathematical entities (if there are such), concepts, and perhaps values. However, it can be said that all things as things display a greater or lesser tendency to be what they are, and therefore to be "identical" in the above sense. This tendency to self-identity among existing realities reaches its maximum in inorganic systems for reasons that should now be moderately clear. It is much less perceptible in organisms, insofar as these are in the process of becoming what they are according to temporal and cyclical patterns. Nevertheless, all beings are in some ways what they are, even if at times their being is, to use the well-known Aristotelian expressions, a "coming to be" and a "passing away."

In a way, the term 'selfhood' purports to designate a type of attribute similar to the one designated by the term 'ipseity.' Furthermore, if we define 'selfhood' as "being itself" or as "becoming itself," then 'selfhood' is just another name for 'identity.' Thus, we may conclude that all realities, insofar as they are identical with themselves, possess the attributes of ipseity and selfhood.

Unfortunately, all these terms behave like the meshes in Eddington's fishing net: they let some interesting fish escape easily. At any rate, they let human reality quickly jump into the sea again. This happens in particular with the terms 'identity' and 'ipseity.' Does it also happen with the term 'selfhood'? Not necessarily, provided that we employ it the way scientists and, above all, philosophers handle a number of expressions—by twisting or, at least, stretching their meanings.[13] 'Selfhood' may mean more than just "being itself"; it may mean "being oneself." It may serve as a formal answer to the question: "Who is it?" rather than an answer to the question: "What is it?" In this sense it may describe a specifically human attribute. In order to avoid confusions, however, I propose the following terminological device: whenever 'selfhood' is used to refer to human beings, I will replace it by 'property,' in a sense of 'property' which I will soon clarify.

Besides being denounced as barbaric, the proposed vocabulary will in all likelihood be declared superfluous. Why not use in this connection the more respectable terms 'spirit' and 'person,' already tested through centuries of philosophical experience? The term 'person' in particular looks quite handy. Yet, I prefer to avoid it, or rather, to use it only after it has been purged of many of its traditional connotations. Should the occasion arise we could, if we really wanted to, use the terms 'spirit' and 'person,' provided that the two following conditions were fulfilled: First, that these terms would not refer to any realities absolutely transcendent to human life, and still less running counter to the material—inorganic and organic—constituents of human life. Second, that they would not designate any indissoluble and inalienable attributes, namely, any supposedly eternal predicates which man would, so to speak, "share" and of which he could be definitely assured. By the way, similar reservations could be made when the attributes called "rationality" and "emotivity" (some higher forms of emotivity) are chosen as denoting specific characteristics of human existence.

At most I will agree to say that man *becomes* personal and *becomes* spiritual, without ever completely succeeding. Man is making himself constantly as man, and that is what I meant by saying that he makes his own life. A certain biological structure and a number of psychological dispositions are in this respect necessary conditions. They are in no way merely contingent facts, purely circumstantial elements which man can take or leave as he pleases. A certain human body and a certain human mind are also a certain given man. Each man thus makes his own life with his body and his mind, which are not solely "things," but basic elements of man's existence.

Here lies one reason why human beings are not identical with, even if in some respects they are comparable to, servomechanisms. It is quite probable that the more we know about the structure and behavior of nervous systems—and above all, about the structure of the human central nervous system—the more similar they will appear to a complex servomechanism. The psychosomatic structure of human beings can be explained largely in terms of complicated mechanical states in stable equilibrium. The so-called "organic self-control" (homeostasis) can be described as a kind of thermostatic control. We may even go so far as to admit that servomechanisms can think, remember, learn, and so on. When all is said, however, there still remains the problem of whether a servomechanism, no matter how human-like we imagine it to be, can indeed perform operations of a really human character. Professor Mario Bunge has pointed out that "irrespective of their degree of automatism [computers] are all characterized by the fact that *they do not perform mathematical operations,* but only physical operations which we coordinate with mathematical ones." [14] Computers "do not add pure numbers; they add turns of cogwheels, electric pulses, etc." [15] That some functions can be described in terms of automatic control operations is one thing; that they are identical with such operations is another. In any case, it would be pure fantasy to claim that servomechanisms make themselves the way human beings do; that, therefore, they belong to themselves. This does not mean that servomechanisms could not in principle "think" or even reproduce themselves (if von Neumann's blueprint for a self-reproducing machine proves feasible, we will eventually witness such a stupendous ceremony); [16] it only, but significantly, means that their reality will never be *theirs,* but something else's, and actually, someone else's reality.

"Man belongs to himself" is a way, albeit a rather awkward one, of saying that man is his own property. I mean not only the fact that the body and the mind of human beings belong to them, instead of being something alien and contingent. I mean also, and above all, that men possess their own lives, so that they are ontologically, and not only morally, responsible for themselves. Man is not a being *that* lives; he is *his own* living. However, since man is not anything definite except the constant effort to become man, it may even be risky to say that he is his own living; let us then say that he constantly tries to make his living his own. Making one's own life—for this is ultimately what all this boils down to—is then something different from, although somehow correlated to, the biological processes of growing and developing. What such "self-making" most resembles is a series of efforts to reach and, as it were, to conquer one's own reality while stumbling all along the way.

The above may cast some light on the perplexing paradox of

man as a free being. On the one hand, man as man is necessarily free. The arguments adduced in favor of this view by authors such as Ortega y Gasset [17] and Sartre [18] are quite pertinent, even if they are not always altogether convincing. On the other hand, freedom is not given to man in the sense in which it might be given to a thing as one of its unassailable, or at least normal attributes. As a consequence, the paradox of freedom is still more puzzling than it has been claimed. Let me put it this way: man acquires his own freedom insofar as he freely develops as man. Thus, freedom is a requisite for the existence of man—who must himself provide this requisite. Man is that type of reality that can make itself while it can also unmake itself. Man, in short, has the possibility of being himself, and of not being himself, of appropriating himself and of alienating himself.

Human reality is, therefore, a "being for itself" in a much more radical sense than the being for itself proper to organisms. No organic reality as such can move away from itself. Ceasing to be itself is for such a reality equivalent to becoming another. To use, and by the way to distort, the Hegelian vocabulary—to which I and many others are indebted nowadays, no matter how much we try to put this fact out of our minds—an organic reality is never an *Anderssein* and can never become, strictly speaking, an *Aussersichsein*. If we persist in applying the expressions 'being for itself' and 'being other' to the behavior of organic realities, we should give them quite different meanings from the ones just intimated. To the extent that we are taking an ontological point of view on human reality, we are not interested in forms of being as being but rather in ultimate possibilities of existence. Whereas organic reality can be in many different ways, it never ceases to be what it is. On the other hand, man can cease to be himself and, as a rule, never becomes entirely himself. Yet, not being himself is also one of the ways of being a man. The reason for this paradoxical condition of human existence is, again, that man is never "a thing that is."

It may now be contended that I have gone too far in my atttempt to deny that man is a "being" or a "thing." First, man is obviously also a thing, an organic thing and many inorganic things together. Second, we may view man, from the religious angle, as a creature, and therefore as a type of reality that could never make his own existence, or even simply exist, unless God produced him, and perhaps helped him to exist. Such claims are not lightly to be dismissed. The former is based upon facts; the latter is founded on a belief. Nevertheless, I need not consider these claims as unduly embarrassing. The first claim I have already rebutted; although man, through his body and mind, is a fact, or a collection of facts, what makes him a man is not these facts but what he does with them. In human life it is the meaning of the facts that counts. As to the second claim, it is sufficient to say that even if man received his being from God it could still be argued that he is not properly speaking a man unless he maintains himself in existence. If man is a created being, he is such in a sense quite different from the one in which we say that things, or for that matter, pure spirits, are created. The freedom that constitutes man and by means of which he constitutes himself must be his very own. To express it in Nietzsche's words: man is an acrobat walking over an abyss; [19] it is up to him to fling himself down or to keep his balance. In order to be able to walk over the abyss with a reasonable degree of poise he does all sorts of things; for example, he creates "culture" and "history." There is little doubt that "part of every culture is 'defense mechanism,'" and that "the function of culture and psychosis alike is to be 'homeostatic,' to maintain preferred equilibriums." [20] But this is only part of the story. As I have tried to establish, culture is also, and above all, the result of the attempt to make man's world an objective world, independent from, albeit attached to, his basic drives and instincts. There is no harm, however, in admitting that man is fundamentally a cultural and historical being. He does not produce culture and history just because he finds it fun, but because he desperately needs them. But this question leads us to the heart of our present problem: the problem of "where" man is heading.

24
THE DEFINITION OF MAN

Let me briefly recapitulate my argument. The concepts "being" and "becoming" apply to human reality only insofar as this reality is part of a continuum—the "continuum of Nature." I have never denied, but rather emphasized, that man is also an inorganic and an organic being, to the extent that he really *is* a body. But as we wish to distinguish human reality ontologically from other realities of the said continuum, the ontological vocabulary must be stretched when it is not twisted. Thus, terms such as 'selfhood,' 'property,' and others come to the rescue in order to allow us to have a glimpse of what it means to say such odd things as "man is not a being, but a maker of himself."

I could have also said that the reality of human life is, properly speaking, the meaning of human life if I had been given the opportunity to introduce the term 'meaning' (or perhaps 'sense') with any likelihood of not being utterly misunderstood. I will confine myself to a less controversial vocabulary, and will say that human reality is "intentional" in character. 'Being intentional' here means "going toward, wending or directing one's course." But a question now arises: "Where" is he going? "To what" is he wending or directing his course?

If I say "toward something outside him," or "toward something inside him," I will not go very far indeed. To proceed to the outside is tantamount to adapting to the surrounding world —a world in turn constantly shaped by the adaptive efforts. To proceed to the inside is tantamount to self-regulating the individual structure. In both cases we are talking about biological and psycho-biological processes. These have, in man and in higher animals, a firm basis in two types of nervous systems:

the cerebro-spinal nervous system, which coordinates the knowledge and action relations with the external world; and the sympathetic nervous system, which regulates the so-called "inner processes" of the organism and which is split into as many independent systems as prove necessary for the proper functioning of the various parts of the organism. Where, then, does man as man proceed to? No doubt, we can still use such expressions as 'toward the ouside' and 'toward the inside,' but the terms 'outside' and 'inside' acquire quite a different meaning here.

The "outside" toward which human beings proceed is the world as a world, namely, the world as an objective reality, independent in principle from strictly biological and psychobiological needs. This "intentional openness" to the objective world, as phenomenologists would put it, is the foundation of knowledge. To be sure, men know and think to some purpose. But the contents of thinking and knowledge must be objectively valid, and not only subjectively useful. Human beings project themselves toward a world outside that transcends any subjective purpose. Human beings may have, so to speak, invented and promoted knowledge for the sake of "life, of "human *praxis,"* and so on. But here we can modify a celebrated formula: *propter cognitionem cognitionis perdere causas;* we must sacrifice knowledge (knowledge as a vital tool) for the sake of knowledge (knowledge as an end). Or, rather, we must promote the former only because we hope to reach the latter. This does not mean, of course, that knowledge as an end is necessarily incompatible with knowledge as a tool; after all, action has often been all the more successful when disinterested contemplation—or so-called "pure theory"—has preceded it. On the other hand, knowing is not the only possible intentional attitude; acting and evaluating are also important, and sometimes even more so than knowing. In any case, man exists as man insofar as he fulfills himself, not by directly responding to the challenges of the environment, but by making the environment an objective world. Therefore, when man proceeds toward an outside, he does not confine himself either to adapting to it completely, or to refusing it completely. He goes back and forth from subjectivity to objectivity—which helps explain why the cultural world, which man creates as he springs up from the natural world, is at the same time a world which he must objectively recognize.

On the other hand, the "inside" toward which man wends his way is not only the inner biological or psycho-biological structure. It is not equivalent to, even if based on, the process of self-conservation and self-regulation of the organism, but rather to some sort of reality which may be called "oneself," "one's own reality," and "one's authenticity." There is also a projecting movement here. But man does not project something; he rather projects "someone"—namely himself. When he thus projects himself, man searches for—without necessarily finding—his "authentic being," or, as it has also been called, somewhat pathetically, his "destiny." To be sure, all realities, and in particular all highly developed organisms, exist in some way as self-fulfilling and self-projecting entities; they all are, consciously or not, intent on realizing themselves. But whereas the pattern for self-realization is given to them in the forms and/or laws of nature, man is not given any such definite pattern. Each one of us, whether he knows it or not, or even cares for it or not, is on the lookout for his own pattern, without knowing whether it will ever be discovered, or even whether there is one. All realities, except man, can be, or can become, in the sense of 'being something' or 'becoming something.' Man can, besides, cease to be, in the sense of 'ceasing to be himself.' Here is why the concepts "being" and "becoming" have proved inadequate to describe ontologically human reality. In that sense Sartre was correct when he contended that human life—or "consciousness," the "being for itself"—is not what it is, and is what it is not. In view of this, we could now assert that man is not even doomed to be free. Man is not, properly speaking, doomed to anything, not even to be man. This does not necessarily mean that freedom is neither good nor bad. In fact, unless he is, or rather, struggles to become, free (in many senses of 'free,' including 'morally free,' 'free from alienation,' etc.), man is not worthy of being called a human being. But he does not receive his freedom ready-made; he must make it. Or, more precisely, he makes it as he (freely) makes himself. This is no doubt, a deplorably vicious circle, for it amounts to saying that only freedom makes a certain type of reality, which makes itself through freedom. But I see no way of escaping this circle. It may well happen, as we have already pointed out (§ 8), that some vicious circles are philosophically inevitable. On the level of the ontology of human life, we must often acknowledge that some consequences may play at the same time the role of principles.

Human life can be defined as a kind of unceasing march toward oneself, which can often become a march against oneself. Paradoxically, not being oneself is as good an attribute of human life as being oneself.

This is the meaning of the attribute called "property": that human life is always man's *own* life. Man owns his life even when he seems to be on the verge of annihilating himself as man, whether going back to his purely animal living, or transcending himself and becoming, as it were, ecstatic in front of pure objectivity. This last point deserves brief elucidation. Let us imagine that man consists, as some say, in being a spiritual substance, and that such a substance is defined as the possibility of bowing to objectivity—to objective reality and to objective values. Even in such a case, spiritual reality cannot be conceived except as *existing*. And in order to exist it must undergo all sorts of experiences, private and public, personal and historical, individual and social. To live as a man is to undergo what makes one be what one is. As a consequence, man as a personal reality tends to yield to the impersonal, but he is no longer a man when he yields to the impersonal to the point of fusing with it. This is, of course, another paradox which, I am afraid, must be allowed to remain. Let me simply say that man continually hesitates between the realm of pure objectivity and the realm of pure internal experience. He cannot come to a halt in his constant shift from one extreme point to the other. Reality and values are objective to man only insofar as they are subjectively experienced. Human experience, on the other hand, is lived through what some philosophers have called "situations." And since situations, whether individual or collective, are historical in character, human living is always historical, namely, irreversible, and in some sense at least, "dramatic," Anything done, thought, or felt by man in order to live authentically is irretrievable. It may be claimed that some acts or decisions sink so deeply into the living root of human reality that they transform it from the ground up. As an example I may cite repentance, usually followed by some kind of conversion (in various senses of 'conversion,' the religious sense being extremely important, but by no means unique). In contradistinction to mere remorse,[21] repentance makes possible some sort of rebirth, traditionally, but not always aptly, called "spiritual rebirth." The past is not actually wiped away, but it becomes so transfigured by the present as to make it appear entirely different from what it was. Yet, even these "extreme situations" are possible only because the facts which they transform have existed the way they did. In other words, for repentance to be even conceivable, something to repent from is necessary. The very possibility of a fundamental change in human life is based on life's basic irreversibility. No human act is entirely alien to man. Hence the dramatic character of human existence. I do not inject the word 'dramatic' here just because I wish to make readers shudder, for I feel certain that readers, if they happen to be philosophers, will hardly shudder. I use the term 'dramatic' only to emphasize the temporal, experiential, and historical character of human reality. To say "life is a drama," on the other hand, is one of the ways of saying "life is mine." No drama is such if it is not the exclusive property of the character who displays it.

The source out of which the "dramatic" actions and decisions of human individuals spring, is therefore, not of a purely spiritual nature, nor is it of a permanent nature. Ortega y Gasset has pointed out that human life is at all times "circumstantial"; [22] each man does what he does, or abstains from doing what he abstains from doing, in view of specific and very concrete circumstances. I must say that I agree, but with one important reservation. Ortega y Gasset thought, as did Sartre later, that the body and mind (the character and temperament) of man belongs to the circumstances of human life, so that man makes his choice with, and, if necessary, against his own body and mind. If such were the case, however, the human reality would boil down to pure nothingness. The body and mind of an individual would never be his own. He would become a disembodied ghostly "chooser." Furthermore, he would be an infinitely plastic and malleable reality. By dint of making every natural reality in him appear as a purely contingent "facticity" (as some philosophers have put it), the very human reality would entirely dissolve. By means of depriving man of everything, he would not even be someone who would act with, for, or against any circumstances. On the other hand, if we conclude that only man's body and mind constitute man, we again risk making man a thing among other similar things. I will now turn to this difficulty.

Some philosophers have tried to determine "who" ultimately man is as distinct from ascertaining "what" he is. A few have contended, moreover, that man is his irreducible "authenticity," his "inner call," his "destiny." And they have added that we may choose to be faithful or not to our "incorruptible (in the sense of 'absolutely reliable and unchangeable') core." Theirs is an exquisite and refined doctrine. It is not, however, a very illuminating doctrine. To say that "whoness" (if I may be allowed to use this word) is equivalent to authenticity and nothing else is to put forward a purely nominal definition of the expression 'oneself.' It is equivalent to saying that one is (at bottom) what one (at bottom) is. No consequences, moral or otherwise, ensue. It may be argued that in view of the above difficulties it is preferable to subscribe to a more traditional definition of man—at any rate, to a formula defining man as a really permanent "someone." But when philosophers have started defining or describing this supposedly more enduring reality, they have been caught in the trap of all classical substantialist theories. They have been compelled to define man as some kind of "invariable nature," and often as someone possessing a "rational nucleus." In other words, they have again defined human reality in terms of such categories as "thing" and "being" which I have taken so many pains to discard.

Is the question at all solvable? The general ontological framework that supports the philosophical views brought forth in this book comes to the rescue. In this ontological framework no "Absolutes," and hence no absolute modes of being, are allowed. Each reality is supposed to bend toward some of the so-called "Absolutes" without ever reaching any of them. Now, the infinite plasticity and malleability of the human reality, on the one hand, and its invariable and permanent character, on the other, are absolute modes of being. As such, they must be viewed only as limiting realities describable by means of limiting concepts. We can talk about them, but only if we are careful enough to allow them a mere quasi-existence. Thus, concrete human reality perpetually oscillates between two ideal poles. Man is not to be defined either as a pure possibility of choice or as a purely invariable entity; he unceasingly rebounds from one to the other in order to make himself. Human reality is not like an unbordered river. Neither is it comparable to a waterless riverbed. It is not pure nature. Neither is it pure history. It is both, but in a constantly shifting—perhaps I should say, "dialectical"—way.

In some respects I have tried to put traditional metaphysics and modern ontology together. The former insisted on substance; the latter has emphasized function. The former argued in favor of a "rational" core of man; the latter has underlined "history," "experience," "drama." If we now reintroduce the time-honored term 'person' and try to put it to some use, would we not say that the unforeseeable and irretrievable history of the human being is inscribable within the frame of the notion of person? We would not then say that man is a person having a history, but rather a person constituting himself historically. According to a celebrated formula, the human person is "an individual substance of a rational character," [23] subsisting in its own right. Provided that we interpret the term 'substance' in the light of the preceding considerations as a self-making reality, we can conclude that man is "an individual substance of a historical character." [24] It is most improbable that my formula will ever become as influential as Boethius'. But perhaps it is only because nowadays philosophers are much harder to please.

25
A BUDGET OF PARADOXES

We have assumed (§ 9) that to be real is to be mortal, in a very broad and, indeed, "analogical" sense of 'mortal.' The converse is, of course, true: to be mortal is to be real. Furthermore, we have assumed that for any given reality, R, the nature of R is parallel to the type of mortality—or, in general, "ceasability" —of R. In other words, R is what it is because of the way in which it ceases to be, and R ceases to be in such and such a way because R is what it is. These assumptions we have consistently maintained throughout our elucidation of the nature and mode or modes of cessation of inorganic and organic realities. The same must be the case with human reality.

The philosophical anthropology sketched above (§§ 20–24) is meant to convey the idea that, although man is also an inorganic reality (a cluster of inorganic systems) and, to be sure, a biological organism, his existence is not entirely explicable in terms of purely inorganic and organic substances. As a consequence, man's mode of cessation—his peculiar kind of "mortality"—should not be entirely explicable in terms of the modes of cessation of such substances. It is now the moment to show that man's peculiar mode of cessation confirms, as well as supports, the main results of our philosophical anthropology. To this question we will devote the remaining sections of the present chapter.

Before we proceed to scrutinize in more detail the nature of human death, we wish to call attention to a few paradoxes, as startling as they are enlightening.

1. On the one hand, human death—which we will henceforth simply call "death"—seems to be so deeply embedded and, as it were, "internalized" in the human being that we are tempted to conclude that man is an essentially mortal being. In other words, to die seems to be something truly "inherent" in the human reality. This aspect of human death we will name "the interiority of death." In addition, death seems to "belong" to the very nature of man, so that it can be concluded that the death of any given man is truly "his own"—or otherwise said, that death is man's inalienable "property." On the other hand, men often act and think as if it were their aim to overcome death at all costs; after all, man is the only being who has ever dreamed that he could become "immortal."

2. On the one hand, death is an event which possesses the same meaning, or, as the case may be, the same lack of meaning, for all men. On the other hand, human death is an event which is strictly individual or, more precisely, strictly personal.

3. On the one hand, death seems to make its presence felt only "at the other end of life"; thus, death emerges truly "outside of," and has little to do with, human life. To be sure, some thinkers have surmised that man is, as it were, perpetually dying, for he begins to die from the very moment when he

begins to live. Yet once a man is dead, his death is, in fact, "beyond his life." Death is not simply dying, but "that which has died." Hence to die is, as Paul Ludwig Landsberg has put it, "to set foot into the ghostly, chilly world of absolute death." [25]

From this point of view, we are able to say little, if anything at all about death. 'Death' is a name which merely designates the complete absence of life. Since the complete absence of life (or, for that matter, of anything) is nothingness, it would seem only wise to abstain from talking about it, for nothingness is not a proper subject of meaningful talk.

On the other hand, death "refers to"—in the senses of 'points at,' 'calls attention to'—life, even if it is only "a life that was." Something remains for a time after death which can be regarded as "that which death has left behind": the "dead one," the corpse. Thus, it is hard to believe that death refers to nothing; as the saying goes, it "preys upon" *living* beings.

Now, the expression 'death refers to life' can be given two meanings. First, the expression in question may describe the trivial fact that death is, in every case, the end of life. Second, it may imply that death is somehow inherent in—and thus "internal to"—life. 'Being inherent in life' may again have two meanings: (1) It may mean that 'death' describes or designates the culmination of the biological process called "aging," at least in highly developed organisms. (2) It may mean that human life calls for and, as it were, necessarily implies death, which is nearly the same as saying that human life would become meaningless without death, and indeed without "his own" death.

In what follows I will take the above "paradoxes" and "contradictions" into account. In tune with a form of thinking on which nothing less than a general ontology is based, I will not try to avoid, but will even occasionally emphasize, a number of conflicting statements and positions. Thus, it will be shown that each man dies for himself, but at the same time that the death of each human being can be taken as a symbol of human mortality in general. It will also be shown that death is an event internal to man's life while not being ever *completely* "his own." It will be shown finally that the predicate 'is basically mortal' is not necessarily synonymous with the predicate 'is (or exists) unto death.'

26
THE INTERIORITY OF DEATH

The expression 'the interiority of death' is meant to describe the following state of affairs: death is not simply the end of life but an event which shapes and constitutes life. Correspondingly, the expression 'the exteriority of death' is meant to designate the fact that death falls outside the scope of life. Now then, it is my opinion that no matter how much death may belong to man as his "property," it is never completely interior (or, as we shall also say, "internal") to man's life. If such were the case, man's life would be explicable solely in terms of his death. On the other hand, I maintain that a complete exteriority of death with respect to life is most improbable and, indeed, inconceivable, for in this case human death would be an entirely meaningless event. We must assume, then, that death is partly internal, and party external, to human life. The question is now, to what degree does the interiority of death noticeably prevail over its exteriority in human beings?

The answer is, to a considerable degree. As has been shown in the preceding chapters, cessation is not equally fundamental and significant in all types of realities. We have been able to disclose that even within the sole realm of organic beings, some entities are "potentially immortal"; for them, cessation is primarily, although never entirely, external and, therefore, primarily, although never entirely, accidental. In highly developed organisms, death seems to be more deeply anchored in their existence; they inevitably die, or nearly so. Now, the death of highly developed organisms is biological death; it is a fact but has yet no meaning, or, more precisely, if it has a meaning it is not yet meaningful enough to be seriously taken into account. This is, of course, due to the fact that even highly developed organisms are (at least relatively) value-free—which is, of course, different from saying that they are valueless. At any rate, their value and, consequently, their meaning is not sufficiently internal to their being. Thus, death puts an end to these organisms but does not "realize" or "fulfill" them; they are not made what they are because of the way in which they happen to die. In fine, for any purely biological organism, O, the fact that O dies is always more important than what it means (or may mean) for O to die. In human beings, on the other hand, death is already an essentially meaningful event; it not only puts an end to their existence but, as intimated, it constitutes their very existence to a considerable extent.

Highly developed organisms can be said to be potentially mortal. Death is, therefore, internal to these organisms—not, of course, completely, but, so to speak, sufficiently. If we now claim that death is internal to human beings, and add that it is not completely so, then we might seem to be led to conclude that human beings are also potentially mortal. Accordingly, it would seem that there is no difference worth mentioning between biological organisms as such and human beings, at least insofar as their degree of mortality is concerned: both are potentially mortal, and death is internal to both of them. Yet we persist in affirming that, although human death is also in a high degree biological death, the former is not entirely reducible to the latter.

The above puzzle can be solved as soon as we realize that we have been surreptitiously identifying the meaning of 'potentially mortal' with the meaning of 'death is internal to life.' Now then, these expressions are far from having exactly the same meaning. To say that death is internal to life is not in the least like saying that death is in life potentially, for instance, as "that which is bound to happen sooner or later." If a being is potentially mortal, then it is potentially mortal. Being potentially mortal means only that death is contained, as it were, in life, perhaps in the manner in which an organism is contained in its seeds. Only in a very metaphorical sense can we affirm that death is then internal to life. On the other hand, although it is true that, as a biological organism, man is also potentially mortal, it is no less true that death is not merely contained in this existence. Death, as potential death, brings pressure to bear upon man's life, and so becomes a decisive factor in it.

We can thus affirm that death gives human life not so much its being, as that which constitutes it primarily, although not, it must be acknowledged, exclusively: its meaning, or, to say it another way, its being as meaning. For human life exemplifies superlatively that form of reality in which meaning predominates over being—over facts as facts—to such a degree that it may even be said that facts exist for man only to the extent that they possess meaning for him. This is only another way of saying that death constantly "points at" life. Thus, death truly "belongs" to human life, which is the same as saying that it makes it posible for human life to achieve its own reality.

In his "metaphysics of death" Simmel pointed out that a distinction must be made in human life between "process" and "contents." [26] The term 'process' designates the course of life and, therefore, its pure and simple temporal development. The term 'contents' designates all that is, or can be, experienced in the course of life: feelings, thoughts, judgments of value, and so on. Now, according to Simmel, it would be totally impossible to distinguish between "process" and "contents" if life had no end. If a life continued endlessly, none of its "contents" would make any great difference, and, therefore, all the "contents" would become identified with the "process." It would be all the same if one embraced this or that particular thought, made this or that particular judgment of value, underwent this or that particular experience. In fact, no thought, no feeling, no experience would be "particular" at all; they would all be the same and, as a consequence, they would all be "indifferent." Now, if we wish each and all of the contents to have a meaning, we must assume that life is not endless but always limited and bound by death.

It is then the continual presence of death in life, its "hidden presence," which makes all the contents of life, and life itself, meaningful. This is why, as Simmel indicated, we do not die at one particular moment; death is not, properly speaking, an event but an "element" continuously shaping our existence. Death may not be the only thing that really matters, but in any case, nothing matters very much without it. We can thus conclude that death is internal to life in a sense of 'being internal,' which is not to be confused with the sense of 'being potentially mortal.' The expression 'the interiority of death' has a definite and more precise meaning now; it means that in human life, death is not only a limit (no matter how inevitable) but also a kind of "dividing line." This "line" performs two functions: it puts an end to a process, and gives this process a meaning. Now, if having some meaning is what specifically differentiates man from all other kinds of reality, then it can be said that an adequate understanding of human life depends, *a tergo,* on death. To express it in plain language, human death is a fact—or an event—that really counts.

27
THE EXPERIENCE OF DEATH

To say that death is—or, more precisely, tends to be—internal to human life is, of course, a very general statement. In point of fact, it is so general as to be quite unenlightening. In order to make it more specific, and thus more informative, we must have recourse to what is often called the "experience of death."

To be sure, we all know what we mean when we use such expressions as 'X is mortally ill, and is about to die,' 'X died yesterday,' and so on. But, although we know that there is such a thing or such an event as death, that death is inevitable, that we all must die, and so on, we still do not realize in full measure what death is and what it means until we somehow "experience" death.

Now, how is an "experience of death" ever possible? We can "see" that people die; we can think of our own death as an event which will take place sooner or later, but we do not seem to be able to experience death in the same way as we do other "events" such as pleasure, pain, good health, illness, senility. All we can "see" of death is its "residue," for example, a corpse. Even a corpse is not only, or exclusively, a testimony of death, for it may equally well call attention to life. A corpse is not only a reminder of "that which is no longer," but also a reminder of "that which was." Thus, death as such seems to be outside all possible experience. As Karl Jaspers has written, "death as an objective fact of existence is not itself a limiting situation." [27]

According to Heidegger, we cannot experience another's death, or what is sometimes called "the death of the Other"; at most, we can "witness" it.[28] Death cannot be "substituted," "replaced," "transferred," "interchanged." No one can die in lieu of another. Although one can "die *for* another"; this does not mean that one can take the Other's *own* death.[29] It is characteristic of the *Dasein*'s death that each *Dasein* assumes it *a radice* for himself.

Heidegger's ideas in this respect should be understood in the light of his famous contention: the being of *Dasein* is a "being unto death." [30] Further on (§ 29) I shall explain more in detail why I disapprove of Heidegger's views on this question, or why I disapprove of them while considering them acceptable when duly integrated with other, seemingly contrary, views. Now, to reject *prima facie* Heidegger's contentions would seem to imply an acceptance of the criticisms against them which were formulated by Sartre.[31] Such, however, is not the case. Sartre points out that, if it is true that one cannot die for another, it is equally true that one also cannot, for example, love for another.

He further maintains that, far from shaping and completing the being of human life, death completely alienates it and turns it into a sort of "prey of the living" [32] —of those who may survive the dead person. Accordingly, it is not we ourselves who are mortal; it is "the Other" who is mortal "in his being." [33]

Now, whereas there is considerable truth in Sartre's views, they lead us, paradoxically enough, to conclusions very similar to those of Heidegger. If death were, as Sartre puts it, a "pure event," an "absolute contingency," something purely and simply "given," then it could not be experienced in any manner whatsoever, except perhaps as the absurd *par excellence*. Must we then resign ourselves to saying nothing about death because it is either absolutely one's own or absolutely another's? Is there no possibility of integrating these contrasting views so as to give each one its due?

The pages that follow are an attempt to give the latter question a positive answer. We shall endeavor to prove that we can indeed cast some light on death—to begin with, on the basis of the experience of another's death. I therefore agree with Gabriel Marcel's contention that the death of a human being, in particular the death of a loved one, cannot be considered as a purely external event; in some manner, it metaphysically affects the one who loves. "One can only lose," Marcel writes, "what one owns. Was this 'Other' *mine*? In what sense? Is my fellowman mine? He is with me; that is his way of being mine." [34] The relation to which Marcel refers does not need to be restricted to the relations "lover–beloved," "friend–friend," and so on; it can be extended to all human beings, and thus it becomes the general, but still very concrete, relation "fellow–fellow." Now, if such relationships are possible, then, it is also possible that the "complete disappearance"—the death—of one member of the relation can be experienced by the other member. As Roger Mehl has written, the experience of another's death "exhibits an aspect through which it is converted into an experience of one's own death," for "the Other's presence is never a quality that belongs exclusively to him." [35] Granted that such an experience is far from yielding a direct and complete grasp of the nature of death. But we should be reasonably satisfied with the possibility of drawing some inferences, which is exactly what I shall try to do in the pages that follow.

28
THREE CASES

The following three descriptions are to be taken as examples of another's death. They cover "cases" which, as happens in legal matters, can be considered "precedents."

The first "case of death" I witnessed was that of my maternal grandmother. She was not "just a relative." I was bound to her not only by blood but also by "togetherness," in the original, and hopefully deeper, sense of this much too dilapidated word. We had lived under the same roof, often seen the same objects, talked about the same persons, followed similar schedules. All this I call "participation in (or sharing) the same circumstances" or, more plainly, "sharing things in common." Now, to participate in the same circumstances means that some part, large or small, of the experience of one person is shared by another. But if one of the "participants" can no longer "share things in common" because he is dead, does, then, the participation of the survivor become exclusively *his own?* No doubt, this is the case to a great extent, and this explains, by the way, the "feeling of loneliness in the very presence of death" to which I shall later refer. Nevertheless, I find it difficult to believe that when a member of what I may be allowed to call "a community of participation" dies, the survivor is merely "present" at his demise. What was shared in common—objects, persons, even feelings and projects—still remains, often for quite a long period of time. It is still what it was, but at the same time it is no longer exactly what or how it was. It has been, as it were, "amputated," and, as happens with some physical amputations, a deep pain is felt where there should be no pain at all.

It may be argued that all this is a "mere question of feelings," and, thus, something "purely subjective." The deceased person is, indeed, deceased, namely, is no longer. On the other hand, we are still alive. Can it be said then that we are, or have been, "experiencing" his death in the sense of somehow "sharing" it? It would be preposterous to give this question an affirmative answer if the death in question were a "purely external event." Now, such would be the case if the deceased person carried with him, so to speak, to the grave whatever he had shared with another person. It is not the case, however, because, as intimated above, "what was shared" still remains—and it remains precisely as "something which we had shared with the deceased person." Therefore, there are times when we are not merely "watching" someone die but we are, or are also, "sharing" his death—at least to the degree in which we had "shared things in common." The obvious fact that we are not dead, but alive, does not in the least indicate that we have been totally unaffected by the beloved person's death. It is not, however, a "mere question of feelings"—such as sadness, anguish, resignation, despair, and so on—but a more fundamental question. Something which belonged to us—we may call it "a common stock of experiences (including projects of further experiences)"—is now irrecoverable and, for that matter, objectively, and not only subjectively, irrecoverable. To conclude from this that we are actually "sharing" another's death would be to go too far. But we may be allowed to say that we have in many cases an experience of another's death which is not reducible to the sheer fact of "just being there" when the beloved person died.

An experience of another's death is a complex affair. In fact, it is made up of a number of contrasting, or seemingly contrasting, elements. Thus far we have emphasized "what is left behind," even if, as has been surmised, "what is left behind" has been "amputated." Yet it is also characteristic of death to be final and irrevocable. To experience a beloved person's death is like a departure. Now, human existence is made up to a considerable extent of situations in which we depart, or someone departs and takes leave of us. As a rule, departures are only temporary and seem to be somewhat fictitious. One takes leave of a lover whom one will see soon again. One sees a child off to school, and expects him to return home early in the afternoon. But, are departures and "leave-takings" always temporary? As a rule, we are certain that they are not—so certain, indeed, that we do not even raise the question of whether the person whom we left will be seen again; confidence and routine take care of the question. Nevertheless, as soon as we think about it, we realize that any departure could be final. One leaves behind the house where one has spent his childhood. One wonders whether one will ever see it again. In some cases it looks extremely improbable, but then uncertainty—a different kind of uncertainty—floats before the eyes; won't there be a possibility of coming back and taking one more, perhaps final, look? All is possible, which means that all is uncertain. Now, leave-taking is final, and truly definitive, with those who die. Farewells are farewells; no matter how final they may seem, they are never definite. Therefore, those who take leave do not feel their being diminished insofar as their relation with whoever is left behind is concerned; after all, there is always the possibility that a personal relationship among living persons can be resumed. With that final and irrevocable "farewell" called "death," however, there is no such possibility. As a consequence, the being of the person who is "left behind"—in the present case, the "survivor"—is irretrievably diminished, and thus actually diminished. Not even the aforementioned possibility of continuing to share what remains of the personal community, of the "common stock of experiences," compensates for the absence of that person. Continuing to live in the deceased person's house, continuing to see the same people he knew, remembering him, paying homage to his memory, and so on, prove to be poor consolations, for in no case will the deceased person "return." This is one of the reasons why death seems to be so incomprehensible, so "unreasonable," even so "unnatural." It is not perhaps an unfathomable mystery, but it is certainly a most disquieting puzzle.

To be sure, habit and common sense soon come to the rescue. There seems to be nothing more "natural" and "reasonable" than for someone to die, especially when, as in the case I am now trying to elucidate, the deceased person had reached an advanced age, and the premonitory signs of her impending death were unmistakable. There was no doubt that her "hour" had come. But, why precisely *that* hour? This is what seems "unnatural," inexplicable, and, of course, "unreasonable." In order to explain why such and such a person died last Monday rather than last Tuesday, at eleven o'clock in the morning rather than at noon, many reasons can be adduced and many causes can be listed: the remedy did not produce the desired effect, the heart was too weak, and so on. None of these reasons and causes can completely obliterate the "surprise" caused by the person's death. Could not death have taken place some other day, which is the same as saying any other day, which in turn may mean no day in particular, that is to say, never? Perhaps this is not what we "should" think, but this is what we actually do think. Death was expected, and yet not expected, but when it finally took place, it was really and irrevocably "the end."

The experience of another's death is tinged with the idea of finality and irrevocability. It may be contended that such is not always the case. For those who believe in an eternal life, in which they will rejoin their loved ones, there seems to be nothing "unreasonable" in death. Death can be explained, and justified, as the "wages of sin," but also as a necessary condition for a later reunion free from any further partings. Yet it is far from true that the belief in an eternal life, even when such a belief is firmly and deeply rooted, not a half-hearted conviction or a search for comfort, solves the puzzle of death for those concerned.[36] Whether he believes in an eternal life or not, the person who experiences another's death cannot repress a feeling of bewilderment: death is obvious, yet elusive; it puts an end to the life of "the Other," as well as to something in us—our "common participation in life."

Among the teachings we derive from the experience of a beloved person's death is an understanding of the peculiar relation between the deceased and what we may be allowed to call "his world." This world does not solely consist of the objects which had surrounded him, for the manner in which he was related to them also make up his world. Since a living and changing relation is no longer to be expected, everything that had surrounded the deceased appears to be temporarily immobilized. On the one hand, things still seem to respond to the presence of the deceased. This strange feeling has been described by Jules Romains in his *Mort de quelqu'un*. "When the janitor, discovering Godard lying in bed, is about to draw the window shades, an impression crosses his mind. A gesture coming from the dead man had drawn the shades. He was not, then, completely dead, for things happened because of him." It may be argued that this is only metaphorical, and that, in the last analysis, inanimate things may produce similar effects. We could say, for instance, "I drew the window shades because of the wet paint in the room; too much sunlight might damage it." Now, although there is no real difference between the effects, there is in their meaning. We expect nothing from the deceased and yet we are ready to accept certain changes as taking place because of his former living presence. On the other hand, from the moment a person dies, the things—and, in general, the "circumstances"—which had surrounded him begin to fade away. This explains, by the way, the very common wish on the part of those who survive the loved one to keep, at least for a while, things the way the decedent had kept them, or to leave them the way they happened to be placed during his last moments, as if this could delay the final separation. The survivors would not act in this way if they considered such things as "mere objects," if they did not look upon them as a world of meanings. Thus, the actual displacement, removal, and dispersion of things symbolizes the demise and is, in some respects, a kind of delayed reenactment of it. For this reason, the experience of another's death may continue for some time, until the experience itself fades away.

The experience of death just described awakened, among others, the feeling of loneliness; I felt I was, as it were, "alone with death." Nevertheless, it did not produce the bewildering feeling of solitude which emerged so forcefully on another occasion, when I witnessed the sudden death of a man whom I did not know personally and who was, therefore, "just a fellow human being." It happened one day when, in the midst of battle, I saw the body of a man fall, mowed down by a bullet. I experienced neither grief nor—except in a very general way —anguish. It would seem then that another's *death* was merely the death of *"the Other."* Something happened "outside there," something, so to speak, "objective," a mere fact. Was it not, to begin with, only the body of an unknown fellow creature that fell, like a marionette whose strings had suddenly been cut, with a dull and muffled thud, on the stone covered field? Enhancing this impression was the somewhat dramatic setting in which the event occurred: the dim light of dawn, the abrupt crack of rifle fire, the desolate landscape, and, within my gaze, as if lit by an invisible projector, the quiescent shape of the fallen man. Ever so gradually, there arose in my mind a myriad of impressions and thoughts which began to give meaning to the event just witnessed. There was no grief striking and gripping the soul, no anguish rising in the throat and rendering one helpless, yet the death of a nameless stranger was as enlightening as that of a close relative. In a way, it was even more enlightening. Paradoxically enough, that sudden death seemed entirely meaningless. The life of the unknown man had been snuffed out during a skirmish, in precisely that moment when it displayed unusual strength: when fighting. The fallen man had rushed—unless he had been rushed—into battle; he had probably hoped that he would weather the storm of steel and fire and come out alive. Strength and hope were imprinted on his body during and after his brief agony: the former showed in the compulsive twitching of his hand clutching the rifle; the latter in the remarkable serenity of his face. His fall gave the impression of having been at once expected and unforeseen; it had taken place in the course of a battle where life is always at stake, and yet it seemed to be the result of chance. This death left me perplexed. I experienced it as an event at once totally alien to me and in some ways also "mine." He had died; *I* might have died instead. I saw his death as a symbolic threat to my own life. I looked upon it as the death of a "martyr," that is to say, of a "witness" testifying to the universal and overwhelming presence of death. Precisely because he was no man in particular, he was a symbol of all human beings as mortal beings.

Yet, no matter how "symbolic" this death may have seemed, it was still meaningless. Let it not be said that his death could be accounted for in terms of a "cause," good or bad, for which the man, either voluntarily or by compulsion, gave up his life. Such "causes" can explain perhaps man's history, but not, or not entirely, man's existence. At most, one might know *from* what he died but not *for* what he died. Thus death appeared "unfair"— just ashes, dust, and silence. In the presence of this death, I felt more alone than ever, as if face to face with death itself, pervaded with disquietude and perplexity.

The meaninglessness of this death was revealed to me primarily in the form of a question: "Death, what for?" Such a question became even more pressing when I witnessed another death—or rather, many deaths—as a consequence of an air raid. I saw an indeterminate number of anonymous human beings slaughtered by an equally anonymous force which, seemingly, was directed against no one in particular and which could therefore be supposed to be directed against everyone. Death loomed strange and uncanny, almost without warning or, at best, with too sudden a warning, and hence with no time for anything other than fear and trembling, fright and flight. In this sense, this anonymous death in pursuit of an anynomous human multitude was unlike my grandmother's and even very different from the fighting soldier's. There was neither expectation nor commitment on the faces of the countless victims buried under the rubble. Resignation, distress, even pain—all had given way to an overwhelming and omnipresent sensation of terror, the terror felt when one is faced with impersonal mass extermination, the kind of death that gives no warning, neither choosing its victims nor making any distinction between them. It could not even be said that the rush to escape was the result of cowardice, for the latter is usually manifested before "something" or "someone." On the other hand, this was the terror before pure and simple annihilation, the kind of annihilation that leaves behind no trace, neither sorrow nor anguish, but only destruction. The air raid victims were not "martyrs," "witnesses." They were not "ready to die," but they died nonetheless—fortuitously, indiscriminately, meaninglessly.

In such a case, can we still speak of an "experience of another's death"? It would seem that we cannot, for here death was truly faceless and anonymous. To be sure, I knew little about the relation between my grandmother and *her* death, and still less about the relation between the man shot down in battle and *his* death. My experience of these "cases" was, therefore, considerably limited. As to the air raid victims, my experience of *their* death was so restricted as to raise the problem whether there was any experience of another's death at all. Nevertheless, I think that not only was there an experience but a particularly enlightening one: it was the experience of the bewildering meaninglessness of death.

The moment has now come to ask this question: Can the various experiences of another's death yield some general idea which can apply to all possible cases of human death? The answer is, "Yes," provided that such an idea is supported by experience and can eventually apply to further experiences. I now proceed to unfold this idea.

From the experiences described and analyzed we can conclude that human death is meaningful—in varying degrees—insofar as we view it as an event capable of molding some fundamental structures of human life. This is not to say that death completely determines life, because if it did there would be no difference between life and death: to live would be, in the last analysis, to die, which is manifestly gloomy; and, conversely, to die would be to live, which is notoriously absurd. It is only to say that death must partly shape and complete a person's life. The adverb 'partly' must be taken literally. In fact, death never completes anyone's life; otherwise, everyone would die "at the right moment," and, as far as I know, no one ever does. On the other hand, death is never entirely alien to life as if it were something totally external to it, as a more or less deplorable "accident." Sartre was correct when he pointed out that we should not compare death to the final note of a melody.[37] He was only wrong in adding that, whereas the final note of a melody is not absurd, death is. To be sure, there are cases when death seems completely absurd. I have described and analyzed one such case, that of the victims of the air raid. But this was so because we were unable to discover any relation between the victims and their death: the anonymity of the deceased made death equally anonymous and thus engendered the impression of meaninglessness. It did not seem to be their death, but death purely and simply. Now, a death which is not the death of anyone is not, properly speaking, death but only "cessation."

In other words, human death is never completely meaningful, nor is it entirely meaningless. It is meaningful and meaningless in varying degrees. Insofar as death, or rather its possibility, is meaningful, it leads us to understand it. Insofar as it is meaningless, it leads us to rebel against it. Now, understanding of, and rebellion against, death are equally significant ingredients in human life. We may choose the ingredient we like best, or the one we dislike the least; in any case, our choice will disclose the basic structure of our existence, which includes our attitude before the possibility of death. As far as I am concerned, I hold that life would be scarcely worth living were it not for the hope of being able to fight against death. On the other hand, I believe that such a hope would be mere wishful thinking if we did not realize that, when all is considered, death still remains one of the possibilities of human life. Human life is largely, if not exclusively, made up of projects with which life anticipates itself. Nevertheless, these projects are constantly threatened by the possibility of remaining unfulfilled. Indeed, they are projects only insofar as they might not be accomplished. We have already intimated that human existence—and perhaps all reality—must be finite in order to be meaningful. Furthermore, human existence is finite not only "externally" (by circumstances, chance, and natural causes) but also "internally" (by the very nature of the human projects). As a constant possibility, death molds our behavior, whether we know it or not: anything we want to do must be accomplished within a certain, constantly decreasing, period of time.

Curiously enough, the basically finite character of human life helps to destroy the idea that the human person is, ontologically speaking, a thing of naught, a kind of "incarnated nothingness." For death bestows upon the human person a unique nobility. "The dead," says one of the characters in Marcel Aymé's novel, *La rue sans nom,* "have the right to have done all sorts of things. A dead man is not something to be cheerful about; nothing is left in him except what he has done." This idea is, by the way, the reason behind the respectful attitude in front of the dead adopted by the survivors. To be sure, sometimes the survivors despise, ridicule, discredit, or desecrate the dead. But then it is because they do not look upon the dead as dead but regard them as if they were still alive, as is the case with men who died in the name of a still vehemently hated cause. As a rule, however, all of a person's most objectionable deeds are forgotten the moment he dies. A unique nobility then emerges: the nobility which consists in having lived and "accepted," whether consciously or not, the possibility of death (§ 29, *ad finem*) —having "accepted" it while rebelling against it, for what is "accepted" here is not so much the sheer fact of death as the human condition which carries with it the possibility of mortality.

29
"LITERARY" TESTIMONY

The author's own experiences of another's death are, of course, limited in number and scope. For a more ample understanding of the nature and forms of human death we must have recourse to some accounts of other, similar experiences. We can find them in "literature," and thus we can speak of "literary testimony." [38]

In Book IV of his *Confessions*, St. Augustine describes his state of mind upon hearing of the death of a friend in Tagasthe. He informs us that everything he had experienced in the company of his friend suddenly acquired the opposite value. What had been happiness was turned into grief. "All that we had done together was now a grim ordeal without him." [39] Everything seemed intolerable and hateful in a world from which his friend was absent, because (as Landsberg has noted in his analysis of this passage) [40] his friend's death was to him not a mere absence but a symbol of the universality and omnipresence of death. "Wherever I looked," St. Augustine writes, "I saw only death." [41] As is often the case with St. Augustine, his account of a personal experience is permeated by metaphysical preoccupations. Thus, in the present case not one particular man but man as such appeared to St. Augustine illuminated by some kind of soul-subduing mystery. To be sure, in the mind of St. Augustine this "mystery" already had an explanation: it was not a matter of raising philosophical questions but of testifying to the existence and glory of God.[42] Yet in the experience of another's death St. Augustine could not help toppling over some kind of "existential mystery": death made its appearance under the guise of an *atrocissima inimica,* as something unjust and "unfair," without which, however, life itself could not be adequately explained. Furthermore, in experiencing the death of his friend, St. Augustine experienced at the same time the possibility of his own death. Witnessing another's death seemed to drain him of his own vital form and substance. Hence, the death of "half his soul," in the words of Horace, was to St. Augustine a step toward the experience of the death of any man, including, of course, himself. At some point Augustine felt that death served no purpose. Later on he was convinced that he had found the ultimate reason for death: when he was able to view his friend's death, or for that matter any death, as the result of a decree of the true God, who should not be questioned but worshiped.

According to St. Augustine, only after God has become manifest and the human heart purified can the death of a friend, as well as human death in general, acquire its true meaning. Grief and anguish should then be relinquished as manifestations of selfishness. As a result it becomes possible to love men, not only individually but humanly—*humaniter.* Such is the insight gained from the experience of another's death: each and any man can "be," at a most decisive moment, "everyman." Viewed in this manner, death is absolutely personal and yet completely universal; it is a fact, a symbol and a meaning all in one.

A similar insight can be found in a more recent "literary testimony." André Gide also described the death of a friend. He begins by warning us that "this time it is not the same thing," because the one who passed away was "somebody *real*." [42] His friend's death was for Gide, as it was for St. Augustine, a crushing experience. He describes it in his own style, clearly and serenely. "There he lies, so small on a large linen sheet, dressed in a brownish suit; very straight, very rigid, as if waiting for a call." [44] The mere presence of the body, so quietly stretched out in repose, generates an enormous and overwhelming vacuum. Around it, all emotions and gestures crystallize—grief, depression, despair, the urge for an impossible dialogue. These emotions and gestures are as individual and interchangeable as the very friend who has passed away. Some consolation is sought by substituting the environment of the deceased for the deceased: this house was *his* house; this town, *his* town; this table was the table where *he* worked. Can we, then, speak of a man and his death instead of referring to a particular man and his particular death? Gide seems at first to oppose such a suggestion, and yet he ends up by fully accepting it. "I hardly admire those who cannot bear definition, who must be deformed by being seen askance. Philippe could be examined from all points of view; to each of his friends, to each of his readers, he seemed *one,* but not the *same one.*" [45] Thus, the late friend was truly a human person and, as such, he could not be replaced by any other person. At the same time, he had something disturbing and surprising within him which Gide describes as "something lasting." We can give it a name: "his attestation of human death as a human being." Upon his death, Gide's friend ceased to be a particular person in order to become a symbol —paradoxically, "a living symbol"—of man as man.

We do not fall short of "literary testimonies" of human death, but the two above will suffice for our purpose. As we go over other "literary descriptions" of someone's death, we notice that they often exhibit a most characteristic feature: they serve as points of departure for gaining an insight into the meaning of human death in general. The same happens with many descriptions of different "types" of decedents and "kinds" of deaths. Sometimes it is the death of a relative, a friend, or a stranger. Sometimes death is described as caused by illness, at other times as caused by an accident. The "type" described may have faced death with resignation, repentance, fear, even (as if abiding by the rules set up by many eighteenth-century "libertines" in order to "enjoy a good death") with arrogance and a hint of irony. In all these typical cases, the description of human death serves as the basis for an understanding of the nature of death in general. It is not surprising, then, that most authors agree in the main points.

Two points of agreement are quite obvious. On the one hand, there is a tendency to regard death as a sort of "fulfillment of life," even when death is considered premature and, as it were, "unfair." Before it occurs, and often immediately afterwards, death seems to be incomprehensible and meaningless. But once it is accepted as a *fait accompli,* against which there is no appeal, it tends to be regarded as one of the inalienable "possibilities" of human existence—a possibility which is both immanent and imminent. On the other hand, there is a tendency to view the death of any person as an event so truly "ultimate" as to be capable of investing the deceased with a certain irretrievable dignity: the dignity usually ascribed to a "martyr" in the original sense of a "witness." The deceased person testifies, willingly or not, to the constant presence of death as the setting of human life.

It would be unwise to consider any descriptions, and subsequent analyses, of human death as strict "proofs." They are not, however, entirely worthless. Reduced to their essentials, they make us notice the paradoxical character of human death: it is absurd, unjust, inexplicable, and yet it is somehow inherent in life, molding it. The conflicting statements of Heidegger and Sartre (§ 27) can now be reconciled and integrated. Death itself is meaningless, and yet it endows life with meaning. Death is, to a considerable extent, a "pure fact," totally contingent and completely outside my scope, and yet without it my life would not exhibit "contents" (thoughts, actions, decisions, etc.) essentially different from the mere "process" of living. It is not necessary to be always on the brink of death, or to be "unto death" in order to live authentically, but neither is it necessary to "choose" the moment in which our life will end in order to acknowledge that death belongs to us. Life does not derive its full meaning from death, but neither does life lose all meaning because of death. Death, in short, is one of the "possibilities" of life, but to live is obviously not the same as to die.

30
THE ATTITUDES REGARDING DEATH

Up to this point we have described and analyzed experiences of another's death. Is it possible to discourse on the experience of one's own death, or, as it is sometimes said, "my death"?

Death is the suppression of life and consciousness. It is obvious that no person has an experience of his own death. Nevertheless, in some sense we can speak meaningfully of "our own death." First, we can "anticipate" our death insofar as we can think of it, and even "imagine" it. Second, we can use analogy, and conceive of our death in terms of another's death. "Everything that applies to me," Sartre has written, "applies to the Other." [46] If we turn this sentence around, we obtain the following plausible statement: "Everything that applies to the Other applies (or can, in principle, apply) to me." Finally, and above all, we can tackle the problem raised here within the framework of our ontology. According to this ontology, there is no clear-cut distinction between "Absolutes," for the simple reason that there are no such "Absolutes." Accordingly, we must refuse to admit that there is "something" called "pure (or absolute) subjectivity" and, of course, that there is "something" called "pure (or absolute) objectivity." Another's death is both a subjective and an objective event. The same must be the case with one's own death. Therefore, if it is true that we cannot experience it exactly in the same sense in which we can experience love, friendship, sorrow, and so on, we can place ourselves, so to speak, in front of it (of its possibility). This I call "an attitude regarding death." A description and analysis of some typical attitudes regarding death can then cast some light on our subject.

Many of the attitudes regarding death are the product of reflection. A case in point is Epicurus' well-known argument against the fear of death: when death exists, we no longer exist; when we exist, death does not.[47] Epicurus seems to deny that there can be any experience of one's own death; the total impossibility of such an experience is precisely what makes it possible to face death fearlessly. Yet there is no denial of the fact that Epicurus is describing a (possible) experience of one's own death: the experience of a death without fear and trembling.

Another attitude regarding death ensues from the feelings experienced by those who have been on the point of dying: those who have been on the verge of drowning, those who have faced a firing squad, and so forth. It has been said that during the moments immediately preceding death (or at least its imminence) there is something like an automatic release of memories, as if his whole life were passing before the person concerned in rapid cinematographic succession. Without necessarily subscribing to Bergson's theory of memory, we could certainly explain, or at any rate discuss, the aforementioned automatic release of memories in terms of the relations between consciousness and life. It seems quite probable that, when consciousness is on the point of losing its foothold on life, it becomes particularly receptive to memory. Thus, one attitude regarding death may consist of what we may call "a recapitulation of one's own life." To be sure, such a recapitulation may not take place. The moments immediately preceding impending death may very well demand all of a man's vital energy. Instead of despair, abulia, indifference, paralyzing fear, recapitulation of memories, and so on, there may be a renewed, and maximumly increased, "will to fight." But then we would still be confronted with an "attitude regarding death." No doubt, an "attitude" is not exactly the same as an "experience." We are not claiming, therefore, that we can have a direct experience of our own death—that we can, for instance, "see" death in the same way in which we "see" a shape, a color, and so on. We are merely claiming that we can conceive, even if it is *a tergo,* of an experience of the possibility of our own death. We see our death somehow from the outside, but 'somehow from the outside' is not the same as 'completely from the outside.' In some respects we are looking at our death (or its possibility) from the inside; otherwise, we could not even take "an attitude" in front of our death (or its possibility).

Some readers will argue that we are going too far in examining the (possible) experience of one's own death from the point of view of the (possible) attitude regarding one's own death. Some readers, on the other hand, will complain that we are not going far enough. Among the latter are those who surmise that we can experience our own death by simply being always "prepared" to die, living as if each moment were the last moment. Stoic and Christian thinkers have developed this theme with verve and vehemence. Thus, for instance, Seneca wrote that death merely interrupts our life without taking it away from us. According to many Stoic philosophers, "the door is always open," so that the wise man can reasonably step across the threshold when the burden of life becomes intolerable.[48] Many Christian writers tell us that our death is in the hands of Providence, so that there is nothing for us to do but await it with both resignation and hope, endeavoring to live in such a manner that we will always be ready to face the fatal yet unpredictable moment. Curiously enough, similar attitudes have been adopted, or at least preached, by writers who have been neither Christian nor Stoic, as is the case with those who have relied on reason—some kind of "Universal Reason"—to convey the idea that death is always "around the corner," so that "the reasonable man calmly walks down the gentle, easy slope which should lead him to eternal rest." [49] Bertrand Russell has come close to the idea that death is, so to speak, "constantly approaching." The best way to face death, Russell argues, is to convince yourself that with advancing age one's interests gradually become less "individual" or "personal" and more "general." Russell compares individual life to a river which at first rushes violently from its narrow source, and finally overflows, thus abating as it flows into the proverbial "sea of death." [50] We may not think of "preparing for death" when we are young, but as soon as we grow old, or simply suspect that we are, we cannot help but conclude that death and life are beginning to walk hand in hand.

This brief examination of various attitudes regarding death has had a twofold purpose: first, to show that, properly speaking, one cannot have an experience of one's own death; second, to surmise that, when all is said, one can have an experience of the possibility of death, and thus, to a certain extent, of the imminence and immanence of death. The problem remains now whether we can talk meaningfully about an individual's death as "his own."

31
THE PROBLEM OF ONE'S OWN DEATH

As a natural being, as a member of society, as part of a social, family, or community group, man never dies completely alone. Furthermore, man's actions and, above all, man's creations—his "cultural achievements"—often endure and, as it is said, "transcend" his life and, consequently, his death. Therefore, when we use the expression 'one's own death' we do not thereby imply that a human being is an "impenetrable" and "incommunicable" monad; we confine ourselves to pointing out that the death of a human being is "his own" in the sense at least that it is—or, more cautiously, constantly tends to be—a truly personal and nontransferable event.

Since there is no scarcity of reflections on the theme that "the death of a human being is his own," we do not have to restrict ourselves to quoting Heidegger or Kierkegaard. We can go as far back as Seneca, who writes to his friend Lucilius, "Be convinced that all ignorant men err when they say, 'It is a beautiful thing to die your own death,' for there is no man who does not die his own death (*Nemo moritur nisi sua morte*). Besides which, you can reflect on the following saying: No one dies in any but his own way [in his own day: *nemo nisi suo die moritur*]." [51] Granted that Seneca does not interpret "his own way" in the manner of many modern philosophers. After all, Seneca's main purpose is to convince his friend and, through him, all men that "to live in conformity with Reason (and Nature)" is the same as "to relinquish everything that does not belong to me." Thus, all the so-called "external goods" (including our own body, with the exception of its basic needs) must be forsaken in order to prepare ourselves to become one with the Cosmic Soul, the all-pervading *pneuma*. Nevertheless, we find in Seneca, as well as in other ancient writers, a penetrating insight into the nature of human death as "our own," that is to say, of human death as man's inalienable "property." One does not simply fuse with the Cosmic Soul or Universal Reason; one joins it by incorporating *oneself* into it and by the acceptance of one's own death.

In addition to philosophical reflections, and at times even more enlightening, are "intuitions" of human death as "one's own." Many writers, and in particular poets, have touched upon the subject. In an imaginary conversation with his late friend Seytres, Vauvenargues writes, "Death slid into your heart, and you carried it in your breast." [52] The first part of this phrase refers to the ineluctability of death; the second, to its "authenticity." Many contemporary poets have been more explicit and vehement than the concise and often elliptic Vauvenargues. Jules Supervielle, for example, writes, "The death which I shall become already moves in me freely." [53] García Lorca describes a bullfighter who walks courageously to meet *his* death, "Ignacio goes up the gradins / His death so heavy on his shoulders." [54] Whether for reasons of literary technique or of poetic "vision," death is portrayed in the last two examples as "someone" who is waiting outside, as a "thief"—a "thief of human life"—who is easily recognizable and whose presence is accepted without questioning. A poetic vision of human death as a more internal "reality"—or "event"—is found in a poet who is particularly fond of "things," "objects," namely, Pablo Neruda. He has compared death with "an inward shipwreck"; death is "like drowning in our hearts / Like falling from our skins into our souls." [55] Although death "moves inward," it is still seen as a "subtle thief"; it glides silently with its "green face" and its "green look," "with its penetrating dampness like that of the leaf of a violet / And its somber color like that of an exasperated winter." [56] The "vegetality" of death does not, however, impair its "inwardness." After all, man's nature is also somewhat "vegetal"—comparable to a plant, to a leaf, to a tree—so that man and his death finally sink into the same abyss. Death, writes Neruda, "lives recumbent, and suddenly exhales." [57] Not recumbent, however, outside, but within man, like ivy twining around the human tree.

The above are only a few among the many examples of poetic descriptions of "one's own death"; literary scholars are liable to find the subject inexhaustible. These examples would suffice here, however, were it not for the fact that we have not yet said anything about a writer who has been rightly called the "poet of death," namely, Rainer Maria Rilke. A few words on Rilke's views are inescapable.

"I have found it puzzling," Rilke has one of his characters say, "that men spoke about death in a different way from all other events." [58] Death is a very strange thing, but it is not necessarily something sinister or uncanny. It exerts a mysterious attraction, which explains why most men "go somewhere to find it and, unknowingly, load it on their shoulders." Yet, what they look for is not death in general, but a particular death, their own. That is why the poet asks God to give him his own death.[59] In *The Notebooks of Malte Laurids Brigge,* Rilke offers us not only a poetic insight but a detailed description of what he believes to be one's own death. The death of Chamberlain Brigge is not like any other death because, strictly speaking, there is "no death like the others." Even children, writes Rilke, die as what they are and "as what they would have become." For this reason, Chamberlain Brigge "closes in upon himself" in order to die, so that his death and the end of his life can coincide. For Rilke this means that death always comes "in time," since even "what one would have become" or "what one might have become" is, as it were, "compressed" and "abridged" in the instant in which death strikes.

It is most unlikely that Rilke wished to prove that people always die at the very moment in which they "ought to die," so that death would be then thoroughly explained as well as "justified." All that Rilke means is that we always carry death within us, in such a manner that "the solemn death that each of us within him has / That is the fruit around which all revolves." [60] We should not confuse "the right time" with "our own time." No matter when a man dies, even if he dies prematurely, he dies his own death. Death does more than simply end a man's life; it realizes his life and reveals its ultimate structure. If this self-realization and self-revelation discloses a person's being as free, then it can be said that one's own death brings one closest to freedom.

32
THE ESSENCE OF HUMAN DEATH

The foregoing descriptions and reflections are as enlightening as they are provocative. They help us to realize to what an extent the death of each human being is, whether he knows it or not, his own death. Nevertheless, these descriptions and reflections must be taken neither literally nor unconditionally. We should avoid the temptation of thinking that the nature of each human being can be grasped fully only in terms of his death, for we would end by concluding that there are no bonds linking each man to his fellow man, as well as no bonds between humanity, as a whole, and Nature. This conclusion would be totally incompatible with our philosophical system, which strongly emphasizes both the peculiarity of the human being and his "continuity" with the rest of reality.

If the degree of mortality runs parallel with that of "inwardness," there is little doubt that the highest degree of mortality and the highest degree of "inwardness" coincide. On the other hand, since "maximum inwardness" is equivalent to "property" in the sense of 'property' discussed above (§ 24), it can be concluded that man, as the most mortal of all realities, is a being whose death is maximumly "his own."

Now, as I have so often remarked, inwardness is never absolute. First, there are no "Absolutes," and hence no absolute properties. Second, if death were absolutely "internal" in each human being, it would end up by being completely external to him. In dying his own death, and nothing but his own death, it would seem as if each person achieves absolute freedom. But what kind of freedom is it that forces us to die our own death? It can only be an external compulsion and, for that matter, a general or universal type of compulsion, not an internal and completely individual property.

If I accept the idea of human death as "one's own death," I do so with important reservations. Some of these I will now point out.

First, the characteristic of human death called "property" does not stem solely from the supposedly unique and totally autonomous character of human life. Human death is ontologically linked to other forms of cessation; indeed, cessation "culminates" in human death. Therefore, the cessation of nonhuman realities can cast some light on human death. The reverse is, of course, also true: the phenomenon or process called "human death" can cast some light on other modes of cessation, including that of inorganic nature. Inorganic, and even organic, entities do not cease to be in the same manner as man does; their cessation is, to a considerable extent, external to them. It is not, however, completely external, and in this sense we can say that nonhuman entities die, however minimumly, "their own death" or, more properly, "undergo their own type of cessation." The intercrossing of two ontological directions (§ 9) is here apparent. From the point of view of inorganic entities, man ceases to be maximumly. From the point of view of man, inorganic entities cease to be minimumly. All entities, however, whether human or nonhuman, cease to be within a "continuum of cessation" which is strictly parallel to the "continuum of reality." Thus, the characteristic of human death called "property" *also* stems from some of the characteristics which we ascribe to "cessation as such."

Second, the idea that each human being is in possession of his own death—the idea, namely, that death is man's "property"—must be understood in the light of the meaning of 'property' to which I have referred at the beginning of the present section. Thus, to say that man achieves his very being by means of his death is not to say that his being is only, or even primarily, "a being unto death," as if man's life hinged upon his death and nothing else counted. Nor is it to say that man has his death at his disposal, as a servant whom he can summon or dismiss at will. The apothegm, "Die at the right time," and the eulogy of one's own death as the "voluntary death, which cometh unto me because *I* want it," have little to do with the concept of "property" proposed here. To affirm that death "is mine" simply means that death "belongs to me"; it does not mean that "I belong to death." Only in this sense can it be said that man makes his own death. In fine, man makes his own death only to the extent that he makes his own life.

Third, no human death is absolutely "his own"; it is only a limiting event which he can try to make completely his without ever entirely succeeding. Moreover, the degree of "success" in this respect is not only an individual matter; it is also historical.

As man begins to make himself in the course of his own life, which is historical, he also begins to make his own death historically. At certain periods men have viewed themselves as "duplications" of other men to such a degree that they were not certain of whether or not they were "themselves," and whether or not they themselves had performed such and such actions or had such and such thoughts. Thomas Mann vividly portrayed this uncertainty in the first part of *Joseph and His Brothers,* when he described the Beni-Israel as a people who felt deeply immersed in a tradition created by the entire community and which no one in particular had helped to produce. No one can claim that he, as an individual, has done something all by himself. El Eliezer, Joseph's preceptor, considers himself the same Eliezer who, for Isaac's sake, had gone after Rebecca. There is a startling resemblance between being a member of a closely knit social group and being a member of a biological species. For this reason, the relative "deindividualization" and complete "depersonalization" of death which is characteristic of a biological species seems to reappear in such a social group. Just as in a biological species, the death of an individual seems to be an accident, so in a group or clan, the death of one person may appear as a "repetition," and sometimes as a "rehearsal"; what counts here is primarily the species, the group or the clan, and not the individuals. On the other hand, when a particular death is intimately related to a particular person, then the death of such a person is never a "repetition"; his death is entirely different from the death of any other man. Proust probably had this idea in mind when he wrote: "The death of Swann! Swann, in this phrase, is something more than a noun in the possessive case. I mean by it his own particular death, the death allotted by destiny to the service of Swann. For we talk of 'death' for convenience, but there are almost as many different deaths as there are people . . ." [61] If we keep well in sight the role played here by the adverb 'almost,' we cannot help but acquiesce.

We can understand now why an excessive weakening of what might be called the "human tension"—the effort exerted by each man in order to continue to be a man, and especially a particular man—can result in such a marked subordination of an individual to his group that their ensuing relationship almost duplicates that of an individual organism and its biological species (§ 21). On the other hand, the excessive strengthening of the above "tension" could cause an individual to forsake completely his own humanity for the sake of supposedly impersonal and absolute values. In either case, man would cease to be man, and accordingly would cease to die as such. Now, to live as a man is to exist "between" organic reality and so-called "spiritual reality." The human "tension" that characterizes man's life is similarly reflected in his death.

Can we ever disclose the ultimate essence of human death? If we are asking whether we can ever offer a final and irrevocable definition of 'human death,' then the answer must be negative. Just as with anything real, the nature of human death can be grasped only by means of a "dialectical process" which must continually move from one polarity to another, from one absolute to another, from one limiting concept to yet another, with the hope that they can finally be integrated. Without relinquishing our distrust of "final definitions," we now offer a few conclusions.

Human death includes inorganic cessation as well as biological decease. Man does not die unless his body, and the material systems of which his body is composed, dies. Nevertheless, man's body is not just "a body," but "a way of being a body," (§ 20). To a considerable extent, this way of being a body is made up of "possibilities" which may or may not be fulfilled, but which in any case are "real." Now, a moment may come when all of a human's possibilities become closed to him —which is the same as saying that a man may become aware that he had no future before him. For a few instants the past and all its memories might fill the resulting vacuum. This can happen only because the individual still regards the past as a future or as something which points to the future in some way, "filling it." To live, then, basically boils down to reminiscing about things past. When even the image of the past projected toward the future fades, man has nothing left but his organic existence. When this happens, man ceases to be a man; he is then only a member of a biological species. At this point, then, he dies as a man. In other words, death hovers over us when our possibilities of living as men vanish. The man contemplating suicide, who sees his future as completely devoid of any and all possibilities—who has no future at all, and no longer finds any meaning in his life, or even in his death—does not really need to carry out the final and supreme act: he is already dead before perishing. On the other hand, when new possibilities which transcend biological death—such as creations and "cultural achievements" which are likely to exert an influence upon a future in which we are no longer present—offer themselves, then death seems to withdraw even if it has biologically annihilated us. The paradox is as obvious as it is startling: in some really limiting cases, it is possible to die without ceasing to be, or to cease to be without dying.

FOUR

Death, Survival, and Immortality

33
THE PROBLEM OF IMMORTALITY

Once it has been shown that cessation is coextensive with reality, it would seem pointless to raise any questions concerning "survival" or "immortality." After all, the only type of reality that even seems to approach "immortality" is inorganic reality, not human beings, who have been proven the most mortal of all realities. Thus our investigation seems to have come to an end.

Yet the so-called "problem of man's immortality"—which includes the "problem of man's survival"—cannot be dismissed with a stroke of the pen. To begin with, man's longing for survival and/or immortality is not a mere whim of his, or, if it is, it is such an obdurate whim that it has all the appearance of an obsession. It is, then, only reasonable to try to clarify its nature and meaning, perhaps as a preamble to a more chirurgical undertaking. The "hunger for immortality," to use Unamuno's vigorous expression,[1] is strong enough to require either satiation or outright elimination. Second, the immortality of which men have spoken so often has little, if anything, to do with the "immortality" or "quasi-immortality" of inorganic entities. Whereas the latter simply tend to persist, human beings hope that they can truly "survive" or that there is something in them capable of "surviving" and thus reaching a final stage called "immortality" or "eternity." To persist maximumly for an entity whose nature is to endure, is one thing; to survive for an entity whose nature is to be maximumly mortal, is quite another. Therefore, we will do well to examine whether man's plea for immortality is or is not well grounded.

It will be noted that I have been using the terms 'survival' and 'immortality' interchangeably. I am aware that their meanings do not always coincide. The term 'survival' is normally used to refer to a supposedly indefinite enduring of human life in whatever form it may take. Survival is conceived then as a temporal prolongation, either finite or infinite, of human life. The term 'immortality,' on the other hand, often refers to the peculiar way in which a certain reality in man—such as his soul or spirit—continues to exist beyond the normal period of human life.[2] 'Immortality' can designate, in principle, a temporal (infinite) perdurability, but it ordinarily designates an "eternal life" transcending all temporality.

Now, a too sharp distinction between the meaning of 'survival' and that of 'immortality' would do more harm than good here, for there has always been a great deal of ambiguity in the use of these terms. A detailed history of man's beliefs in survival and/or immortality might well supply evidence for concluding that there is a tendency to start with "rough" and "primitive" ideas of survival and gradually reach the notion of "immortality" as "spiritual immortality." In some ways, then, we could speak of a "development and growth of the idea of survival" until it evolves into an idea of "pure immortality." Since it is difficult, however, to know exactly where the notion of survival ends and that of immortality begins, it is wise to continue using the terms 'survival' and 'immortality' somewhat ambiguously. It will not be difficult for the reader to see which meaning is being discussed or emphasized.

The sections that follow can be divided into two parts. The latter part (§§ 38–40) is the only one which is philosophically relevant, for it is concerned with the so-called "proofs of immortality," or, more precisely, with the "arguments to prove the immortality (of the soul)." It will be seen that these arguments are as interesting as they are deceptive. The reason for this state of affairs is simple enough: the arguments in question fail to prove whatever it is they meant to prove, while they succeed in proving something other than what they meant to prove. Now then, the meaning of these arguments can be understood more clearly once we have grasped the nature of the "subject matter." This "subject matter" unfolds through a number of ideas, beliefs, or, as they are also called, "representations," in the course of history; hence, we will devote the former part (§§ 34–37) to a historical elucidation.

Some preliminary remarks on these historical sections will help put things into focus.

Two factors that contribute to the development of many of the ideas of human survival must be kept in mind. On the one hand, these ideas can arise as a reaction against the fear of dying. Schopenhauer made this point clear when he wrote that religious beliefs as well as philosophical systems are "the antidote secreted by reason against the idea of the inevitability of death." [3] On the other hand, such ideas can emerge as an attempt to explain and justify death, especially in relation with the notion that "existence [human existence] is not self-sufficient." [4] These two factors crisscross each other frequently: the attempt to explain and justify death can be a consequence of the fear of death, while at the same time this fear often helps to bring about all sorts of explanations and justifications.

The negation of survival sometimes has the same origin as its affirmation: a reaction against the fear of death as well as a desire to explain and justify death. An outstanding example of this interlocking of an affirmation and a negation of survival is found in the Epicurean argument (§ 30): we ought not to fear death, and, consequently, we ought not to fear survival either —and vice versa. Some claim that death is only an "accident," entirely "outside of life"; some say that life is sufficient, or ought to be sufficient, for man; some affirm that man "conquers" or "overcomes" death simply by contributing to the life and happiness of those who follow, or by leaving his imprint on history, or by creating timeless values, and so on. In all these ideas and arguments we find the expression of a desire to account for death, similar to the desire felt by those who proclaim their belief in a life "hereafter." A complete history of the ideas and beliefs concerning survival should take into account such negations of survival and/or immortality, but we will merely emphasize what we may call "positive" rather than "negative" ideas on the subject.

Many beliefs in survival are intimately related to the consciousness that "one must die," and above all to the consciousness that "I must die." As far as we know, this awareness of one's own impending and inevitable death is characteristic only of human beings. It has sometimes been said that a number of highly developed biological organisms possess at least some (instinctive) premonition of death, as is shown by the fact that some animals can distinguish between living and inanimate beings or, what is even more interesting, or at any rate suggestive, that they seem to "lie down to die," as the saying goes. Bergson contended that some animals could even "play dead." These claims do not seem to be well founded. On the basis of behavioral studies Jules Vuillemin has shown that no animal "plays dead," for the environment of an animal is not a world of objects but only a field of relatively variable psychophysiological forces.[5] An animal is incapable of symbolization, which can come into being only when intelligence is liberated from its biological servitude. Therefore, "animals are unaware of death because death is a symbolic form." [6] As Xavier Zubiri would point out, animals, including the higher vertebrates, are totally incapable of "formalizing" death.[7] If man's idea of death is, as Freud suggests,[8] the result of an instinct contrary to the drive for pleasure and at the same time transcending it, this is only insofar as such an instinct has already undergone a process of symbolization and conceptualization.

For the sake of clarity, I shall classify the ideas, beliefs, and "representations" concerning survival and/or immortality into four headings: the "primitives," the "ancients," the "Christians," and the "philosophers." To be sure, these terms are to a great extent conventional labels. In fact, there are not a few "primitives" and "philosophers" among the "ancients," many "philosophers" and of course "ancients" among the "Christians," and numerous "ancients" and "Christians" among the "philosophers." Furthermore, in some cases the same label covers vastly different conceptions. For example, the label "ancients" includes ideas as diverse as those of "shadow" and "soul." For the sake of simplicity, I shall henceforth omit the quotation marks in the use of the above labels. Needless to say, it is not my intention to write a "history," however brief, of even the most important ideas and beliefs concerning survival and/or immortality. The pages that follow are highly selective. For example, I shall almost completely omit any reference to a number of important ideas and beliefs concerning the development of this subject in China and India. Hebrew conceptions will be simply included within one section (§ 36), which is not meant to lessen their significance or their influence. For my limited purpose, however, my "selective history" will, I hope, suffice.

34

THE PRIMITIVES

Much has been written concerning whether there have always and everywhere been ideas and "representations" of human survival. The usual opinion is to affirm, at least *grosso modo*, their universality. This opinion has given rise to two contrasting views: some authors claim that it is this very universality that proves the truth of survival, while others maintain that the only thing such a universality can prove is that man is ensnarled in superstitions until he realizes that he is a truly rational being. A number of writers, however, flatly deny that beliefs concerning immortality are, or have ever been, "universal." According to some of these writers, belief or lack of belief in human survival is a "cultural," if not a purely "racial," matter. Outstanding among the latter writers is Spengler. In his opinion, only the "Nordic races" consider "life" really worth living, which explains why the "Northern Eurasian man," from the primitive Chinese to the modern Germans, has never been concerned with his destiny after death. On the other hand, the less vital and "decadent" Southern races, spread out between Egypt and Ireland, have always lived under the obsession of a "hereafter." Spengler himself must admit that there are exceptions among "Northern Eurasians": the ancestor cults in China and Rome; the Zoroastrian doctrine among the Vedic Aryans and the Iranians; the Greek Olympus; the Germanic Valhalla, and, on the other side of the fence, a total lack of belief in a life after death among the Hittites. Too many exceptions, as a matter of fact, but Spengler is not easily discouraged. Some of the above exceptions are, he is ready to admit, "real exceptions"; such is the case with Zoroastrian theology. Some of the other so-called "exceptions" are, he claims, not exceptions at all, provided they are given the right interpretation. Thus, the ancestor cults are only a manifestation of race worship; Olympus is a *tableau poétique;* Valhalla is a fantastic image created by the Skalds during the Viking era, etc. Furthermore, when the "exception" is obvious, the belief in an afterlife can always be blamed on "Southern influences." It is always the "South," cunning and superstitious, that tries to stab the stalwart, but excessively ingenuous, "North" in the back.[9]

Spengler's views on this question are interesting, but they are at least as fantastic as, in his opinion, the Valhalla of the Skalds is. However, even if we assume that many "cultures" have never been concerned with the problem of a hereafter, the fact remains that many other "cultures" have been almost obsessed by the idea of a life after death. We shall examine briefly some of their beliefs and ideas concerning survival.

There is, indeed, a great variety of what we may call "primitive representations of survival." An outstanding feature of such representations is the idea of a "minimum survival." We find here no belief in an eternal life nor even in an infinite (or indefinite) temporal perduration; in fact, there is hardly any idea of another life which is really "other," namely, different, from "this life." Death is not seen as a dividing line between the living and the dead. Many primitive cultures believed, and still believe, that the deceased continue to live in their tombs; that they descend into the ground and possess, or retain, a certain amount of sensitivity; that they exist and wander as "shadows," "simulacra," or "images"; that they inhabit a place (usually underground) where they associate with other "shadows"; that they preserve their former habits and utilize the tools and implements which are interred with them. Curiously enough, when cremation is practiced instead of burial, the ideas concerning the dead remain very much the same. The earth shelters, but it also "oppresses," the dead. Therefore, even to this day, the hope is expressed that "the earth may be light upon them."

These primitive representations and ideas emphasize the close relationship between this life and the hereafter. The deceased continues to enjoy the same social position and to perform the same tasks as in his "former life." Accordingly, those who have passed away do not subsist on an equal footing; "a kind of [social] hierarchy is often established among them." [10] This "hierarchy" is usually based on two factors: the occupation formerly practiced by the deceased, which determined his "social status," and the time that has elapsed since his death. It is supposed, moreover, that not all the deceased survive for an equal length of time or even with equal "strength." They are, so to speak, more or less "mortal" and, therefore, more or less "immortal." For example, it is thought that the survival of those who have recently died is the longest; it is shorter for those who have been dead for some time, and practically nonexistent for those who have already "crumbled to dust." [11] This variation, and inequality, in the degree of survival can be explained by the ties that bind the living and the dead within the clan, the tribe, the community. Since these ties can likewise be explained in terms of the nature and forms of survival, it is possible that both factors are causally related to each other.

It may be noted that the above ideas of survival as "minimum survival" are similar to some notions wrought by common sense and by "reason." For example, it has often been said that whatever "survival" there is depends on the "preservation in memory" of the defunct. This is equivalent to saying that the "reality" of the dead is in the hands—or in the heads—of those still living. Some have reached the conclusion that the best, if not the only, way to "survive" is to leave the strongest possible imprint on the memory of future generations. Unamuno referred to this side of the problem when he equated the desire for fame and renown to the longing for immortality. Some writers have even regarded the conception of "survival" based on the remembrance of the dead as a kind of basic core around which many ideas concerning survival have grown.

It would be unwise, however, to emphasize solely the dependence of the dead upon the living in primitive representations of survival. Somehow the dead acquire a "life of their own," and so become more and more independent of the living and of their former life on earth. This passage from (relative) dependence to (relative) independence can be observed in various wide-spread conceptions of survival. Thus, the ancestor cults (as manifested, for example, in complicated Chinese rituals [12] or those honoring the Roman *lares* and *penates*) show that the dead are no longer viewed as "just the departed ones," namely, as those who simply continue in "another world" the kind of life that they had led on earth. In many primitive representations the dead are seen as "shadows," but as "powerful shadows" capable of haunting the living. The "shadow" remains a weakened image of the earthly life, but in many cases it seems to behave as if it were an "autonomous reality," moved by an "autonomous principle." As an example of the latter conception we may mention the distinction between the *Kra*, as the principle of life, and the *craman*, as the spirit of a dead human being.[13] All these ideas seem to gravitate toward a certain still tepid form of dualism, which becomes the basis for not a few conceptions of survival as an endless chain of reincarnations. The doctrine of reincarnation has, of course, many variants. Some of them are intimately related to, if not based on, lofty moral considerations. The ancients, among them the Indians, elaborated these doctrines of reincarnation in great detail. The only aspect which is of interest here, however, is that which emphasizes the greater "permanence" of the dead, and indeed of the souls of the dead, in a realm of their own which is not independent of the realm of the living but only insofar as it imposes itself constantly upon the latter. The spirit of a dead person is supposed to have the power to absorb or "inhale" the principle of life. Among the primitive cultures where this belief is prevalent, an individual lives in constant fear that his own "shadow" will suddenly disappear, snatched away by the spirits of the dead.[14] This fear is dispelled only when the doctrines of survival are rationalized, and hence made less uncanny and forbidding, either by means of a moral interpretation of the concept of "shadow" or by a metaphysical and religious elaboration of the belief in reincarnation. In many primitive representations of survival we find a slow but constant passage (and progress) from the notion of "shadow" to that of "soul." The ancients were to become keenly aware of the importance of this tranformation.

35

THE ANCIENTS

I have pointed out (§ 33) that there are a considerable number of "primitive" elements in the ancients' ideas and representations of human survival. As a matter of fact, during many periods of what is commonly (although very imprecisely) called "ancient history"—the history of the Semitic and Indo-European communities which developed in southern Russia, Persia, Babylon, Asia Minor, continental Greece, Italy, and so on—the differences between the ancient conceptions and the primitive ones were imperceptible. Franz Cumont has noted [15] that the so-called "ancient beliefs," especially the early Hellenic beliefs, were superimposed in a series of layers, which makes it difficult to establish clear-cut separations between them. In fact, we find (1) the idea that the dead live in their tombs with their own clothes and utensils and frequently even with food and drink, which are periodically replenished for them; (2) the idea that the shadow-corpses descend into the innermost recesses of the Earth (Hell, Avernus, Hades, Tartarus), where they live with the other shadow-corpses in a vast subterranean realm; (3) the idea, which has arisen in opposition to the previous ones but which at the same time would be difficult to grasp without them, that there is some kind of "airy soul" (conceived by analogy with the human breath). Often accompanying the latter idea is the belief in "airy demons" personifying actions and forces; (4) the idea of astral immortality, often derived from the belief in daemons, which, from the early Persians and Babylonians until the Greeks (the Pythagoreans), was more of a "learned" doctrine than a popular belief. Quite possibly it was even tinged with a shamanistic flavor.[16] The last idea is associated with beliefs which were held and debated by many thinkers of antiquity, especially those of Platonic and Neo-Platonic persuasion. In this manner, ideas which could hardly be labeled "primitive" penetrated into the various layers described above and often permeated them entirely. At first the "new ideas," deeply metaphysical and highly ethical, appealed only to a small number of people, who became "initiates," but they gradually gained wider acceptance. In time, the belief spread that the "shadow" was really a "soul" and that the soul was ultimately a spiritual reality.

The most primitive (earliest) layers contain representations which can be called "magical-natural." Bruno Snell has pointed out that in Homer there is no word which designates the spirit or soul as opposed to the body, life, or breath.[17] This distinguished Greek scholar has gone too far in this respect, for in Homer the term ψυχή designates not only breath and "life," but also a kind of incorporeal shadow or "image," εἴδωλον which is "seized" by those who have departed from this world.[18] Even so, we admit that there is still a strong "naturalistic" tendency in Homer. The world of the shadows and that of living beings seem to be overlapping or, in any case, intertwined. Yet in Homeric, and even pre-Homeric, descriptions of a life after death there is already a glimpse of certain distinctions that will be of great consequence. Especially important in this respect is the distinction between an individualized "breath," the ψυχή and an "impetus" spread throughout all living things, the θυμός. The former is ultraterrestrial or, as the case may be, subterranean, whereas the latter is strictly terrestrial and earthly. Some writers believe that such a distinction is common to most ancient conceptions of man and, in general, of ancient conceptions of living nature.[19] I am not qualified to pass judgment on this matter. But I am reasonably sure that as soon as the distinction in question is enlarged and refined, ideas of survival arise which are of a much less "primitive" character— ideas which are often considered "philosophical." Religious motives and rituals, such as the Dionysian and Orphic cults, are often conjoined with arguments of a cosmological, metaphysical, and moral character—the type of arguments which we find in the writings of some Pythagoreans. At first, the more intellectually sophisticated "new ideas" retained a number of rather crude and primitive representations of human survival. The continued presence of primitive representations in the new ideas can explain the tendency to distinguish between the initiates and the uninitiated. Only the initiates possess a spiritual life; the uninitiated are flung into the pale and shivering semi-life of the shadow world.[20] As the new ideas became purer, the primitive representations gradually vanished.

Plato accomplished this transformation and made it a cornerstone of his philosophy. His ideas concerning the soul and its survival (or immortality) are too numerous and subtle to be examined here. Contrary to what is sometimes believed, a pure and simple dualism of body and soul is not found in the writings of Plato;[21] whenever such a dualism raises its head, an attempt is immediately made to fustigate and decapitate it. Hence the so-called "Platonic conception of the soul" can be adequately described only by means of an intricate dialectic. What is of interest here, however, is not so much "what Plato really thought" as the manner in which he stated the problem and transmitted it to the intellectual tradition of the West. From this point of view—purposefully simplified—it can be said that Plato originated the conception of the soul as a divine element or "daemon," and consequently as a substance "imprisoned in the body," which means that the body is "the tomb of the soul."[22] More important to our purpose is the fact that Plato tried to conceive of immortality as eternal life. Hence Plato's conception of the soul's divinely immortal "vital force." Souls long for immortality, ἀθανατον ἐρῶσιν,[23] and it is precisely by cultivating and fostering this longing—usually revealed in the desire for pure knowledge—[24] that the soul becomes able to conceive of, and prove, immortality.

The above ideas raise many problems. Plato was well aware of them. Is the soul completely separated from the body? If it is not separated, then is it not necessary to reintroduce the idea that the soul is the principle of the body and, in general, of everything alive? If the soul is a "harmony," is it not necessary to conclude that it perishes when the various parts which it holds together are separated? If the soul is identified with the purely rational element, how can it influence bodily movements and "passions"? If the soul is not a simple and independent substance, how can its immortality ever be demonstrated? Doesn't the existence of the soul depend completely on the existence of an ideal world—the "world of Ideas," often called the "intelligible world"—where it can live as if in its own domain? If that is the case, how are we to account for the individuality of a soul? Etc. Almost all the Greek schools, Platonists, Stoics, Aristotelians, Neo-Platonists, discussed the above questions eagerly and endlessly. The Stoics, as usual, sought a compromise. They claimed that the soul is a reality, but an "impassive" one: the soul is the thinking side of Nature. It is a compound, but one which is strongly unified by a superior hegemonic force. Ultimately, the soul returns to where it essentially belongs: to "Nature." Therefore, death is only a "restitution"; so-called "immortality" is a kind of "fusion." Aristotle and his followers tried to preserve both the rationality and the substantial individuality of the soul. The soul, then, is "like the principle of life"; it is "the form of a natural body having life potentially within it." [25] The human soul is not, of course, corporeal; yet it belongs to the body, σώματος δὲ τι. Can it be said then that the soul is part and parcel of the ideal (intelligible) world? If we answer affirmatively, will it not be necessary to admit that what is intelligible in the soul is something essentially "passive"? The problem of the relation between the passive intellect and the active intellect becomes an unsolvable puzzle. To emphasize the passivity of the soul is equivalent to denying its individuality. In such a case, the immortality of the soul will never become an individual immortality; only the active intellect, which is the same for all souls, will become immortal. Aristotle himself was never too clear on the subject. On the other hand, Alexander of Aphrodisias—and later,

Averroës—identified rationality and intelligibility; as a consequence, the soul was robbed of all possibility of becoming individual and, *a fortiori*, individually immortal. All the efforts made with a view to "purifying" the soul seemed to have been in vain. The difficulties inherent in the Platonic conception of the soul seemed to lead to quite "un-Platonic" conclusions.

Most Neo-Platonists tried to go back to a more Platonic, or supposedly Platonic, point of view. The soul, these Neo-Platonists claimed, very closely resembles an "Idea." But it cannot be reduced to a pure Idea, for only from the outside does the soul offer a "static appearance"; seen from within, it is a dynamic reality. In fact, the soul is the only reality which is truly dynamic, for it alone can "ascend"—and, of course, "descend"—the "Great Ladder of Being." Doubtlessly, nothing so closely resembles the intelligible world as the soul. In the few extant fragments of Porphyry's *Treatise on the Soul,* we read that the soul's reality—and hence its immortality—is based on the fact that it "seems divine by virtue of its likeness to what is intelligible." [26] Thus the intelligible world and the possibility of its direct contemplation, primarily by means of mystical communion, is the only point of view from which the purely intelligible reality of the soul can be understood.[27] In short, the intelligible world not only "practically" (as in Kant) but also and above all "theoretically" postulates the existence and immortality of the soul. For most Neo-Platonists, the intelligible world is not simply a hierarchy of ideas, principles, and laws; it is also the way in which "Life" unfolds, 'Life' meaning here "divine Life," or the unique source of all life, including that of Nature. Thus, the concept of the soul, without losing its basic spirituality and "intelligibility," has been "revitalized" and, as it were, "existentialized." This is the reason why, in the last analysis, it does not matter that the soul is, *in fact,* a prisoner of the body. What really matters is that it acts *as if* it did not live within the body; as if it were, even while on earth, a citizen of the world of ideas.[28]

36
THE CHRISTIANS

To a considerable extent, Christian conceptions of human survival are linked to the representations of it in Scripture. A thorough examination of Scripture would be an indispensable preamble to an adequate historical study of the Christian conceptions. Also, it would be extremely helpful to scrutinize other beliefs, such as those of the Ahura-Mazda. It is not our plan, however, to undertake a historical study of the Christian conceptions of human survival, much less an adequate historical study. A number of crucial references will suffice for our purpose.

It has often been said that only in Daniel (12:13), 160 B.C., do we find the notion of personal resurrection. Neither in Ezekiel (37:1–14) nor in Isaiah is there any hint of it. Not even in Daniel is the conception of the resurrection for all men clearly expressed. We must wait until the Ethiopic book of Enoch (31:1), and possibly until Ezra (24:35) to find the idea which is so familiar today.[29] For many years, the Hebrew notions of human survival resembled the representations which I have labeled "primitive" (for example, the notion of the "eternal mansion" of the dead or the distinction between those chosen by God, who rise from the dead, and the others, who sink into nothingness). Furthermore, among the Hebrew conceptions were many primitive ideas concerning the "other world" and the "afterlife" which were patterned upon earthly existence. Examples of such primitive ideas can be found in many of the representations of *Sheol* as a place of "rest" (similar to the idea of Ahura-Mazda's *Khsazra,* or *Yannat* in the Koran), and of Gehenna as a place of punishment and torture. Now then, in the Hebrew conceptions a most interesting notion begins to develop: the idea of the resurrection of the body. It took a long time for this idea to join the notion of the immortality of the soul.[30] Even in the Acts of the Apostles (26:32) the "resurrection of the body" and the "immortality of the soul" are sharply contrasted. The contrast weakened and, finally, vanished when a number of Christians tried to provide a philosophical foundation for their beliefs in human survival. Thus, the Christian doctrine of immortality is indebted to two apparently contrasting views: one which strongly accentuates the vital–personal aspect of immortality, and one which emphasizes no less strongly its spiritual–intellectual component.

The term 'Christians' designates here a group of thinkers who seem to be unable to disentangle themselves completely from the "ancients," and especially the "ancient philosophers." At times, it seems as if Christian speculations merely reflect the manner in which a particular problem was treated by many members of the traditional philosophical schools, in particular Platonists and Neo-Platonists, but also to a considerable degree Aristotelians, Stoics, and even Skeptics. This can be seen very distinctly when we consider the following question: Is the soul "divisible" or is it completely "undivisible"? One of the most widely accepted answers claimed that the soul is an entity which occupies a unique position, intermediate between indivisible essence and divisible essence, so that its divisibility can be understood as the possibility that the whole soul is present simultaneously in all the singular parts of the body. Now, both St. Augustine and St. Thomas Aquinas seemed to agree with this answer.[31] Therefore, they seemed to accept unreservedly Plotinus' suggestion that the indivisibility in question is not comparable to that of a point, but rather to that of a singularly "concentrated" and almost unimaginably "tense" reality. We must conclude that there is no fundamental distinction between most of the ancients and most of the Christians concerning the nature of the soul and its immortality.

Nevertheless, there is at least one very fundamental aspect in the Christian conception of the soul which cannot be reduced to, or even compared with, the conceptions of the ancients. Let us point it out briefly.

Plotinus and the Neo-Platonists never succeeded in avoiding the confusion between the soul and an "idea." Perhaps they were secretly in love with this confusion, and hence did not try too hard to avoid it. This can be seen most clearly in Plotinus' writings. So eagerly did Plotinus maintain the idea of the "intelligible character" of the soul that he even denied it self-consciousness. When dwelling in its own domain, the intelligible world, the soul does not even have a memory of its own being.[32] Once the soul has ceased to spread and disperse, a process of self-concentration starts. The final aim of this process is not to achieve maximum awareness of itself but rather to cast off all self-awareness in order to become one with the world's soul.[33] What, then, is the individual life of the soul but a constant and dangerous impoverishment? The only experience which might (and then only relatively) fulfill the life of the soul would be a purely "negative" experience, the longing to escape its temporal prison so as to become a truly impassive reality. Now, in contradistinction to this view, the Christians tended to conceive of the soul as "life," in the sense of "innermost life." No doubt, many Christian ideas concerning the nature and destiny of the soul were developed with the help of concepts contributed by Greek and Hellenistic philosophers. We need only mention two "traditions" in Christian thought: the Platonic–Augustinian–Bonaventurian tradition, and the Aristotelian–Thomistic tradition. In both traditions, Greek and Hellenistic ideas loom large. But once the Christians' indebtedness to the "ancients" is duly acknowledged and even praised, a number of basic and, it would seem irreducible, differences between Greek and Christian remain. At certain very crucial points, Christian intuitions concerning the soul go far beyond Greek concepts. At any rate, the Christian idea of the soul, whether Augustinian or Thomistic, does not fit within a strictly "intelligible" framework. The very being of the soul is never seen as independent from its most profound experiences. Thus, for instance, the body may be regarded by Christians as an obstacle, but never as a curse. No Christian would accept the idea that the body is something with which we may be able to live but which we must treat *as if* it scarcely existed at all. Simplifying matters we may conclude that the Platonic tradition was much too "spiritual-minded," even for St. Augustine. On the other hand, the Aristotelian tradition was much too "corporeal-minded" even for Thomas Aquinas. The constant presence of many ancient ideas in Christian thought should not make us forget these basic facts.

The reasons behind the Greek–Christian cleavage are numerous. One is the Hebrew tradition, or the fragment of the Hebrew tradition, already mentioned, which not only contributed to the "scandalous" and "foolish" notion of the resurrection of the dead, but also gave a strong "historical" bias to the Christian conceptions. The problem of the immortality of the soul is thus inseparable in Christianity from the problem of anthropogenesis. In this light, we can grasp the nature and meaning of certain Christian ideas, which are as remote from naturalism as they are from "Platonism." For example, it is said that the body of Adam was mortal according to its nature but could achieve immortality by a gift of grace.[34] Only with sin is mortality introduced into the body of man. This mortality, however, is never absolute, for the body may be resurrected and may even become a "glorified body." Christians also speak of two kinds of death; the first death is of the body, while the second is of the soul. It is believed that there is a difference between death itself and the uses to which it may be put. For just as the godless make bad use not only of evil but also of good, so the righteous make good use not only of good but also of evil: "as the wicked make an ill use of the law, which is good, so the good make a good use of death, which is an ill." [35] Corresponding to these two kinds of death are two kinds of life. The first life is that of

Adam before the fall; the second is that of mankind after the fall. The death of the body becomes that of all men at the end of their life; the second kind of death is that of the sinner. The Spanish mystic, Master Alexo Venegas, even claimed that there are three kinds of life and three kinds of death: the life of nature, which is opposed by the death of the body; the life of grace, which is opposed by the death of the spirit through mortal sin; and the glorious life, which is opposed by the infernal death. "These three deaths," he writes, "are reduced to two: the death of the body and the death of the spirit; because the second death is followed by the third death, just as the life of grace is followed by the life of glory." [36] That is why the death of sinners is not the same as that of the just man or that of the saints; in the death of the latter, ". . . what was originally ordained for the punishment of the sinner, has been used for the production of a richer harvest of righteousness." [37] Death, "wages of sin," and "enemy of life" can become an "instrument of life." [38]

I have lingered over these considerations—a mere drop in a vast ocean—because I wished to emphasize the fact that the "spiritual atmosphere" in which the Christians conceive their vision of death is quite different from that in which the ancients conceived theirs. The Christian vocabulary includes words such as 'sin,' 'righteousness,' 'punishment,' 'reward,' 'salvation,' 'damnation,' and so on. Of course, these words have a moral meaning, but it is not the decisive meaning in this context. Much more important than the moral meaning is the personal and "experiential" significance that these words possess within an anthropological and religious framework. Christians often speak of the soul, and insist on its spiritual nature. But the soul to which they refer is never a purely passive and "intelligible" entity. It is an aggregate of dramatic experiences which unfolds in the course of a personal history. For the Christian, man is neither a purely natural object (no matter how eminent) nor an image of the intelligible world: he is a creature of God, made in his image. Thus, man's reality is never an answer to "What is it?" It is an answer to "Who is he?" Anxiety, love, hate, hope, and so on are of paramount importance in any "definition" of man's existence. For this reason, the kind of eternity that he may achieve is everlasting life, eternal life. Everlasting and eternal, to be sure, but also *life*. Although the Christian is unable to describe what such a life really is, he is still convinced that his conception of it is "more real" than any other notion of survival and immortality. If there is a "progress" in the development of the idea of survival, then, to the Christian, eternal life is its very culmination. At any rate, he is convinced that only eternal life can defeat the "ultimate enemy": death.

37
THE PHILOSOPHERS

The label 'philosophers' is in the present context even more inadequate than the other labels thus far employed. After all, nearly all the writers of antiquity, as well as most Christians who have been concerned with our subject, can be called "philosophers." Hence, if I use this word with a somewhat conventional meaning, it is because I wish to emphasize certain differences. The principal difference is a certain "intellectual atmosphere." "Philosophers" may be believers or skeptics; they may be profoundly influenced by religious dogmas or totally indifferent to them. In any case, their mode of thinking is in principle independent from the strictly religious "atmosphere."

There are, of course, many philosophers in the above sense. Moreover, many of the Christians have often adopted a "philosophical attitude." For reasons of brevity, however, I shall limit myself to three examples.

I have already mentioned the opinions of the Epicureans concerning death and survival (§ 30). In short, they assert that death does not exist for us, or more precisely, that it does not exist for *us*, because it does not exist for *each one* of us. When we believe that we have thought about death, we have only imaginatively anticipated it. In order to think about it truly, we must experience it, which is utterly impossible. The only thing we *know* about death is that others have died. The so-called "experience of death" is only the experience of another's death, which, in turn, is simply our observation of the death of others. According to Epicurus, death is nothing for each of us insofar as we are living beings; while we are alive, we are not dead. Nor is it anything for each of us when we die; once dead, we have not the slightest experience (or "feeling") of it. If death does not exist, neither is there any survival in the ordinary sense of this word. The only thing that there is for each one of us—and for all other human beings endowed with consciousness—is life.

These Epicurean opinions have been dismissed either as merely trivial or as thoroughly mistaken. The Epicureans themselves are to be blamed if their opinions have been treated rather cavalierly; after all, they formulated such opinions not as philosophical theses but as words of solace and comfort. The Epicureans' opinions on death were meant to serve as a lenitive to those who live in constant fear of survival, in fear of the sinister world of shadows and demons which haunted the nights, and sometimes even the days, of the "excessively pious." Since this lenitive did not prove to be very effective, the failure of the Epicureans to convince their contemporaries was attributed to the weakness of the Epicurean arguments. Yet, there is something truly profound in these arguments: the idea that the pure and simple fact of living and, in general, of existing surpasses all death and all cessation. The Epicureans did, in fact, deny survival. In principle, they held that living is, in the last analysis, surviving.

Another typical example of a purely philosophical mode of thinking concerning death and survival is found in the writings of Spinoza. Spinoza's thought is, of course, more complex and subtle than that of the Epicureans, but it will serve our purpose to emphasize one basic point: the idea of existence as necessary existence. This idea is often expressed by means of negative terms: [39] necessary existence is in-finite (not finite) and immortal (not mortal). To speak of reality (true and necessary reality) as if it were mortal is, then, a contradiction in terms. The body may be mortal, but then it is mortal in a sense different from the ordinary one: "There is no reason," Spinoza writes, "which compels me to maintain that a body does not die, unless it becomes a corpse." [40] A real change is only a change into "something else." Apart from it, there is something in the human mode that is not mortal: the soul, which is "like an idea to be found in the thinking thing." [41] What could destroy such an idea? It is able neither to destroy itself nor to begin to be while it is still existing. Nor can God, the absolutely real and necessary Being, be destroyed, for "God, the sole cause of his own essence, would also be the cause of his non-essence, thus undergoing transformation and perishing, if the soul were to perish." [42] Therefore, the human spirit "cannot be absolutely destroyed with the body, but there remains of it something which is eternal." [43]

It would seem that we have here a reassertion of the traditional doctrine concerning the spiritual nature of the soul and its immortality. At most, it might be said that the difference between Spinoza and "traditional spiritualists" is that, while the latter indorse the idea of the immortality of the soul as a personal reality, Spinoza subsumes the soul and with it the human person under a single unique reality: *the* infinite, necessary, and eternal Substance which we can call "God or Nature." In short, we seem to have here an uncompromising version of classical pantheism. In this respect, Spinoza might be considered an "ancient" and, even in some fundamental aspects of his thought, a "Neo-Platonist." [44]

Now then, although the above interpretation of Spinoza's

thought is not completely misleading, it fails to notice in it a most original attempt to tackle the problems of death and survival. In the final analysis, Spinoza claims that, insofar as we are real, we are immortal. Since our real being is measured by the idea (in the Spinozistic sense of this word) of our being, then it follows that a reality endures insofar as its idea endures. To make endurance (or persistence) real it is only necessary that we look at the (enduring or persisting) existence from the point of view of the eternal. This is precisely what the "free man" does when he has reached the highest level of knowledge. In this state, the free man no longer thinks about his death.[45] Such a thought would be meaningless; indeed, it would be no thought at all. To think of one's own being is to think of it as immortal. In point of fact, not even "thought" is necessary; only being is necessary. True thought and true being are one and the same thing. Thus we are able to experience ourselves as eternal, which is equivalent to saying that we can experience being from one, and only one, point of view: that of eternity.

My third and last example is drawn from a book by a contemporary philosopher. In his doctoral dissertation, Professor José Echeverría has offered a series of "reflections" on the problem of death in the light of the idea that 'being' is synonymous with 'being as consciousness.' Professor Echeverría's ideas are not, despite appearances, a mere reformulation of the Idealist position, but they are nonetheless an attempt to base the distinction between the subjective and the objective on "being as consciousness." As a consequence, Professor Echeverría is led to reject any metaphysics admitting a (hypothetical) "cosmic observer"—and, therefore, the type of metaphysics outlined in the present book. According to Professor Echeverría, objectivity (for any given consciousness) ensues only from being as consciousness.[46] It is not the right moment to submit Professor Echeverría's ideas to criticism, my present concern being only to divulge some interesting views on the problems of death and survival contained in his dissertation.

As Professor Echeverría himself admits, there is something in his position which is reminiscent of Epicurean thought. Nevertheless, in many respects he goes beyond the Epicurean tenets and, in the final analysis, definitely rejects them. According to Professor Echeverría, it is a sheer mistake to view death from the angle of a hypothetical "cosmic observer"; death can only be viewed by, and in, the consciousness of a mortal being. Now, to die is to disappear for (or from the point of view of) another consciousness; it is not to disappear for (or from the point of view of) myself. Thus, I am dying for another, not for myself, and, therefore, I am immortal in my own eyes.[47] "To be dead" and "to be a man" are, then, mutually exclusive concepts when I am *myself* at stake. This means that at the level of one's own reflective consciousness, the concepts "death" and "immortality" are not necessarily contradictory, for "the reality of death for a spectator does not entail the nonreality of immortality for the dying subject."[48] It could be argued that it is not fair to disregard the experience of aging, which leads us to conclude that we will eventually die. But to conclude, on the basis of our temporal lives, that we will inevitably die is not irreconcilable with the evidence that we are immortal in our own eyes. The end of our temporal existence "does not have and cannot have the meaning of 'a death,' of a 'being no longer,' unless it is in terms of our desire to continue living: it is the question of an experience in which time plays no part, in which we do not have a future but only a past filled with all the events that we have experienced."[49] Hence, neither the fact that each of us "really dies"—that is, disappears for the others—nor even the fact that our time has come to an end contradicts the idea, or more precisely, the experience, of our "immortality for ourselves." As Professor Echeverría writes, *"in death, I do not die; it only happens that time dies in me."* [50]

38
RATIONAL PROOFS

Many of the opinions outlined above (§§ 34–37, and especially §§ 35–37) go hand in hand with attempts either to prove survival or to refute it. In many cases the nature of the arguments adduced in the proof are closely related to the type of survival which is to be defended. In the pages that follow I will consider the proofs themselves independently from the type of survival which they are supposed to uphold. The term 'proof' will often be used as an abbreviation for 'arguments to establish a proof.'

I shall divide the proofs (and hence the corresponding arguments) into two types: rational and empirical. This division is somewhat artificial, for none of the proofs presented thus far is either exclusively rational or totally empirical, but it has the advantage of clarity. It may be argued that there is a type of proof which is difficult to classify: the so-called "moral demonstration." Nevertheless, I shall set it aside, because it is not, properly speaking, a proof but rather a postulate, in the sense of the well-known "moral postulates" in Kant.

The rational proofs are almost always based on certain previous conceptions concerning the nature of the soul. Let us consider a typically rational proof: Plato's third proof for the immortality of the soul in the *Phaedo*.[51] According to Plato, realities can be either simple (indivisible) or composite (divisible into their constituent, simple elements). Simple realities are imperishable; only composite realities perish, from the separation of their constituent parts. The soul is simple, hence imperishable, that is, immortal.

Plato's proof is irrefutable only if we accept the definition of the soul as a "simple reality." If the soul is simple, and if 'simple' means both "indivisible" and "immortal," then there is no doubt that the soul is immortal. But the proof is deceptive insofar as it says very little, if anything at all, about the soul. What does it mean to say that a given entity is simple? Only that it is not composite. We have demonstrated that the soul is immortal, but we wonder whether we have even talked about a soul; we might just as well have talked about a geometrical point.

Plato was extremely eager to prove that the soul is immortal, but he was no less eager to prove that he was talking about something *real*. Thus, he tried to base his proof on some kind of "experience." To say that the soul is "simple" is not enough; when all is said there remains a great deal of complexity in "simplicity." It is, therefore, necessary to understand what 'simple' means, and to that effect it is necessary to have some "experience" of "simplicity" and, *a fortiori,* some experience of the "simplicity of the soul." We can gain this experience when we contrast the soul with the body. Sometimes we feel that our bodies are, so to speak, "alien to *us,*" that they are like an "obstacle," that they drag us down, and so forth. The body may obey *me* or it may not obey *me,* but in either case I must acknowledge that I am not the body, or cannot be identified with the body.[52] It may be argued that these are only "negative experiences" and that they only prove that I am *not* the body. Plato realizes that "positive experiences" of the soul are necessary if the soul is to have a reality. An example of "positive experience" is the soul's access to those realities which are neither given to the senses nor inductively derived from sensation, namely, ideas. In other words, Plato tries to enrich his conception of the soul as much as he can, but in so doing he loses sight of the idea of simplicity. The simpler a reality is, the more immortal it is, but then it seems to become less and less real, so we may be tempted to conclude that an entity is immortal only to the degree that it is not real.

Plato's predicament reappears in the great majority of rational proofs for the immortality of the soul. Many philosophers, Greek, Arabic, and Christian, ancient, medieval and modern, have followed in the steps of Plato. Thus, Malebranche wrote that "we must exist eternally in order to behold divine perfection, because a finite spirit requires infinite time to see an infinite being." [53] Here we have a number of concepts which are not, strictly speaking, Platonic, such as the concept of the infinite on the one hand, and that of an infinite personal God on the other. Malebranche believed that an infinite God has created a spirit so that he can eternally contemplate God's works. Nevertheless, the arguments adduced by Malebranche are, at bottom, Platonic. There we can see a constant oscillation between the concept of "simplicity" and the concept of "richness." The case is the same with those philosophers who have "expanded" simplicity into a number of properties, the "properties of simplicity." For example, it has been said that the soul possesses at least six attributes: divinity, immortality, intelligibility, indissolubility, permanency, and identity.[54] What was originally absolutely simple has now become extremely complex. We have spoken of the "complexity of simplicity"; we could likewise refer to the "simplicity of complexity."

To be sure, not all the rational proofs are Platonic, much less dualistic. Let us briefly consider the Aristotelian–Thomistic proofs. According to St. Thomas Aquinas, man is composed of spiritual substance and corporeal substance.[55] The spiritual substance or soul must be considered not only in its being or essence, but also in its potencies and in its operations. Even if the two substances in question are simple, the relations between them are complex. From the point of view of its operations, the spiritual substance is (intrinsically) independent of the corporeal substance (or matter). On the other hand, from the point of view of its being, the soul is not intrinsically independent of matter. It is also possible to speak of different kinds of "soul." Furthermore, the human soul is sensitive and vegetative as well as intellective. If it were not, it would either form an intrinsic unity with the body or it would exist entirely separated from the body. But none of these statements implies that such a soul is not immortal. Its object—and its happiness—are not found in this life but in an afterlife, where it can participate in the vision of God.[56] Consequently, the soul's ultimate destiny is immortality through participation—which is not to be confused with the immortality that pertains to God, and God alone, through his essence. "The intellectual principle," writes Thomas Aquinas, "which we call the mind or intellect, has essentially an operation in which the body does not share. Now only that which subsists in itself can have an operation in itself . . . We must conclude, therefore, that the human soul, which is called intellect or mind, is something incorporeal and subsistent." [57]

The Thomistic proofs are vastly more complicated than the preceding paragraph suggests. Furthermore, they evince a remarkable effort to resolve—and dissolve—"dualism" without falling prey either to a corporalistic monism or to a radical spiritualism which dispenses with any kind of body or "matter." In this sense, they are both interesting and enlightening. Nevertheless, they possess a characteristic which is common to the "Platonic arguments": the arguer knows beforehand that the entity whose immortality is to be demonstrated is immortal. Therefore, there is some justification in considering the "proofs" in question as examples of paralogisms, which is exactly what Kant did.[58] The paralogisms of substantiality and simplicity are particularly obvious. To be sure, these proofs are not completely divorced from "intuition," in the Kantian sense of 'intuition.' But their "intuitive basis" is too narrow and too unstable to make them effective. In the last analysis, what is proved true is what it was assumed to be true.

The circularity of the rational proofs for the immortality of the soul becomes extreme in Wolff's *Psychologia rationalis*. Here we can see with utmost clarity that underlying the rational proofs is a substantialist realism. Either these "rational arguments" prove only what they had previously assumed or else there is something in what they had previously assumed which they are not able to prove.

39
EMPIRICAL PROOFS

The difficulties inherent in the rational proofs have often led philosophers to rely on the so-called "empirical proofs." Some thinkers, to be sure, have concluded that no empirical proof is possible, but this conclusion scarcely accords with a truly empiricist attitude. It would seem more reasonable to acknowledge simply that a convincing empirical proof has not yet been devised.

A careful analysis of psychic experience shows, according to Fechner, that the denial of human survival is a mere prejudice of modern natural science. Fechner claims that science insists on presenting only a "nocturnal conception" of reality, the conception which holds that reality possesses exclusively material attributes. If psychic or psychical-spiritual phenomena cannot be derived from material phenomena, it is concluded that they do not exist. But the fact is that psychic and psychical-spiritual phenomena overflow the narrow riverbed of purely material phenomena. Instead of continuing to subscribe to a "nocturnal" (negative) conception of reality, we should turn to a "diurnal" (positive) conception. Then we would realize that, while psychical-spiritual phenomena cannot be derived from material phenomena, the latter might be derived from the former. In order to understand this possibility, we only need to avoid identifying psychic and psychical-spiritual activity with sensation. Sensation is not the foundation of psychic activity; it is often a screen that comes between consciousness and reality. If we pierce this screen we come up with a vision of reality which is not dependent upon sensation. From the new point of view thus gained, what is called "death" is only the cessation of sensory perception but not, or not necessarily, that of psychical-spiritual activity. In point of fact, death enables man to concentrate on his own psychic core, on the "invisible center of primeval force, full of spiritual energy, where everything assembles, engendering thoughts in other spirits by means of reciprocal communications." [59] Nature itself can then be seen in its ultimate reality, which is a psychical-spiritual reality. Instead of moving from the exterior to the interior, from nature to the soul, one can—and, indeed, should—move from the interior to the exterior, from the soul to nature. The "Platonists" had claimed that the body can be compared to a prison in which the wailing soul is incarcerated. They did not realize that the body is the necessary condition for the birth, life, and development of the soul. But the body is not only the carrier of the soul; it is the living vehicle of the soul in the sense that it is constantly "vivified" by the aforementioned psychical-spiritual core. Just as the caterpillar and the chrysalis do not perish when the butterfly is born, but "attain a higher and freer form through the butterfly," [60] so, too, the organic body of man does not perish with his death, but is transformed into a soul. In this sense, both the soul and the body are immortal. The body has not been resurrected; it has been elevated by the soul to the level of spiritual life.

Fechner's "diurnal" views are themselves "nocturnal," that is to say, obscure. Nevertheless, in their dim light we can catch a glimpse of some of the basic assumptions made by those who insist on the possibility of an "empirical proof" of human survival.

A great majority of parapsychologists, metapsychologists, advocates of "psychical research," and so on follow in the steps of Fechner insofar as they claim that psychic phenomena are not entirely contained in, or dependent upon, physiological phenomena. Some authors have even claimed that we can "communicate with the dead," but here we shall abstain from even indulging in critically considering such fantasies. We shall confine ourselves to a brief examination of the philosophical assumptions underlying "psychical research," as it has been carried out by such authors as W. Carington,[61] J. B. Rhine,[62]

D. J. West,[63] and others. Since the aforementioned philosophical assumptions were already made explicit by William James, we shall refer to him in particular as the "philosopher of parapsychology."

It is common to all psychical researchers to admit that in psychical research we deal primarily with phenomena which are accessible to perception but which cannot be accounted for in terms of "normal" psychological, psycho-physiological, or neuro-physiological laws. It is also common to all psychical researchers to postulate, or at least hint at, the existence of some "psychic energy" or "psychic substance"—sometimes abbreviated as *psi*—which "exceeds" biological, physiological, and neurological processes and activities.[64] This last point is the most significant for our purpose. If, in fact, *psi* exists, then we can assume that, although channeled and organized by living systems, it is capable of existing independently from its organic support. In short, we can assume that there is, or can be, a psychic "residue" which may persist even after its organic support has vanished. Psychical researchers themselves are unwilling to reach such conclusions. But a "philosopher of parapsychology" like William James seemed to be more interested in the conclusions to be drawn from psychical research than in the research itself.

James holds that thought (or psychical activity at large) can be a function of the brain (or of the nervous system in general). Now, the fact that there is a functional relationship between thought and the brain does not mean that thought is produced by the brain. There are, James contends, various types of functional relations. One is the relation which is made apparent when the brain exerts a merely "permissive" or "transmissive" function.[65] Let us imagine that behind the cosmic workshop which we call "Nature" lies a vast deposit of psychic energy which enters the moment a "window" is opened. The "window" in question could consist of individual organisms, endowed with brains and nervous systems capable of letting this psychic energy "go through," and even capable of really "transmitting" this energy. The brain, far from being a producer of psychic phenomena, has become merely an organ of transmission and communication. If psychic energy is, at least in principle, independent of the organ which transmits it, it is not illogical to conclude that this energy can persist even after the organ of transmission has ceased to function. Furthermore, transmission of psychic energy can be effected in two ways: one based on combination; the other on separation.[66] In the first case, it is supposed that psychic energy (or "consciousness") preexists in the form of scattered particles. The function of the brain is then to assemble such particles into "unitary conciousnesses." In the second case, it is supposed that psychic energy preexists in the form of vast units, or perhaps in the form of a single, undifferentiated reality. Under these circumstances, the function of the brain is to "channel" psychic energy. Because James seems to favor the first hypothesis, his theory can be called the "transmission-channel theory." James feels that in this manner three momentous problems can be resolved. First of all, the problem of the relation between heterogenous entities, such as the physical and the psychical, has been solved; instead of supposing that one type of entity produces the other, it is postulated that they are related through transmission. Then there is the problem of the specific manner in which this transmission is effected. There is no need to imagine the existence of a universal "psychic substance"; one can simply suppose that there are, so to speak, particles of psychic substance which are channeled by the brain. Finally, there is the problem of human immortality; once the foregoing has been admitted, it is not unreasonable to conclude that psychic substances can survive.

Let us assume, then, that psychic phenomena are not "mere epiphenomena" of physical and organic processes, but a reality even more enduring than those we call "natural." Unfortunately, even then we do not see the end of our troubles. Why should such a reality manifest itself through the human brain? If the brain is its natural organ of transmission, how could we ever dispense with it? Aren't the psychic processes coextensive with the organic? It is most unlikely that doctrines such as those of William James, or other philosophers who have endeavored to provide a conceptual framework for psychical research, can satisfactorily answer the above questions. Yet let us be tolerant, and let us assume that they have given these questions a satisfactory answer. A most embarrassing problem concerning human survival still remains. Let us state it briefly.

If psychical reality survives organic processes, the former can be said to be, to some extent, immortal. But do human beings as such really survive? In a preface to the second edition of his famous lecture on human immortality, William James candidly acknowledged that this is a very tricky question. Nevertheless, he cleverly avoided the issue by stating that his doctrine does not entail "psychic pantheism," because one can easily imagine not that man simply channels a psychical world, which is in principle a unique and vast "deposit," but that one's own consciousness may be "an extract of another greater and truer personality which has remained behind the veil." This is not, in our opinion, a solution but at most a pious desire. A philosophical interpretation of parapsychological data only allows us to admit the possibility of "something psychical," but it does not guarantee the existence of what we normally call "a human person." Let us assume that psychical reality survives. Does this mean that we survive as persons? Even if we accept the idea of survival, the question still remains: *whom* does it affect?

There is little doubt that in the above conceptions, the personal unity called "I," "myself," is always dissolved in a whirlwind of "mental images" which, only provisionally and momentarily, are organized in "personal unities." Thus, the mental images cannot be the manifestations of a personal unity unless we further assume that such a personal unity preexists—which is to assume as much as is assumed by the metaphysics of the soul discussed in the preceding section. Carington has clearly admitted that such is the case. According to this author, the only thing that can be said, and empirically proved, concerns a system of *psycha,* a "psychon-system." [67] Therefore, even if the empirical proofs do prove something, in no way do they prove what they claim to prove. They do not prove the survival or the immortality of the human person unless we supplement the empirical proofs with rational arguments which, as we have indicated, also prove something other than what they meant to prove.

40
FURTHER ATTEMPTS

We can conclude that there is no completely adequate or reasonably satisfactory proof of human survival. It would be wise, therefore, to end this chapter if some further attempts had not been made which, without being, strictly speaking, "proofs," allow us to catch a glimpse of possibilities of survival scarcely touched upon in the foregoing sections.

The attempts to which I refer are based on an analysis of self-awareness, and sometimes of the so-called "inner sense." A few examples will suffice.

St. Augustine insisted upon the possibility of an experience of a personal intimacy which transcends the "natural" being of man. When we turn our glance inward, St. Augustine has often declared, we see not a simple being, nor even a mere living being, but rather an activity which consists in "tending towards" —*intendere*. Such an activity makes little sense unless we think of it as a bundle or system of spiritual acts tied together by the three basic modes of temporality: the memory of the past, the perception of the present, and the expectation of the future. This bundle or system of spiritual acts we may call "the self." Now, our awareness of our self reveals to us a type of existence which surpasses the modes of being characteristic of purely natural objects. This same awareness also reveals to us a type of existence which is not self-sufficient. Thus, it becomes necessary to transcend not only nature but one's own conscious reality.

Then we will discover in our innermost depths a deeply rooted truth which we may call "eternity," and which is like a reflection in us of the Life of God. Therefore, the eternity of Truth constitutes a "proof" of the eternity (immortality) of the self (or the soul).[68] In several of his early Christian writings, St. Augustine insists on the Platonic notion that the soul is the subject of a "reason" that does not change.[69] In his later writings, however, the experience of self-consciousness as inward life—*se ipsa vita*—takes precedence over a purely "intelligible" existence. Augustine claims that the soul "is wholly throughout the body," and even that "the supreme immortality of any human being is the perfect health of his body." [70] Therefore, when he states that the soul is immortal because it is subject to immortal (eternal) laws, he does not mean that the soul is only a rational principle of the body but rather that 'soul' is the very name of "our life." Human life as it is experienced in the consciousness of our own self is not, therefore, merely subjective. But neither is it merely objective. Its being is not exclusively for itself or for another; it is a being that continually transcends itself. In this sense, it cannot live without simultaneously surviving itself.

Starting from a psychological analysis of the "self," Maine de Biran claims that the experience of personal life is reducible neither to a natural phenomenon nor to an epiphenomenon (of a natural process). "After abstracting all the accidental impressions," Maine de Biran writes, "and admitting only the potency of the force which is exerted on the different parts, both inert and movable, of one's own body, there will always be the same, immediate feeling of personal existence or of a duration, which may be considered the vestige of a force which flows uniformly." [71] The fact that the self is not a substance does not mean, then, that it is only a system of mental images; it may well mean that it is some kind of nucleus which is fundamentally dynamic.

Thoughts similar to those sketched above can be found in the writings of some twentieth-century philosophers: for example, in Bergson, with his examination of the experience of duration; in Max Scheler, with his thesis that an autonomous, and eternal, spiritual lawfulness supports the manifestations of human life as personal life; in Simmel, with his doctrine which holds that the "I" can always fall back on, and as it were "collect," itself, thus revealing itself as a reality capable of dissociating the "contents" of life from the "process" of life (§ 26, above). In all these doctrines a view, or rather a vision, of the "I," "soul," "self," "selfhood," "consciousness," "person," and so on is offered, which is not based on a rational analysis of the notion of substance. Consequently, these doctrines cautiously avoid proclaiming that there is something immortal in man only because there is something substantial in him which is, by definition, immortal. But since the existence of the "self," as a reality ascertained by purely empirical means, is not thought to be sufficient to constitute personal life, it is concluded that human beings as persons display properties which neither "pure souls" (not to say "ideas") nor natural entities can ever possess. The personal life of man, according to the above authors, could not be conceived if it were not existent—if it did not exist at least as "something" that is present to itself and lives for itself. Hence, it could be said, in agreement with Professor Echeverría, that no "self" can die for itself, even if it can die, and in fact does die, for everyone else.[72]

41
CONCLUSION

The foregoing attempts are of considerable interest particularly if we relate them to a realistic theory of values, on which they all probably depend to a greater or lesser degree. Unfortunately, they rely on an ontology based on the notions of consciousness and self-consciousness—the type of ontology we have rejected as "one-sided." Therefore, they are subject to all the objections we have raised against such a type of ontology.

To conclude, I will confine myself to making a few suggestions on the topics discussed in §§ 38–40.

1. The systems of "mental images," to which we refer in § 39, seem to indicate that there are certain aspects of psychic acts, in particular, self-reflection, which are difficult to reduce entirely to natural phenomena or to modes of behavior which can be described by means of an intersubjective language. But such systems of "mental images" cannot be equated with any of the types of reality called "soul," "I," "the self," "selfhood," "person," and so on.

2. The philosophical speculations on the substantiality and simplicity of the soul, to which we refer in § 38, are interesting and, at any rate, thought-provoking, insofar as they seem to intimate the existence of a realm which, like that of values, can be supposed to be eternal—or a realm which, like that of God, must be declared eternal. But such speculations, especially when they are clothed in arguments of a more or less "Platonic" character, fail to emphasize the reality of a truly intimate and personal life.

3. If both the rational arguments and the empirical proofs are rejected, the result is clear enough: there is no such thing as human survival. On the other hand, if the rejection of any one type of proof gives us a better understanding of whatever interesting points may be contained in the other type of proof, a form of thinking emerges which is circular without being necessarily otiose. Thus, for instance, the systems of mental images whose existence is revealed by the empirical proofs are unacceptable unless supplemented by an ontology of the human person as an enduring (although not forcibly substantial) reality. At the same time, the type of reality described by the metaphysics of the soul and, in general, by "personal realism" is unacceptable unless supplemented by a philosophy which emphasizes the importance of both experiment and experience.

We can thus say that no type of proof is sufficient in itself, so that we are forced to shift from one to the other constantly, without, to be sure, admitting any of them completely but also without committing them entirely to the flames.

4. In his *Second Meditation,* Descartes wrote: "I have been plunged into so many doubts by this meditation that it is no longer in my power to forget them; nor can I see by what means they might be resolved. I am as confused as if I had suddenly fallen into deep water and was able neither to plant my feet on the bottom nor to swim to the surface again." I heartily acquiesce with what Descartes said—and most probably did **not mean.**

NOTES

ONE

Death in Inorganic Nature

1. I. Kant, *Untersuchungen über die Deutlichkeit der Grundsätze der natürlichen Theologie und Moral* (1763). Zweite Betrachtung.
2. *Vera philosophiae methodus nulla alia nisi scientiae naturalis est* (F. Brentano, *Ad Disputationem qua Theses* . . . [Aschaffenburgii, 1866], in F. Brentano, *Über die Zukunft der Philosophie nebst an* . . . *den 25 Habilitationsthesen,* ed. Oskar Kraus [Leipzig, 1929], p. 136).
3. José Ortega y Gasset, *La idea de principio en Leibniz y la evolución de la teoría deductiva* (Madrid, 1958), § 4, p. 33.
4. *Ibid.,* § 4, p. 45.
5. See Alphonse de Waelhens, *Existence et signification* (Louvain and Paris, 1958), pp. 7–29, and Ludwig Landgrebe, *Der Weg der Phänomenologie. Das Problem einer ursprünglichen Erfahrung* (The Hague, 1963), *passim.*
6. See José Ferrater Mora, *Philosophy Today* (New York, 1960; second printing, 1962), pp. 159 ff.
7. See Max Scheler, *Philosophische Weltanschauung* (Bonn, 1928), pp. 1–14, and *Schriften aus dem Nachlass,* vol. I (Berlin,

1933); 2d edition in *Gesammelte Werke,* vol. 10, ed. Maria Scheler (Bern, 1957), pp. 301–302. Similarly, Heidegger points out that reality is not "subjective" any more than human existence is "objective." (Cf. *Sein und Zeit* [Halle a. d. S., 1927], § 2, pp. 5 ff.)

8. See Dominique Dubarle, O.P., "L'idée hylémorphique d'Aristote et la compréhension de l'univers," *Revue des sciences philosophiques et théologiques,* 1e année, No. 1 (1952), 3–29; 2e année, No. 2 (1952), 205–230; 3e année, No. 1 (1953), 1–23. See also Jean Daujat, *Physique moderne et philosophie traditionelle* (Paris, 1958), pp. 61–83; and Henry Margenau, *Thomas and the Physics of 1958: A Confrontation* (Milwaukee, Wis., 1958) [Aquinas Lecture, 1958].

9. E. R. Peierls, "The Atomic Nucleus," *Scientific American,* vol. 200, no. 1 (Jan., 1959), 75, 82. See also Louis de Broglie, *Introduction à la nouvelle théorie des particules de M. Jean-Pierre Vigier et de ses collaborateurs* (Paris, 1961), especially on the "goutelette fluide en rotation" model.

10. Henry Margenau, *The Nature of Physical Theory* (New York and Toronto, 1950), pp. 1–11.

11. Gustav Bergman, "Physics and Ontology," *Philosophy of Science,* 28 (1961), 1–14.

12 Émile Meyerson, *De l'explication dans les sciences* (Paris, 1927), p. 350. Also by Meyerson, *Identité et réalité* (Paris, 1908), pp. 257–268, 362, and *Du Cheminement de la pensée,* vol. I (Paris, 1931), p. 91; vol. II, p. 488.

13. Norwood Russell Hanson, *Patterns of Discovery: An Inquiry into the Conceptual Foundations of Science* (Cambridge, England, 1958), p. 120.

14. See José Ferrater Mora, *Diccionario de filosofía,* 5th ed. (Buenos Aires, 1965), entry for "Fenómeno."

15. See Andrew G. Van Melsen, *From Atomos to Atom* (Pittsburgh, Pa., 1952; reprinted New York, 1960), p. 95.

16. The problem of the "particle-wave duality" is the subject of considerable debate among physicists. Some authors shun duality in favor of "complementarity" (the Copenhagen school); some others affirm that there is neither duality nor "complementarity" but "unity," which is accounted for in terms of symmetry, continuity, and so on. (See Alfred Landé, *From Dualism to Unity in Quantum Physics* [Cambridge, England, 1961], *passim.*)

17. Jean-Paul Sartre, *L'Etre et le Néant* (Paris, 1943), p. 12.

18. It should be pointed out that not even Wolff went so far as to claim that all logical principles are at the same time ontological principles, and that all truths of fact are deductively obtained from truths of reason. According to Wolff (*Ontologia*, §§ 29–32; 175–178; 180–186; *Cosmologia*, §§ 302–303), some truths of fact are disclosed by means of experience and "induction" (as well as by means of "mathematics and experiment"). Nevertheless, these truths are never "merely probable statements," nor are they in any sense incompatible with truths of reason and, therefore, with "ontological principles."

19. See Badi Kasm, *L'idée de preuve en métaphysique* (Paris, 1959), pp. 224–226.

20. M. Heidegger, *Sein und Zeit* (Halle a. d. S., 1927), § 2, p. 7.

21. Norwood Russell Hanson, "Copenhagen Interpretation of Quantum Theory," *American Journal of Physics*, 27 (1959), 1–15; reprinted in Arthur Danto and Sidney Morgenbesser, eds., *Philosophy of Science* (New York, 1960), pp. 288–312.

22. G. F. W. Hegel, *Encyclopädie der philosophischen Wissenschaften*. Zweiter Teil. Einleitung, p. 247.

23. Jean-Paul Sartre, *L'Etre et le Néant* (Paris, 1943), pp. 30–34.

24. See Milič Čapek, *The Philosophical Impact of Contemporary Physics* (Princeton, 1961), p. 290. Whatever stands for 'time' in physical equations is, of course, the subject of much debate among some physicists and most philosophers of science; in any case, it would seem that 'time' in physics does not mean the same as 'time' in "common sense." (See Hans Reichenbach, *The Direction of Time* [Berkeley and Los Angeles, Calif., 1956], *passim*; *The Philosophy of Space and Time* [New York, 1958], *passim*, and especially Adolf Grünbaum, *Philosophical Problems of Space and Time* [New York, 1963], pp. 209 ff.)

25. Cf. Lucretius, *De rerum natura*, I, 149–150: *Principium cuius hinc nobis exordia sumet / Nullam rem e nilo gigni diunitus umquam.*

26. Cf. Ernest Nagel, "Determinism in History," *Philosophy and Phenomenological Research*, 20 (1959–1960), 306–307; and Nagel's *The Structure of Science: Problems in the Logic of Scientific Explanation* (New York and Burlingame, Calif., 1961), pp. 547 ff.

27. See Joaquín Xirau, *Amor y Mundo* (México, 1940), pp. 166 ff.

TWO

Death in Organic Nature

1. Max Scheler, *Der Ressentiment im Aufbau der Moralen,* in *Vom Umsturz der Werte,* vol. I (Leipzig, 1919), pp. 202 ff.; 4th edition in *Gesammelte Werke,* vol. 3, ed. Maria Scheler (Bern, 1955), pp. 127 ff. Originally published under the title "Über Ressentiment und moralisches Werturteil. Ein Beitrag zur Pathologie der Kultur," *Zeitschrift für Psychopathologie,* I (Leipzig, 1912), 2–3.

2. Georg Simmel, *Lebensanschauung. Vier metaphysische Kapitel* (München, 1918; 2d edition, München and Leipzig, 1922).

3. Henri Bergson, *L'Evolution créatrice* (Paris, 1907), pp. 34–35 (*Oeuvres,* ed. André Robinet [Paris, 1959], p. 522).

4. Hans Driesch, *The History and Theory of Vitalism* (London, 1914), pp. 171–172; see also *Philosophie des Organischen* (Leipzig, 1909; 4th ed., Leipzig, 1928), pp. 41 ff. It should be noted that Wilhelm Roux adhered to "strict mechanism."

5. Hans Driesch, *Philosophie des Organischen,* pp. 42–47.

6. Hans Driesch, *The Problem of Individuality* (London, 1914), p. 33.

7. Hans Driesch, *Philosophie des Organischen,* pp. 283–288.

8. *Ibid.,* p. 303.

9. *Ibid., op. cit.,* p. 307.

10. Max Scheler, "Tod und Fortleben," in *Schriften aus dem Nachlass,* vol. I (Berlin, 1933); 2d edition in *Gesammelte Werke,* vol. 10, ed. Maria Scheler (Bern, 1957), p. 32. See also *Der Formalismus in der Ethik und die materiale Wertethik,* 2 vols. (Halle a. d. S., 1913–1916), reprinted in *Gesammelte Werke,* vol. 2 (Bern, 1954), pp. 174–175.

11. Francisco Romero, *Filosofía contemporánea* (Buenos Aires, 1941), p. 193.

12. Max Scheler, *Die Stellung des Menschen im Kosmos* (Darmstadt, 1928), pp. 16–17.

13. Ernest Nagel, "The Meaning of Reduction in the Natural Sciences," in Robert C. Stauffer, ed., *Science and Civilization* (Madison, Wis., 1949), p. 131, reprinted in Arthur Danto and Sidney Morgenbesser, eds., *Philosophy of Science* (New York, 1960), p. 308.

14. Ernest Nagel, "Mechanistic Explanation and Organismic Biology," *Philosophy and Phenomenological Research,* 11 (1950–

1951), 332–333; also in Nagel's *The Structure of Science: Problems in the Logic of Scientific Explanation* (New York and Burlingame, Calif., 1961), pp. 361–364.

15. Ernest Nagel, "The Meaning of Reduction in the Natural Sciences," p. 130, reprinted in *Philosophy of Science* p. 309.

16. Erwin Schrödinger, *What Is Life? The Physical Aspect of the Living Cell* (Cambridge, England, and New York, 1947), p. 1.

17. F. Grande Covián, "La obra científica de Severo Ochoa," *Revista Ybis* [Madrid], año XVIII, no. 2 (1960), 93.

18. Erwin Schrödinger, *What Is Life?*, p. 80.

19. See Nicolai Hartmann, *Der Aufbau der realen Welt* (Berlin, 1940; 2d edition, Meisenheim am Glan, 1949), pp. 188 ff. Also *Neue Wege der Ontologie* (Berin, 1942; 3d edition, Stuttgart, 1949), pp. 33–34, and *Das Problem des geistigen Seins* (Berlin and Leipzig, 1933), p. 15.

20. Xavier Bichat, *Recherches physiologiques sur la vie et la mort* (Paris, 1800; 4th edition [Paris, 1882], p. 2). According to Ludwig von Bertalanffy, the expression 'life is the sum total of the functions which resist death' is a vicious circle, because the concept "death" has meaning only with reference to the concept "life" (*Problems of Life* [London, 1952; reprinted New York, 1960], p.129). Von Bertalanffy's objection would be flawless if Bichat's expression were a real definition instead of only a way of emphasizing the close relation between death and organic life.

21. There is an abundant bibliography on this question. I will single out only a few items (1 through 13 concerning experimental results; 14 through 26 containing mostly theories and interpretations of experimental results):

1. E. Maupas, "Recherches expérimentales sur la multiplication des infusoires ciliés," *Archives de Zoologie expérimentale et générale,* séries 2, VI, 2. *2.* E. Maupas, "Le rajeunissement kyrogamique chez les ciliés" *ibid.,* VII. *3.* G. N. Calkins, "Studies in the Lifehistory of Protozoa," *Archiv für Entwicklungsmechanik,* 15 (1902), 139–186; *Biological Bulletin* (1902), 192–205; *Journal of Experimental Zoology,* I (1904), 423–461; *Biological Bulletin,* 11 (1906), 229–244; *Journal of Experimental Zoology,* 10 (1906), 95–116. *4.* L. L. Woodruff and R. Erdmann, "A Normal Periodic Reorganization Process Without Cell Fusion in Paramecium," *Journal of Experimental Zoology,* 17 (1914), 425–518. *5.* L. L. Woodruff, "The Problem of Rejuvenescence in Protozoa," *Biochemical Bulletin,* 4 (1915), 371–378. *6.* L. L. Woodruff, "The Present Status of the

Long Continued Pedigree Culture of *Paramaecium aurelia* at Yale University," *Proceedings of the Natural Academy of Sciences,* 7 (1921), 41–44. *7.* E. G. Conklin, "The Size of Organisms and of Their Constituent Parts in Relation to Longevity, Senescence, and Rejuvenescence," *Popular Science Monthly* (August, 1913), 178–198. *8.* O. Enriques, "Duemila cinquecento generazioni in un infusorio, senza coniugazione nè partenogenesi, nè depressioni," *Rendiconto delle Sessioni della Reale Accademia di Scienze dell'Istituto di Bologna* (1916). *9.* M. Hartmann, "Über die dauernde rein agame Züchtung von *Eudorina elegans* und ihre Bedeutung für das Befruchtungs- und Todproblem," *Sitzungsberichte der königlichen Akademie der Wissenschaften* [Berlin], 52 (1917). *10.* B. Slotopolsky, "Zur Diskussion über die potentielle Unsterblichkeit der Einzellingen und über den Ursprung des Todes," *Zoologischer Anzeiger,* 51 (1920), 63–71, 81–91. *11.* A. Carrel and A. H. Ebeling, "The Multiplication of Fibroblasta in vitro," *Journal of Experimental Medicine,* 34 (1921), 317–337. *12.* A. Carrel and A. H. Ebeling, "Age and Multiplication of Fibroblasta," *ibid.,* 34 (1921), 599–623. *13.* Joachim Hämmerling, "El problema de la muerte natural," *Revista de Occidente,* 37 (1932), 311–328; 38 (1932), 54–68.

14. August Weismann, *Über die Dauer des Lebens* (1881). *15.* A. Weismann, *Über Leben und Tod* (1884). *16.* I. I. Metchnikov, *Études sur la nature humaine* (1903). *17.* I. I. Metchnikov, *Essais optimistes* (1907). *18.* C. M. Child, *Senescence and Rejuvenescence* (1915). *19.* H. J. Jennings, *Life and Death, Heredity and Evolution in Unicellular Organisms* (1920), especially pp. 34–37. *20.* Raymond Pearl, *The Biology of Death* (1922). *21.* E. Korschelt, *Lebensdauer, Altern und Tod,* 2d ed. (1924). *22.* S. Metalnikov, *La lucha contra la muerte,* trans. (1940). *23.* Various authors, *Studium generale. Zeitschrift für die Einheit der Wissenschaften im Zusammenhang ihrer Begriffsbildungen und Forschungsmethoden,* Heft 10, IV (1951), especially D. Kotsovsky, "Gibt es spezifische Alterungsveränderungen?" *24.* K. Friedrichs, *Lebensdauer, Altern und Tod* (1959). *25.* Alexis Comfort, "The Life Span of Animals," *Scientific American,* 205, no. 2 (August, 1961). *26.* Nathan W. Schock, "The Physiology of Aging," *Scientific American,* 206, no. 1 (January, 1962).

22. Joachim Hämmerling, "El problema de la muerte natural," *Revista de Occidente,* 37 (1932), 317.

23. *Ibid.*, pp. 317–318.
24. *Ibid.*, p. 321.
25. Ludwig von Bertalanffy, *Problems of Life* (London, 1952; reprinted New York, 1960), p. 48. See also Henri Bergson, *L'Évolution créatrice* (Paris, 1907), p. 13; reprinted in *Oeuvres,* ed. André Robinet (Paris, 1959), pp. 504–505.
26. *Ibid.*
27. Jean Rostand, *L'Homme* (Paris, 1963); see also Eugène Mannoni, "Quand Jean Rostand imagine l'évolution biologique de l'homme," *Le Monde* [Paris], March 21, 1956, p. 9.
28. Joachim Hämmerling, *op. cit.*, p. 312.
29. Alexis Comfort, "The Life Span of Animals," *Scientific American*, 205, no. 2 (August, 1961), 118.
30. E. Metchnikov, *Études sur la nature humaine* (Paris, 1903), pp. 201 ff.
31. Juan Rof Carballo, *Cerebro interno y sociedad* (Madrid, 1952), p. 12.
32. Raymond Pearl, *The Biology of Death* (Philadelphia and London, 1922), pp. 46–47.
33. Numerous cases of fallibility in determination of "clinical death" have been described by C. S. Birukhonenko and V. Negovsky.
34. M. D'Halluin, *La mort, cette inconnue* (Paris, 1940), quoted by Paul Chauchard, *La mort* (Paris, 1947), p. 69.
35. André Lalande, *La dissolution opposée à l'évolution dans les sciences physiques et morales* (Paris, 1899), p. 73.
36. A. Draste, *La vie et la mort* (Paris, 1909), p. 307.
37. Oscar Hertwig, *Lehrbuch der Entwicklungsgeschichte des Menschen und der Wirbelthiere,* 5th edition (Jena, 1896), p. 346.
38. Max Scheler, "Lehre von der drei Tatsachen" (written *ca.* 1911/1912), in *Schriften aus dem Nachlass*, I (Berlin, 1933), reprinted in *Gesammelte Werke,* vol. 2, ed. Maria Scheler (Bern, 1954), pp. 431–502, and especially pp. 446–448.
39. *Ibid.*, pp. 475–476.
40. Max Scheler, "Tod und Fortleben," *Schriften aus dem Nachlass*, vol. I (Berlin, 1933), reprinted in *Gesammelte Werke,* vol. 10, ed. Maria Scheler (Bern, 1957), pp. 17, 19–21.
41. See Arnold A. Hutschnecker, "Personality Factors in Dying Patients," in Herman Feifel, ed., *The Meaning of Death* (New York, Toronto, and London, 1959).

THREE

Human Death

1. *De Anima*, II, 1, 412 a 27 ff.
2. *De Civitate Dei*, XXI, 10. See Pascal's comment on this passage in *Pensées*, ed. Jacques Chevalier (Paris, 1936), § 84 (p. 847), and *Oeuvres*, ed. Léon Brunschvicg, XII (Paris, 1925), § 72, pp. 91–92.
3. For instance, in Gilbert Ryle's *The Concept of Mind* (London, 1949), and M. Merleau-Ponty's *The Phenomenology of Perception* (Paris, 1945). Also, but less obviously, in Gabriel Marcel's *Journal métaphysique* (Paris, 1927), 3d edition (Paris, 1955), pp. 224–226, 252, 261–264, and *The Mystery of Being*, vol. I (London, 1950), pp. 148–170. For interesting similarities between the phenomenological approach and the "linguistic approach" see C. Taylor and A. J. Ayer, "Phenomenology and Linguistic Analysis," *Proceedings of the Aristotelian Society*, suppl. vol. 33 (1959), 93–124, and John J. Compton, "Hare, Husserl and Philosophic Discovery," *Dialogue*, III (1964), 42–51.

It should be kept in mind that there is now a tendency among a number of "analytical philosophers" to argue in favor of a (moderate) type of "dualism," or, at least, a tendency to prove that a mild body–mind dualism is no less defensible than an antidualism. As an example of the aforementioned tendency we may mention Anthony Quinton's article, "The Soul," *Journal of Philosophy*, LIX (1962), 393–409. To be sure, the term 'the soul' is made synonymous here only with 'the nonphysical aspect of a person.' It is, in Quinton's words, "an empirical concept of the soul, which, like Locke's, interprets it as a sequence of mental states logically distinct from the body" (*op. cit.*, p. 397). "All I have tried to show," Quinton writes, "is that there is no necessary connection between the soul as a series of mental states linked by the character and memory and any particular continuing human body" (*op. cit.*, pp. 407–408).

4. The terms 'outside' and 'inside' have here, then, a more radical (and hence more controversial) meaning than in Weston La Barre's sentence: "It was the first organism which first brought the concepts of 'inside' and 'outside' into the universe" (*The Human Animal* [Chicago, 1954], p. 2; reprinted in Phoenix Books P45 [Chicago, 1955], p. 2).
5. See Sherwood L. Washburn, "Tools and Human Evolution,"

Scientific American, 203, no. 3 (September, 1960), 63–75.
  6. Cf. Grace A. de Laguna, "The *Lebenswelt* and the Cultural World," *Journal of Philosophy,* LVII (1960), 781.
  7. I use the terms 'community' and 'society' in a sense similar to, although not necessarily identical with, the one proposed by Ferdinand Tönnies in *Gemeinschaft und Gesellschaft. Grundbegriffe der reinen Soziologie* (Leipzig, 1887); 8th edition (Leipzig, 1935).
  8. See Marshall D. Sahlins, "The Origin of Society," *Scientific American,* 203, no. 3 (September, 1960), 76–86.
  9. Max Scheler, *Die Stellung des Menschen im Kosmos* (Darmstadt, 1928), p. 63.
  10. See Pedro Laín Entralgo, *La espera y la esperanza* (Madrid, 1957; 2d edition [Madrid, 1958], p. 479).
  11. M. Heidegger, *Sein und Zeit* (Halle a. d. S., 1927), § 4, p. 13, and § 10, pp. 45–50.
  12. José Ortega y Gasset, *La idea de principio en Leibniz y la evolución de la teoría deductiva* (Madrid, 1958), § 29, p. 339. The distinction between 'ontical' and 'ontological' has been hailed as a useful one by Willard van Orman Quine (*Word and Object* [Cambridge, Mass., 1960], p. 120), but on the basis of a meaning of 'ontological' quite different from Heidegger's.
  13. Twisting and stretching the meaning of terms borrowed from common speech is, of course, only part of the story. It is necessary that meaning-twistings and meaning-extensions should not function *in vacuo.* See, among many other contemporary writings in this respect, H. A. Hodges, *Languages, Standpoints, and Attitudes* (London, 1953), pp. 17–18 (University of Durham, Riddell Memorial Lectures, 24th Series), and in particular A. J. Ayer, *Philosophy and Language* (Oxford, 1960), p. 30 (An Inaugural Lecture, Oxford, Sept. 3, 1960; reprinted in Ayer's book, *The Concept of a Person and Other Essays* [New York, 1963], pp. 1–35). Among classical warnings against *illegitimate* meaning-twistings and meaning-extensions Berkeley is still the most valuable.
  14. Mario Bunge, "Can Computers Think? in *Metascientific Queries* (Springfield, Ill., 1959), p. 129 (American Lecture Series, 41).
  15. *Ibid.,* p. 133.
  16. See John G. Kemeny, "Man Viewed as a Machine," *Scientific American,* 192, no. 4 (April, 1955), 58–67.
  17. José Ortega y Gasset, *The Revolt of the Masses,* James

Cleugh, trans. (New York, 1933), p. 52. On the meaning of this contention in Ortega y Gasset's thought, see José Ferrater Mora, *Ortega y Gasset: An Outline of His Philosophy* (London, 1956, and New Haven, Conn., 1957), pp. 52–53; new revised edition (New Haven, Conn., 1963), pp. 61 ff.

18. Jean-Paul Sartre, *L'Etre et le Néant* (Paris, 1943), pp. 508–642. It should be noted that, despite his adherence to Marxism, Sartre has not changed his views too drastically concerning the "primacy of freedom" in man, even during the so-called "period of exploitation." Sartre limits himself to pointing out that such freedom displays itself "within a certain given conditioning environment"; man is "what he succeeds in doing with what has been done to him" (*Critique de la raison dialectique*, vol. I [Paris, 1960], p. 63). Sartre himself claims that his later opinions can easily be integrated with his earlier ones—a claim similar to the one made by Heidegger with respect to the relation between his "earlier" and "later" philosophies (see *Unterwegs zur Sprache* [Pfullingen, 1959], pp. 85–155, especially pp. 98–99).

19. Literally, a tightrope walker (*ein Seiltänzer*): *Der Mensch ist ein Seil, geknüpft zwischen Tier und Übermensch—ein Seil über einem Abgrunde. Ein gefährliches Hinüber, ein gefährliches Auf-dem-Wege, ein gefährliches Zurückblicken, ein gefährliches Schaudern und Stehenbleiben— . . . eine Brücke und kein Zweck . . ."* (*Also sprach Zarathustra*. Zarathustras Vorrede, vol. 4. *Werke in drei Bänden*, Karl Schlechta, ed., vol. II [München, 1956], p. 281).

20. Weston La Barre, *The Human Animal*, p. 246.

21. On the difference between repentance and remorse, see Vladimir Jankélévitch, *La mauvaise conscience* (Paris, 1951), pp. 94–107, especially pp. 94–95.

22. See José Ferrater Mora, *Ortega y Gasset: An Outline of His Philosophy*, pp. 26–27, 49; new revised edition, pp. 25–26, 58.

23. *Persona est naturae rationalis individua substantia* (Boethius, *De duabus naturis et una persona Christi*, 3 [Migne, *Patrologia Latina*, 64, col. 1345]).

24. Further elucidations on this question and, in general, on "the problem of man" will be found in my article, "Images de l'homme," *Revue philosophique de la France et de l'Étranger*, XC (1965).

25. Paul Ludwig Landsberg, *Experiencia de la muerte*, Spanish translation of a hitherto unpublished German manuscript (México, 1940), p. 71.

26. Georg Simmel, "Zur Metaphysik des Todes," *Logos*, vol. I

(1910–1911), p. 59, reprinted with revisions in *Lebensanschauung*. *Vier metaphysische Kapitel* (München, 1918), 2d edition München and Leipzig, 1922), p. 108, and *Brücke und Tür* (Stuttgart, 1957), p. 31.
    27. Karl Jaspers, *Philosophie*, vol. II (Berlin, 1932), p. 220.
    28. Martin Heidegger, *Sein und Zeit* (Halle a. d. S., 1927), § 47, p. 239.
    29. *Ibid.*, § 47, p. 240.
    30. *Ibid.*, §§ 51–53, pp. 252–267.
    31. Jean-Paul Sartre, *L'Etre et le Néant*, p. 618.
    32. *Ibid.*, p. 630.
    33. *Ibid.*, p. 631.
    34. Gabriel Marcel, *Présence et immortalité* (Paris, 1959), p. 60 ("Journal métaphysique, May 19, 1942").
    35. Roger Mehl, *Le vieillissement et la mort* (Paris, 1955), p. 67.
    36. See Irving E. Alexander, "Death and Religion," in Herman Feifel, ed., *The Meaning of Death* (New York, Toronto, and London, 1959), pp. 271–283.
    37. Jean-Paul Sartre, *L'Etre et le Néant*, p. 431.
    38. The "literary testimony" is only a part, albeit a most significant one, of what we may call "historical testimony." We will not be concerned with the latter, but we will mention a few works in which the reader will find an abundance of historical material: Alfons Schulz, "Der Sinn des Todes im Alten Testament," *Braunsberg Akademie*. Verzeichnis der Vorlesung (1919), 5–41. Alberto Tenenti, *Il senso della morte e l'amore della vita nel Rinascimento (Francia e Italia)* (Torino, 1957), especially about the works concerning the *ars moriendi* and the iconography of death. J. Huizinga, *Hersttij der middeleeuwen* (Haarlem, 1928), chap. 11. Bernhard Groethhuysen, *Die Entstehung der bürgerlichen Welt- und Lebensanschauung in Frankreich*, 2 vols. (Halle/Saale, 1927–1930), part I, chap. 2, § 2.
    39. *Confessions*, IV, iv, 9.
    40. Paul Ludwig Landsberg, *Experiencia de la muerte*, pp. 92, 98.
    41. *Confessions*, loc. cit.
    42. *Ibid.*, IV, vi, 11: *Non enim tempus quaerendi nunc est, sed confitendi tibi*.
    43. André Gide, "Mort de Charles Louis Philippe," in *Journal* [1909] (Paris, 1939), p. 278.
    44. *Ibid.*, p. 280.
    45. *Ibid.*, p. 287.

46. Jean-Paul Sartre, *L'Etre et le Néant*, p. 617.
47. Diogenes Laërtius, X, 127. Also Lucretius, *De Rerum Natura*, III, 830 ff.
48. Diogenes Laërtius, VII, 130. Also Epictetus, *Encheiridion*, 5. The Stoics' fearless attitude in the face of death may conceal a "fear of life." See, on this question, José Ferrater Mora, *Man at the Crossroads* (Boston, 1958), part I, chap. 2.
49. Choderlos de Laclos, *De l'éducation des femmes*, chap. 7 (*Oeuvres complètes*, ed. Maurice Allen [Paris, 1951], p. 419).
50. Bertrand Russell, *New Hopes for a Changing World* (London, 1951), p. 210.
51. *Epistolae morales*, LXIX.
52. *Éloge de Seytres*.
53. *La mort que je serai bouge en moi sans façons* (*Choix de poèmes* [Buenos Aires, 1944], p. 234).
54. *Por las gradas sube Ignacio / Con toda su muerte a cuestas* ("Llanto por Ignacio Sánchez Mejías. 2. La sangre derramada" [1935], in *Obras completas*, IV [Buenos Aires, 1944], p. 155).
55. . . . *como ahogarnos en el corazón / Como irnos cayendo desde la piel al alma* ("Sólo la muerte," in *Residencia en la tierra 1931–1935*, vol. II [Santiago de Chile, 1939], p. 21).
56. . . . *con la aguda humedad de una hoja de violeta / Y su grave color de invierno exasperado* (*loc. cit.*).
57. . . . *vive tendida y de repente sopla* (*loc. cit.*).
58. In the *Geschichten des guten Gottes*.
59. *O Herr, gib jedem seinen eignen Tod / Das Sterben, das aus jenem Leben geht / Darin er Liebe hatte, Sinn und Not* (*Das Stundenbuch* [*Gesammelte Werke*, vol. II, Leipzig, 1927], p. 273.
60. *Der grosse Tod, den jeder in sich hat / Das ist die Frucht, um die sich alles dreht* (*Das Stundenbuch*, p. 273).
61. Marcel Proust, *La prisonnière*, in *A la recherche du temps perdu*, eds. Pierre Clarac and André Ferré, vol. III (Paris, 1954), p. 199.

FOUR

Death, Survival, and Immortality

1. On Unamuno's "hunger for immortality," see José Ferrater Mora, *Unamuno: A Philosophy of Tragedy*, trans. Philip Silver, with revisions by the author (Berkeley and Los Angeles, Calif., 1962), chap. 3, *passim*.

Notes

2. See M. F. Sciacca, *Morte ed immortalità* (Milano, 1959), pp. 178–290.

3. A. Schopenhauer, *Die Welt als Wille und Vorstellung.* Ergänzungen zum vierten Buch, chap. XLI (*Sämtliche Werke,* Julius Frauenstädt, ed., vol. 3 [Leipzig, 1923], p. 529).

4. See Nicola Abbagnano, "Metafisica ed esistenza," in M. F. Sciacca, ed., *Filosofi italiani contemporanei* (Milano, 1944; 2d edition [Milano, 1948], p. 14).

5. Jules Vuillemin, *Essai sur la signification de la mort* (Paris, 1948), p. 9.

6. *Ibid.,* p. 11.

7. For the ontology underlying Zubiri's idea, see Xavier Zubiri, *Sobre la esencia* (Madrid, 1962), *passim.*

8. Sigmund Freud, *Jenseits des Lustprinzips* (Leipzig, Wien, and Zürich, 1920), pp. 34 ff. (*Gesammelte Werke,* vol. XIII, pp. 38 ff.). See also Norman O. Brown, *Life Against Death* (Middletown, Conn., 1959), *passim.*

9. Oswald Spengler, "Zur Weltgeschichte des zweitens vorchristlichen Jahrtausends" [1935], in *Reden und Aufsätze* (München, 1938), pp. 163–166.

10. See L. Lévy-Bruhl, *Le surnaturel et la nature dans la mentalité primitive* (Paris, 1931), p. 145.

11. See Kenneth Scott Latourette, *The Chinese: Their History and Culture,* 3d edition (New York, 1960), p. 67.

12. See Francis L. K. Hsu, *Under the Ancestors' Shadow* (New York, 1948), *passim.*

13. L. Lévy-Bruhl, *L'âme primitive* (Paris, 1927), p. 239.

14. J. G. Frazer, *The Golden Bough,* abridged edition (New York, 1942), p. 192.

15. Franz Cumont, *Lux Perpetua* (Paris, 1949), *passim.*

16. E. R. Dodds, *The Greeks and the Irrational* (Berkeley and Los Angeles, Calif., 1951), pp. 135–156 (Sather Classical Lectures, 25).

17. In a lecture entitled "The Forging of a Scientific Language in Ancient Greece" (at Swarthmore College, March 20, 1960).

18. Isaac Flagg, *A Homeric Dictionary* (Norman, Okla., 1958), s.v. ψυχή, a translation and revision of Georg Autenrieth's *Wörterbuch* (1876, 1901).

19. Walter F. Otto, *Die Manen oder von den Urformen des Totenglaubens* (Berlin, 1923), pp. 47, 63; new edition (Darmstadt, 1957).

20. Erwin Rohde, *Psyche. Seelenkult und Unsterblichkeitsglaube der Griechen* (Freiburg i. B. and Leipzig, 1849), 9th and 10th editions, vol. I (Tübingen, 1925), p. 308.
21. Cf. *Republica*, IV, 436A-B; *Timeus*, 41A.
22. *Phaedo*, 82E: ὥσπερ διὰ εἱργμου.
23. *Phaedo*, 208B-E.
24. *Timeus*, 89B.
25. *De Anima*, B, 1, 402a; 412a-b.
26. Cf. Eusebius, *Praeparatio Evangelica*, XI, 28.
27. Plotinus, *Enneads*, IV, ii, 1; IV, vii (*passim*).
28. See José Ferrater Mora, *Man at the Crossroads*, part I. chap. 3.
29. Franz Cumont, *Lux Perpetua*, p. 451. Cf. Ps. 1:5.
30. Cf. J. Bonsirven, *Le judaïsme palestinien au temps de Jésus Christ*, vol. I (Paris, 1935), pp. 484 ff.
31. St. Augustine, *De Immortalitate Animae*, 16; St. Thomas Aquinas, *Summa contra Gentiles*, II, 72.
32. Plotinus, *Enneads*, IV, iv, 1.
33. *Ibid.*, III, v, 4.
34. *Summa Theologica*, I, q. 97, 1c.
35. St. Augustine, *De Civitate Dei*, XIII, 5.
36. Alexo Venegas, *Agonía del tránsito de la muerte* (1565). Punto segundo, cap. IV (Nueva Biblioteca de Autores Españoles. Escritores místicos españoles, vol. I [Madrid, 1911], p. 122).
37. St. Augustine, *De Civitate Dei*, XIII, 7.
38. *Ibid.*, XIII, 8.
39. *Tractatus de intellectus emendatione*, 89.
40. *Ethica*, IV, prop. xxxix, sch.
41. *Tractatus de Deo et homine ejusque felicitate* [*Korte Schetz*], II, xxiii, 1.
42. *Ibid.*, II, xxxiii, 2.
43. *Ethica*, V, prop. xxiii.
44. Perhaps even a *hermeticus*. Cf. the "Spinozian" Treatise VIII of the *Corpus Hermeticum* (*Hermès Trismégiste*, vol. I, A. D. Nock, ed. [Paris, 1960], p. 89).
45. *Ethica*, IV, prop. lxvii.
46. José Echeverría, *Réflexions métaphysiques sur la mort et le problème du sujet* (Paris, 1957), p. 26.
47. *Ibid.*, pp. 119–132.
48. *Ibid.*, p. 126.

49. *Ibid.*, p. 140.
50. *Ibid.*, p. 142. See also Arnold Metzger, *Freiheit und Tod* (Tübingen, 1955), pp. 188 ff.
51. It should be noted that none of Plato's proofs must be considered in isolation. Plato himself admits that the first two proofs (the one based on the notion of "contraries" and the one based on "recollection") are interdependent (*Phaedo*, 77C-D).
52. These thoughts have found expression in thousands of literary works, particularly novels, as in Alberto Moravia's *La Romana: Soltanto, il mio corpo continuava a vivere, per conto suo, noncurante della mia volontà.*
53. "Lettre de Malebranche à M. de Torssac" (March 21, 1693), *apud* Victor Cousin, *Fragments philosophiques,* vol. IV, 5th edition (Paris, 1866), p. 522; now in Malebranche, *Oeuvres complètes,* ed. André Robinet (Paris, 1961), p. 606.
54. Cf. Olympiodoros on the *Phaedo* (Victor Cousin, *op. cit.,* V [Paris, 1865], p. 468).
55. *Summa Theologica,* I, q. 75, ad 1.
56. *Summa contra Gentiles,* I, 57.
57. *Summa Theologica,* I, q. 75 ad 2.
58. *Kritik der reinen Vernunft,* A 344–371; B 410–412.
59. G. Th. Fechner, *Das Büchlein vom Leben nach dem Tode* (Leipzig, 1836), "Insel-Bücherei," § 187, p. 20.
60. G. Th. Fechner, *Zend-Avesta,* vol. III (Leipzig, 1851), pp. 14–15; 3d edition (Hamburg and Leipzig, 1906).
61. W. Carington, *Telepathy: An Outline of Its Facts, Theory, and Implications* (London, 1945).
62. J. B. Rhine, *The Reach of the Mind* (New York, 1947), and *New World of the Mind* (New York, 1953).
63. D. J. West, *Psychical Research Today* (London, 1954).
64. Cf. F. W. H. Myers, *Human Personality and Its Survival of Bodily Death,* vol. I (New York, 1903; reprinted New York, 1961).
65. William James, *Human Immortality: Two Supposed Objections to the Doctrine* (Boston and New York, 1899), 2d edition (Boston and New York, 1899; Ingersoll Lecture, 1897), reprinted in *The Will to Believe, and Other Essays in Popular Philosophy. Human Immortality* (New York, 1956), *ad finem.*
66. *Ibid., ad finem,* n. 3.
67. W. Carington, *op. cit., passim.*
68. *Soliloquia,* II, 19.

69. *De Immortalitate Animae*, 1.
70. Ad Dyon. Lett. CXVII, iii, 14: *sanitas autem perfecta corporis, illa extrema totius hominis immortalitatis erit.*
71. Maine de Biran, *Essai sur les fondements de la psychologie et sur ses rapports avec l'étude de la nature* (written *ca.* 1811/1812), in *Oeuvres,* ed. P. Tisserand, vol. IX (Paris, 1932), pp. 322–323.
72. José Echeverría, *op. cit.*, pp. 121, 126 (see n. 46 above).

INDEX

Abbagnano, Nicola, 255 (n. 4)
Absolutes: rejection of, 7–8, 73–74, 85–86, 90, 168; talk about, 87–88, 121, 192, 199
Aging: and death, 136 ff., 140 ff.
Alexander of Aphrodisias, 216
Analogia mortis, 20, 52, 64 ff., 89, 169
Appearance: and reality, 55, 56, 58–59; in organic reality, 83
Aristotle, 11, 20; on Being, 13, 89; on matter and form, 20; on motion, 32; on substance, 90–91; on organic reality, 97; quoted, 146; on immortality, 216
Atomic models, 37–38
Atomism, 47 ff., 63; and mechanism, 48 ff.; ontological presuppositions of, 53, 79
Augustine, St.: quoted, 146, 188–189, 238, 253 (n. 42); on the soul, 219, 221, 237–238
Authenticity, 164–165, 167–168
Averroës, 217

Ayer, A. J., 251 (n. 13)
Aymé, Marcel, quoted, 187

Bain, James A., 108
Basic elements, 45–50 *passim;* 52 ff., 59, 63, 78, 80
Becoming: and being, 85, 153 ff. *See also* Change
Beers, C. D., 124
Being, 8, 21; and change, 46 ff.; "in principle" and in reality, 51–59 *passim;* and cessation, 52, 60 ff., 64, 84; and becoming, 85, 153 ff.; and reality, 53 ff.; and meaning, 85–88; analogy of, 85, 89; and natural reality, 154
Being for itself, 113, 115–116, 157
Bergman, Gustav, 244 (n. 11)
Bergson, Henri, 31, 193; on life, 97–98; on death, 207; on survival, 239
Bichat, Xavier, quoted, 121
Biologism. *See* Organicism

Body, the: and the mind, 146 ff.; as a way of being, 147, 202; death of, 202–203; and the soul, *see* Soul
Boethius, 169; quoted, 252 (n. 23)
Bohr, Niels, 112
Brentano, Franz, quoted, 25
Bunge, Mario, quoted, 159

Calkins, G. N., 123–125
Carington, W., 233, 236
Carrel, Alexis, 124–125
Cassirer, Ernst, 31
Cessation: in fact and in principle, 22, 23, 49–50; in inorganic realities, 38–39, 43–45, 78–79; of structures, 43–45, 78–79; and change, 46 ff.; mechanistic view of, 50–51; analogy of, 52; as a real process, 52, 60 ff., 64, 90; degrees of, 64–65, 80–81, 88, 120 ff., 172–173; in organic realities, 83–84; and death, 83–84, 89, 120–123; as related to being and meaning, 88; progression in, 89–91, 142–143, 199–200
Change: meaning of, 22, 23; and being, 46 ff.; and cessation, 46 ff.; and novelty, 50
Classes: and abstract entities, 40; and structures, 41
Classical mechanics, 36, 37, 77, 78
Comfort, Alexis, 249 (n. 29)
Common sense: nature and role of, 32–35; and physics, 33–34
Community, 150
Conklin, E. G., 123
Continuum of reality, 9, 20–21, 92, 199–200; and death, 13, 65 ff., 89, 199–200
Conventions: as points of view, 44–45
Creation. *See* Novelty
Culture, 151, 161–162, 203
Cumont, Franz, cited, 213
Cybernetics, 108

de Laguna, Grace A., 251 (n. 6)
Dead, the: primitive representations of, 210–215 *passim;* as shadows, 212, 214
Death: images of, 1; meanings of the term, 2, 4–5, 17–18; conception of, in the modern age, 3–4; religious conception of, 3–4; as a philosophical problem, 3–5; mechanistic conception of, 5, 63, 122–123; spiritualistic conception of, 5–6; can be said in many ways, 13, 20, 64 ff.; in inorganic nature, 17–18, 45; degrees of, 64–65, 80–81, 88, 120 ff., 132, 142–144, 169; and cessation, 83–84, 89, 120–123; in human reality, 88, 170–171, 202–203; progression of, 89–91, 142–143, 199–200; in organic reality, 92 ff., 172–173; neovitalist conception of, 101–102; Hans Driesch on, 102–103; as an accident, 122–123, 207; in primary organisms, 123–132 *passim;* in superior organisms, 132–139 *passim;* causes of organic, 133–139 *passim;* kinds of organic, 137; as rupture of social bond, 138; as essence, according to Scheler, 141–142; as tendency, 142 ff.; ontology of, 142–143; and individuality, 143–144; paradoxes in human, 170–171; and life, 171; interiority of, 172–175, 187; Simmel on, 174–175; experience of, 175–178, 185–186; Jaspers on, 176; Sartre on, 176–177, 186, 191, 192; Heidegger on, 176–177, 191; of the Other, 176–188 *passim;* meaningfulness and meaninglessness of, 183–188, 191–192; rebellion against, 186–187; anticipation of one's own, 187, 188; St. Augustine on, 188–189; "literary" tes-

timony on, 188–198 *passim;* Gide on, 189–190; kinds of, 190–191; the problem of one's own, 192–194, 195–198, 199–201; attitudes regarding, 192–195; and memory, 193; Epicurus on, 193, 207; Stoics and Christians on, 194; Seneca on, 194, 196; Bertrand Russell on, 194–195; transcendence of, by cultural achievements, 195, 203; poets' descriptions of, 196–197; Rilke on, 197–198; essence of human, 198–203 *passim;* Proust on, 201; fear of, 206–207; idea of inevitability of, 207; Bergson on, 207; Vuillemin on, 207; Freud on, 208; and survival or immortality, *see* Immortality; Survival

Democritus: on atomism, 48, 50, 51

Descartes, René: his view of material world, 49; dualism of mind-body in, 145; quoted, 241

Dialectic, 12, 13, 56–57, 168

Dilthey, Wilhelm, 95

Dombrowski, Heinz J., 125

Draste, A., cited, 138

Driesch, Hans: on notion of entelechy, 100–101, 127; on organic reality, 100–103; quoted, 101; on death, 102–103

Dualism, 66; rejected, 53, 147; types of, 66

Ebeling, A. H., 124, 126

Echeverría, José, 226, 239; quoted, 227

Eddington, A. S., 157

Einstein, Albert, 69

Elements: and structures, 39–45 *passim,* 47–48; structures viewed as, 45

Empiricism, 13, 56–57

Entelechies: Driesch's conception of, 100–101, 127

Epicurus: on death, 193, 207, 223–224, 226, 227

Essences: Husserl and Scheler on, 62; and principles of reality, 62–63; traditional notion of, 62–63; as immutable realities, 63; and facts, 140

Eternal life: belief in, 181–182, 223; as immortality, 215

Ex nihilo nihil fit, 79

Experience: and reason, 47; ontology based on, 67, 68, 87–88

External, the: as ontological pole, 70 ff.; as limiting principle, 71 ff.; definition of, 72; and the Internal, 75 ff., 81 ff., 148; in organic reality, 93

Fechner, Gustav Theodor, 232–233; quoted, 233

Fichte, Johann Gottlieb, 154

Fischer, A., 124

Form and matter, 30

Freedom, 199; paradox of, in man, 160, 161, 164–165

Freud, Sigmund: on death, 208

Functional models, 49

Galilei, Galileo, 33, 153

García Lorca, Federico, quoted, 196

Gide, André, quoted, 189–190

Grande Covián, F., 247 (n. 17)

Haldane, J. S., 104

Hämmerling, Joachim, 124; quoted, 126, 134

Hanson, Norwood Russell, 244 (n. 13), 245 (n. 21)

Hartmann, M., 124

Hartmann, Nicolai, 104, 247 (n. 19)

Hegel, G. W. F., 11; on the real and the rational, 54; on notion of exteriority, 75

Heidegger, Martin, 195, 252 (n. 18); on history of ontology, 55; on vicious circles, 60; on "ontologic realm," 155; on death of the Other, 176–177; on death, 176–177, 191

Heisenberg, Werner, 69, 77

Heraclitus, 48

Hersch, Jeanne: on vicious circles, 60

Hertwig, Oscar, 104; quoted, 138

Historical, the: in organic reality, 84, 128; in human life, 84–85, 150

Homer: life and death in, 214

Horace, 189

Human life: cycles and patterns in, 84; three features of, 84–85; interiority in, 84–85; as maximumly mortal, 88; Ortega y Gasset on, 167; Sartre on, 167. *See also* Man

Husserl, Edmund, 56; on essences, 62

Hutschnecker, Arnold A., 249 (n. 41)

Hylomorphism, 30–36 *passim*

Hylosystemism, 31–32

Ideal being and "reality," 61, 63, 76, 79, 88

Idealism: opposed, 56, 58; phenomenological, 62

Identity, 156–157; and reality, 59 ff.

Immortality: hunger for, 204–205, 211; beliefs in, 205, 208, 218 ff.; meaning of term, 205–206; proofs of, 206; Platonic and Neo-Platonic ideas on, 215–217; Aristotle on, 216; Alexander of Aphrodisias and Averroës on, 216–217; Hebrew conception of, 218–219, 221; Christian conceptions of, 219–222; Epicurus on, 223–224, 226, 227; philosophers' views on, 223–227 *passim;* Spinoza on, 224–226; Echeverría on, 226–227, 239; rational proofs of, 228–231, 240; Aristotelian–Thomistic proofs of, 230–231; Kant on, 231; Fechner on, 232–233; empirical proofs of, 232–237 *passim*, 240; William James on, 234–236; further proofs of, 237–239; discussed, 239–241

Individuality: in organic reality, 113, 118–120, 129–131; degrees of, 119, 130; and death, 143–144

Inorganic reality: changes in, 22–25; nature of, 24–25, 29, 32, 152–154; theses on, 29–39 *passim;* physical and metaphysical statements on, 35; cessation in, 38–39, 43–45, 78–79, 199–200, 204; as elements and as structures, 42; mechanistic-atomistic view of, 49–50; ontological situation of, 76–77; exteriority of, 77; forms of, 77–78; interiority of, 78; individuality in, 83; being and meaning in, 86–87; and organic reality, 93, 97–98, 104 ff.

Integrationism, 6–13 *passim*, 69, 71; as first philosophy, 14; ontology of, 72

Interiority: of inorganic reality, 78; of organic reality, 81–83; of death, 172–175

Internal, the: as ontological pole, 70 ff.; as limiting principle, 71 ff.; and the External, 75 ff., 81–82, 148; organic reality and, 83, 92–93, 148

Ipseity, 156–157

Jacobi, Günther, 104

James, William: on survival, 234–236

Jaspers, Karl: on vicious circles, 60; quoted, 176
Jennings, H. J., 123
Jollos, Victor, 124

Kant, Immanuel, 25, 26, 54, 63, 217, 228; on philosophy, 14; on principles of knowledge and reality, 56; on immortality, 231; quoted, 24
Kierkegaard, Søren, 195
Knowledge: types of, 34–35; principles of reality and principles of, 56; function of, in man, 163
Kornberg, Arthur, 109

La Barre, Weston, 250 (n. 4), 252 (n. 20)
Laclos, Choderlos de, 254 (n. 49)
Laín Entralgo, Pedro, 251 (n. 10)
Lalande, André, quoted, 137–138
Landé, Alfred, 244 (n. 16)
Landsberg, Paul Ludwig, 188; quoted, 171
Language, 149; of philosophy, 14–18, 155
Leibniz, Gottfried Wilhelm, 11, 97
Lévy-Bruhl, Lucien, 255 (n. 10)
Life: Nietzsche on, 95; Scheler on, 95; Simmel on, 95–96; making one's own, 147 ff., 152; and death, 171. *See also* Human life; Man; Organic reality
Limiting concepts, 7, 9, 12
Limiting realities, 7, 9
Loeb, Jacques, 110
Logical principles: and ontological principles, 58
Lotze, Rudolf Hermann, 97
Lucretius, 245 (n. 25)

Maine de Biran, François Pierre, quoted, 238
Malebranche, Nicolas, quoted, 230
Man, 144; and his death, 88, 170–171; and his body, 145–147; as a maker of his own life, 147–148, 159–160, 164–165; as user of tools, 148; and language, 149; and the world, 150, 152, 162–165; as a historical being, 150–152; Scheler on, 151; cultural structure of, 151, 161–162; biological structure of, 151–152; ontological structure of, 154–156; as an "existent," 155; as selfhood and property, 156, 157, 159, 165; as person, 158, 169; and servomechanisms, 158–159; freedom in and of, 160, 164–165; Nietzsche on, 161; in continuum of Nature, 162; "intentionality" of, 162; definition of, 162–169 *passim;* as maker of projects, 163, 165, 187; as a "hesitant" reality, 166, 168, 202; as a "chooser," 167; Simmel on, 174–175; finitude of, 187; survival and immortality in, 204 ff.
Mann, Thomas, 201
Marcel, Gabriel, 250 (n. 3); quoted, 177
Margenau, Henry, 244 (n. 10)
Matter: and form, 30; mechanistic and atomistic conception of, 48 ff.; reduction of reality to, 68–69; and spirit, 70, 90; being and meaning in, 86
Maupas, E., 123–125
Mazia, Daniel, 136
Meaning, 162; and being, 85–88, 161; and cessation, 88
Mechanical models, 49, 79
Mechanism: on death, 5, 63, 122–123; and atomism, 48 ff.; as explanation of nature of organic reality, 93–94, 105–107; discussed, 107–112 *passim*
Mehl, Roger, quoted, 177–178
Melissus, quoted, 48
Merleau-Ponty, Maurice, 250 (n. 3)

Metalnikov, S., 123, 124
Metaphysics: and physics, 24, 35; traditional and modern, 169
Metchnikov, I. I.: on causes of organic death, 134–135
Meyerson, Émile: on Parmenides' "sphere," 46; on reductionism, 54
Mind, the: and the body, 146 ff.
Monism, 66–67, 69, 147; a *sui generis* kind of, 68–69, 72, 90
Moravia, Alberto, quoted, 257 (n. 52)
Mortality: types of, 13; degrees of, 64–65, 80–81, 88, 120 ff., 132, 142–144, 169, 199; and reality, 64 ff., 169; causes of organic, 133–139 *passim;* as a tendency, 142–143. See also Cessation; Death

Nagel, Ernest, quoted, 105, 106, 107, 245 (n. 26)
Neovitalism, 99–103 *passim*
Neruda, Pablo, quoted, 197
Newton, Isaac, 24
Nietzsche, Friedrich: on life, 95; on man, 161; quoted, 252 (n. 19)
Nominalism, 40–41
Novelty: elimination of notion of, 50

Occam's razor, 41, 42
Ochoa, Severo, 109
Olympiodoros, 257 (n. 54)
Ontological directions, 8, 9, 13, 64 ff., 70–72, 74, 82
Ontological principles: discussion of two, 53 ff.; and logical principles, 58
Ontology, 169; "two-way," 9, 64 ff., 72 ff., 90, 121, 200; foundations of a new, 53 ff., 60 ff.; principles of a new, 64–65; two basic types of, 66–67

Organic reality: interiority of, 81–83; specificity of, 82–83; individuality in, 82–83; as "internal," 83, 92–93, 128–129, 148; cessation in, 83–84, 199–200; being and meaning in, 86–87; as "external," 92–93; and inorganic reality, 93, 97–98, 104 ff., 148; doctrines on, 93–113 *passim;* description of, 104–105; mechanistic view of, 107 ff.; characteristics of, 113–120 *passim,* 148–152 *passim;* effect of time on, 128; differentiation, centralization, and specialization in, 135 ff.; and human reality, 147; and organic species, 149 ff.; man's transcending of, 151–152; nature of, 152–154
Organicism: as a philosophy of organic reality, 93 ff.; discussed, 104–107
Organisms. See Organic reality
Ortega y Gasset, José, 26, 160; quoted, 25; on human life, 167
"Oscillation" in organic reality, 113–115, 131–132
Other, the: death of, 176–177, 191, 192; descriptions of death of, 178–188 *passim;* "sharing" death of, 179–180; world of, 182–183
Otto, Walter F., 255 (n. 19)

Parmenides: on what "it" is, 46–47; and his "Way of Truth," 54
Pearl, Raymond, quoted, 136
Peierls, E. R., 244 (n. 9)
Person, 157–158, 169
Phenomena: and things in themselves, 48
Phenomenalism, 29–30, 36, 48, 56–57
Philosophy: as a system, 14; language of, 14, 15, 17–18; as a habit, 15; as "conceptography,"

21; Kant on, 24; and science, 24–29 passim, 155–156; Brentano on, 25; Ortega y Gasset on, 25; coexistence of science with, 26; nature of, 26–28; beginnings of, 53–54; "traditional" and "linguistic," 87
Physical reality: characteristics of, 38. See also Inorganic reality
Physicalism, 29–30
Physics: and metaphysics, 24, 35; as model for philosophy, 25; and common sense, 33–34; knowledge in, 34–35; distrust of "purely mechanical models" in, 49
Plato: on the soul and its immortality, 215, 288–230, 257 (n. 51)
Plotinus: on the soul, 219, 220
Pluralism, 66 ff., 73
Plurality: and unity, 69
Polarities, 7–9, 10, 12, 90. See also Ontological directions; Ontological principles
Polarity: principle of, 11
Porphyry, quoted, 217
Potential immortality: in "primary organisms," 121, 123–132 passim, 172; and potential mortality, 173–175
Potter, van R., 108
Primary organisms, 121; death in, 123–132 passim
Process: and entities, 30, 72; two meanings of, 31; discussed, 37–39; and cessation, 38–39
Processualism: defined, 30–31
Property, 156–157, 165, 199
Proust, Marcel, quoted, 201
Psychic reality: and organic reality, 114 ff., 232–237 passim
Psychical research, 233 ff.

Quinton, Anthony, quoted, 250 (n. 3)

Ratio essendi and *ratio cognoscendi*, 57–59
Reality: and change, 46 ff.; as cessation, 52, 60 ff., 64; meaning of, 53 ff.; and appearance, 55, 56, 58–59; is not "in principle," 55 ff.; principles of knowledge and principles of, 57–59, 60–62; and identity, 59 ff.; and sufficient reason, 61 ff.; and mortality, 64 ff., 169; types of, 65; as grasped in terms of ontological poles, 71 ff.; analogy of, 85, 89
Reason: and problem of change, 46–47; and experience, 47; reductionist tendency of, 54
Reduction: conceptual and real, 94–95, 103–104; according to neovitalists, 103–104, according to organicists, 105; according to mechanists, 110 ff.
Reductionism, 54, 146; and monism, 66, 68; discussed, 67–68. See also Reduction
Reinke, Johannes, 100, 102
Rejuvenation, 126 ff., 132–133, 135, 137
Rhine, J. B., 233
Rilke, Rainer Maria, quoted, 197–198
Rof Carballo, Juan, 249 (n. 31)
Romains, Jules, quoted, 182
Romero, Francisco, quoted, 104
Rostand, Jean, quoted, 132–133
Roux, Wilhelm, 100
Russell, Bertrand: on death, 194–195
Russell, E. S., 104
Ryle, Gilbert, 250 (n. 3)

Sahlins, Marshall D., 251 (n. 8)
Sartre, Jean-Paul, 160; quoted, 56, 57, 75; on human life, 167; on death of the Other, 176–177, 191, 192; on absurdity of death, 186, 191

Scheler, Max, 104; on essences, 62; on life, 95–96; on aging and death, 140–142; quoted, 141; on man, 151; on survival, 239
Schopenhauer, Arthur, quoted, 206
Schrödinger, Erwin, quoted, 108, 111
Science: and Kant on, 24; philosophy, 24–29 *passim,* 155–156; Brentano on, 25; Ortega y Gasset on, 25; coexistence of philosophy with, 26; and magic, 34–35
Self, the: analysis of, 237–239
Selfhood, 156–157
Seneca: on death, 194; quoted, 196
Servomechanisms, 158–159
Sheldon, W. H., quoted, 10
Simmel, Georg: on life, 95–96; cited, 174–175, 239
Situations, 166
Snell, Bruno, cited, 214
Society, 150
Soul, the: and the body, 145–147, 221–222; and its immortality, 215 ff.; Platonic and neo-Platonic views on, 215–217, 219, 228–230; Aristotelian view of, 216, 219; Thomas Aquinas on, 230–231. *See also* Immortality; Survival
Species: and individual organisms, 149–150, 202–203; the world of the, 152
Specificity: in organic reality, 113, 117–118
Spencer, A. G., 124
Spengler, Oswald, cited, 209
Spinoza, B.: on immortality, 224–226; quoted, 225
Spirit, 157–158; and matter, 70, 90; being and meaning in, 86–87
Spontoneity: in living beings, 105, 116–117
Structures, 37–38; and elements, 39–45 *passim,* 47–48; definition of, 39; and sums of elements, 40, 41; as ordered wholes, 41; as "singles," 42; cessation of, 43–45, 59
Substance: and mode, 30, 36; discussed, 36–37
Suicide, 203
Superior organisms, 121; phases in development of, 132–133; death of, 132–139 *passim;* complex structure of, 135 ff.
Supervielle, Jules, quoted, 196
Survival: meaning of term, 205–206; types of belief in, 208; primitive conceptions of, 208–213 *passim;* degrees of, 210–211; Chinese conceptions of, 211–212; Roman conceptions of, 212; Hellenic conceptions of, 213 ff.; ancient conceptions of, 213–217 *passim;* Homeric conceptions of, 214; Fechner on, 232–233; empirical proofs of, 232–237 *passim,* 240; William James on, 234–236. *See also* Immortality
Survivors, 182–183; dependence of the dead on the, 211–212

Taylor, A. C., 106
Thales, 54
Things in themselves: and phenomena, 48
Thomas Aquinas, 146; on the soul, 219, 221, 230–231; quoted, 231
Time: ontological direction of, 77; effect of, on organic realities, 128
Tönnies, Ferdinand, 251 (n. 7)
Totality: E. Nagel on, 106

Ultimate particles. *See* Basic elements
Unamuno, Miguel de, 204, 211
Unity: and plurality, 69; of reality, 89
Usefulness: in organic reality, 113, 115–116

Values, 151–152
Van Orman Quine, Willard, 251 (n. 12)
Vauvenargues, Luc de Clapiers, Marquis of, quoted, 196
Venegas, Master Alexo, quoted, 222
Vicious circles: in philosophy, 60–61, 165
Vieweger, 124
Vitalism: as a philosophy of organic reality, 93–94; radical, examined, 96–99; strict, examined, 98–103 *passim*
Von Bertalanffy, Ludwig, 104, 108; quoted, 130, 131, 247 (n. 20)
von Neumann, J., 159
von Uexküll, Jacob von, 100
Vuillemin, Jules: on death, 207

Washburn, Sherwood L., 250–251 (n. 5)
Weismann, August, 124; cited, 122; on continuity of germinative plasma, 127
Weiss, Paul, 106
West, D. J., 234
Whitehead, A. N., 31, 80
Wittgenstein, Ludwig, 18
Wolff, Christian, 231, 245 (n. 18)
Wolff, Gustav, 100
Woodruff, L. L., 123–125
World: organic and human, 151–152, 163

Xirau, Joaquín, 245 (n. 27)

Zubiri, Xavier, 207